Routledge Revivals

Concept Formation in Social Science

First published in 1983, this book examines the problems of concept formation in the social sciences, and in particular sociology, from the standpoint of a realistic philosophy of science. Beginning with a discussion of positivistic, hermeneutic, rationalist and realistic philosophies of science, Dr Outhwaite argues that realism is best able to furnish rational criteria for the choice and specification of social scientific concepts. A realistic philosophy of science therefore acts as his reference point for the dialectical presentation of alternative accounts.

Concept Formation in Social Science

William Outhwaite

First published in 1983
by Routledge & Kegan Paul Ltd

This edition first published in 2011 by Routledge
2 Park Square, Milton Park, Abingdon, Oxon, OX14 4RN
52 Vanderbilt Avenue, New York, NY 10017

Routledge is an imprint of the Taylor & Francis Group, an informa business

© 1983 William Outhwaite

All rights reserved. No part of this book may be reprinted or reproduced or utilised in any form or by any electronic, mechanical, or other means, now known or hereafter invented, including photocopying and recording, or in any information storage or retrieval system, without permission in writing from the publishers.

Notice:
Product or corporate names may be trademarks or registered trademarks, and are used only for identification and explanation without intent to infringe.

Publisher's Note
The publisher has gone to great lengths to ensure the quality of this reprint but points out that some imperfections in the original copies may be apparent.

Disclaimer
The publisher has made every effort to trace copyright holders and welcomes correspondence from those they have been unable to contact.

A Library of Congress record exists under ISBN: 0710091958

ISBN 13: 978-0-415-61116-9 (hbk)
ISBN 13: 978-0-203-83164-9 (ebk)
ISBN 13: 978-0-415-61126-8 (pbk)

Concept formation in social science

William Outhwaite
Lecturer in Sociology
University of Sussex

Routledge & Kegan Paul
London, Boston, Melbourne and Henley

*First published in 1983
by Routledge & Kegan Paul Ltd
39 Store Street, London WC1E 7DD,
9 Park Street, Boston, Mass. 02108, USA,
296 Beaconsfield Parade, Middle Park,
Melbourne, 3206, Australia, and
Broadway House, Newtown Road,
Henley-on-Thames, Oxon RG9 1EN
Printed in Great Britain by
Redwood Burn Ltd, Trowbridge, Wiltshire
© William Outhwaite 1983
No part of this book may be reproduced in
any form without permission from the
publisher, except for the quotation of brief
passages in criticism*

Library of Congress Cataloging in Publication Data

Outhwaite, William.

*Concept formation of social science.
(International library of sociology)
Bibliography: p.
Includes index.
1. Social sciences – Methodology.
2. Concepts. I. Title. II. Series.
H61.089   300'.1   82-7620*

ISBN 0-7100-9195-8   AACR2

Contents

	Acknowledgments	vii
	Introduction	1
1	Concepts of science	5
2	Concepts in science	24
3	Constitution	68
4	Max Weber and concept formation in sociology	120
5	Concepts of society	135
	Notes	156
	Bibliography	220
	Subject index	244
	Name index	250

Acknowledgments

I am extremely grateful to Tom Bottomore for his patient encouragement during the very long gestation of the thesis which forms the basis of this book, and to my two examiners, Roy Edgley and Anthony Giddens. A number of other people have also made invaluable comments on various parts of the manuscript. I should like to thank in particular Michèle Barrett, Roy Bhaskar, Sue Easton, Peter Halfpenny, Jorge Larrain, Gillian Rose and Norman Stockman.

Introduction

Since the early 1960s there has been a growing interest in examining the concepts used by scientists in general and social scientists in particular. This is part of a more general tendency towards critical self-reflection within science. Just as natural scientists come increasingly to worry about the moral and practical implications of research in nuclear physics or molecular biology, and social scientists worry about their possible complicity in the military-industrial complex or in the reproduction of bourgeois ideology, so their worries also focus, more precisely, on the validity of their own assumptions, theoretical frameworks, etc. These anxieties are perhaps more extreme in the social sciences, where we may wonder, in moments of despair, whether our concepts and theories give us any sort of grip at all on the world. We are told by outsiders that we are neither genuine scientists nor genuine humanistic scholars; that we not only use a hermetic and rebarbative jargon but that this jargon, unlike that of natural science, is also gratuitous because the propositions expressed in it are no more than glorified common sense.

If questions of this sort have a particular poignancy for social scientists, there is by no means an absence of critical reflection on the natural sciences, as is proved by the immense interest in and development of the work of Thomas Kuhn. The social sciences have rarely generated paradigms with the sort of general authority that Kuhn's theory of 'normal science' implies, but the notion that concepts, assumptions, measurement techniques and so on are linked together in a limited set of frameworks is only too familiar in the social sciences, where representatives of alternative traditions have characteristically ignored each other or talked past each other. Durkheim and Max Weber, those two contemporaries, are among the more striking examples.

2 Introduction

The endemic opposition between conflicting frameworks in the social sciences finds a particularly sharp expression in the differences between their terminology. Why is it, for example, that the term 'society', which plays such an important part in Durkheim's sociology, is virtually absent from Max Weber's work?(1) Why is it that the same term, 'social structure', is given a radically different sense by two different anthropologists: Radcliffe-Brown and Lévi-Strauss? For Radcliffe-Brown, 'The (social) structure consists of the sum total of all the social relationships of all individuals at a given moment in time.'(2) For Lévi-Strauss, by contrast: 'The term "social structure" has nothing to do with empirical reality but with models which are built up after it.'(3)

The fact that differences such as these can be assimilated with apparent ease to traditional philosophical oppositions such as those between individualism and holism or between empiricism and conventionalism may lead the social scientist to see them as irresolvable and therefore to avoid any serious examination of them. Durkheim, for example, asserted robustly that 'Sociology does not need to choose between the great hypotheses which divide metaphysicians,'(4) and many sociologists have gone even further and argued, in a way which Durkheim would not have done, that these 'definitional questions' are arbitrary and that the proof of the pudding lies in the predictive-explanatory power of the theories which are generated on the basis of some choice or other of initial assumptions. I shall argue in more detail later than this latter view is one of the more baneful influences of a mistaken philosophy of meaning and science, and that this attitude, at once permissive and dismissive, to alternative accounts of the nature of the social and of our knowledge of it is one cause at least of the intellectual and social disarray in which the social sciences find themselves.

For if social scientists are inevitably pushed into taking serious notice of semantic aspects of their own practice, they are also compelled to adopt positions in the philosophy of meaning and science. They must, for example, support their choice of concepts and the ways in which they choose to specify them (by definition or otherwise), by metatheoretical reflections on the relation between scientific terminology and ordinary language, on the legitimacy or illegitimacy of stipulative definitions, and so on. More precisely, they can hardly avoid rejecting the more vulgar positivist positions on these issues - for example extreme empiricism or operationalism.(5)

A more sophisticated view, which came to predominate within the positivist tradition itself, accepts that theoretical concepts cannot simply be reduced either to observational statements, in the manner of early logical empiricism, or to a set of operations. On this later view, it may be argued that the specification of individual concepts is relatively unimportant. What counts are the theoretical structures in which these concepts are combined. (6) But this view is itself open to an attack from within the philosophy of science which questions how far scientific theories are in fact deductively formalised and argues further that deductive formalisation as an ideal may be less appropriate to the sciences than had previously been assumed.(7) It can readily be seen that this argument, developed from within the second, 'linguistic' phase of analytic philosophy, will apply a fortiori to the social sciences, and indeed there is an important convergence between the analytic philosophy of the post-war period, developing out of logical positivism but increasingly opposed to it, and the earlier continental tradition of hermeneutics,(8) despite the latter's concern with the human sciences to the exclusion of natural science.

The hermeneutic tradition, which I have discussed in my previous book,(9) provides a much more adequate account of the place of language in the social sciences and, in particular, the way in which our access to social reality is mediated through language. There is, however, a problem within this tradition of establishing rational criteria for the choice of concepts and theoretical frameworks - a problem which it shares more generally with conventionalist approaches within the philosophy of science. Rationalist and realist philosophies of science, discussed in chapter 1 of this book, offer a possible solution to these difficulties, and I offer some arguments, there and in chapter 2, for the adoption by social scientists of a realist philosophy of science along the lines developed by Roy Bhaskar.(10) This approach also sheds a new light on the traditional opposition between positivistic and hermeneutic theories of society, the former stressing the essential similarity of the social and natural sciences, the latter asserting their radical distinctiveness. A realist philosophy of science makes it possible to reject positivist versions of naturalism, the thesis of the methodological unity of science, and to develop a new form of naturalism which does justice to the hermeneutic moment in the social or human sciences.(11)

Chapter 1 of this book presents the positivist, hermeneutic, rationalist and realist traditions in the philosophy of science and social theory. Chapter 2 develops the implications of these traditions for concept formation in the social sciences - in particular for the choice of

4 Introduction

concepts, the ways in which they can be defined or otherwise specified, and the relation between social scientific discourse and ordinary language. This chapter raises certain fundamental questions about the relationship between language, science and reality - in particular, the question of object-constitution to which chapter 3 is devoted. Here again the claim is made that only rationalism and realism furnish an adequate account of constitution, if we accept that critical theory has not provided sufficient backing for its own stronger account (and its claim that object-domains are constituted differentially by cognitive interests). Rationalist accounts of constitution are incomplete, in that they lack an adequate theory of society. Such a theory is needed to deal with the ontological sense in which the world is (partially) constituted by human practice; knowledge of this process is required for the reflexive reconstruction of the social base of acts of theoretical constitution, and hence the materialist grounding of theory in relation to past, present or future practice.

Chapter 4 provides negative support for the realist programme by way of some critical remarks about Max Weber. These bear mainly on his metatheory, which was explicitly directed (in part at least) against something like the views advanced in this book. It is suggested that Weber's arguments against these views are not conclusive, given certain antinomies in his own position.

Chapter 5 examines positivistic conceptions of society, which either brush it aside or reify it as a substantive entity, and 'transcendental idealist' conceptions, loosely associated with hermeneutics, which reduce it to a quasi-transcendental postulate or at best a processual tendency. Finally, it is suggested that one particular attempt to develop a realist conception of society converges interestingly with other work in this area and furnishes an attractive research programme in sociological theory.(12)

1 Concepts of science

Having sketched out, in general terms, the conceptual oppositions with which I am concerned, I shall now discuss in more detail three accounts of concept formation. These three (positivism, hermeneutics and various recent forms of rationalist and realist philosophy of science) represent clusters of views rather than clearly delimited and mutually exclusive positions.(1) I shall, in fact, argue that there is a close affinity between traditional Marxism and recent versions of realism and also that important elements of positivism are incorporated into verstehende social science, often in an unacknowledged form. However, I shall also suggest that the hermeneutic tradition encouraged a recognition of the importance of description, and a non-positivist account of explanation(2) which in turn have important affinities with realism.

The following discussion ranges over both the philosophy of science and social theory, as these are conventionally defined. Two points should perhaps be made about this procedure. First, I do not believe that there is any clear-cut difference between the two. Although philosophy is primarily concerned with conceptual questions, and social theory is more concerned with empirical matters, this does not imply a sharp disjunction. Second, and related to the first point, I do not think it is possible to give any single account of the proper relationship between philosophy and social theory. The philosopher, or the scientist engaged in philosophical activity, is neither simply an 'under-labourer', nor a 'master-scientist', (3) nor an apologist for science. He or she may be all of these things, and more. Philosophy should be seen neither as an all-important foundation sine qua non of empirical science, nor as merely a scientific ideology. The concept of ideology is a helpful one here, but it must be used in this context without automatically pejorative connotations and in a way which admits that philosophy can make a genuine contribution to science.(4)

1 POSITIVISM

The term 'positivism' is used in notoriously varied ways. (5) In subsequent chapters I shall use it in a rather broad sense, in which important aspects of the work of, for example, Weber and Schutz can be represented as positivistic. Here, however, I am concerned with the philosophical tradition which grew out of the Vienna Circle and flourished in the Anglo-Saxon countries of emigration.(6) This tradition is sufficiently well known not to require a general characterisation here, and the following discussion is heavily biased towards questions of language and of the logic of the social sciences.(7) The Vienna Circle's attitude to language is best understood from the angle of its critique of 'metaphysics'. This was the mainspring of the Circle's simultaneous emphasis on and depreciation of language.(8) First, scientific theories were to be seen as systems of statements, to be analysed in the 'formal mode of speech'; the philosophy of science was concerned with the syntax of the language of science. (9) Second, this 'linguistic turn'(10) was simultaneously a rejection of much of the language of traditional philosophy, with its oppositions between realism, materialism, phenomenalism, idealism, and so forth. These no longer presented a choice between ontologies but merely between languages whose usefulness was in large part dependent on the particular context. Carnap reports that, while working on 'Der Logische Aufbau der Welt', (11) in discussions with friends he shifted freely between materialistic and idealistic, nominalistic and 'Platonic' kinds of language. 'Only gradually, in the course of years, did I recognise clearly that my way of thinking was neutral with respect to the traditional controversies, e.g. realism vs. idealism, nominalism vs. Platonism (realism of universals), materialism vs. spiritualism, and so on.'(12)

Third, the distinction between good (scientific, logical) and bad (metaphysical) language was applied also to ordinary language. This contains unclear impressions which must be made more precise by being replaced by concepts.(13) At the same time, these must not be reified or rendered metaphysical.(14) The 'search for a neutral system of formulae, for a symbolism freed from the slag of historical languages ... for a total system of concepts' (15) is primarily an attack on metaphysical errors within

philosophy and empirical science, and only secondarily against the confusions of ordinary language. Neurath argued, for example, that the 'purification' of the concepts of the social sciences, although less advanced than in the case of physics, was also(16)
  less urgent perhaps. For it seems that even in the heyday of metaphysics and theology, the metaphysical strain was not particularly strong here; maybe this is because the concepts in this field, such as war and peace, import and export, are closer to direct perception than concepts like atom and ether.
Fourth, it turns out that the 'physical language' proposed by Carnap as the reduction basis for the language of all science is itself reducible to 'thing-language', containing 'those terms which we use on a prescientific level in our ordinary language'.(17)

Underlying this programme of reductionism and linguistic purification was the Vienna Circle's basic conception of an observation-language, grounded in observation, perception, experience and expressed in 'protocol sentences'. Statements in the observation-language make up the base of our knowledge of the world; all other statements must be truth-functional compounds of these. Indeed, the meaning of a statement was identified with its truth-conditions, just as the meaning of a term was identified with its extension - the range of objects to which it applied. What logical positivism aspired to, in essence, was a harmonious fusion of the most advanced theoretical formulations in logic, mathematics and physics, and a relatively straightforward empiricism with a linguistic twist.(18) The origins of this marriage are well enough known; it will, however, illuminate the systematic questions to be discussed in the later chapters if we examine in some detail the strains which caused it to break up.

The Vienna Circle began with a highly favourable view both of theory, which was conceived as a deductive system in the manner of mathematical logic,(19) and of empirical observation.(20) As the above quotations from Carnap indicate, it was at first believed that theoretical terms could be translated into observational terms without loss of meaning. Gradually, Carnap and others began to feel that this did not do justice to the specificity of what came to be called the theoretical language. In what Radnitzsky has called the 'holistic turn',(21) it came to be held that, instead of a direct relation between each theoretical term and a set of observational terms, the best that could be hoped for was a 'partial interpretation' of the former, via so-called 'correspondence rules'. The status of these rules was a matter of considerable dispute, but it was generally agreed that they were not merely definitionally true.

The new position gave a more adequate account of theory, especially the more abstract sort of theory found in contemporary physics.(22) By the same token, however, some suspiciously metaphysical constructs which had been kept out of science by the original postulates of translatability and testability were able to slip back through the broader mesh of the correspondence rules, which applied only to some theoretical terms.(23)

Second, although the revised view allows for some degree of theoretical determination of observational terms, (24) it is not enough to satisfy the very powerful criticisms which have been levelled against *any* hard or fast distinction between observational and theoretical terms. (25) These objections also apply to Karl Popper, and have been raised, in particular, in relation to his account of falsification.(26)

In summarising the criticisms which have been directed at the position described above, it is possible to show that many of them have an added salience for the social sciences. These criticisms have taken four main directions:

1 The first pours cold water on the notion of 'atomic' facts and the idea of a theory-free observation language. For a cogent expression of this view, one need stray no further from the orthodox positivist camp than to the works of Karl Popper.(27) In the case of the social sciences, the idea of an atomic social or economic fact seems, if anything, even less plausible.(28)

2 A second criticism attacks the other end, querying the postulate of theoretical integration and formalisation. There is a tendency for positivist writers to present entire bodies of theory as actual or potential axiomatic systems. The following characteristic criticism again, concerns science in general but has a peculiar poignancy for the social scientist:(29)

> The intellectual content of an entire science can ... be represented in a strictly 'logical' form only in quite exceptional circumstances. More typically, a science will comprise numerous coexisting and logically independent theories or conceptual systems, and it will be none the less 'scientific' for doing so.

3 Third, the connections postulated between theoretical and empirical terms are unsatisfactory and provide no rational basis for theory-choice. Positivists characteristically shore up their own theories by means of simplifying assumptions and ceteris paribus clauses, thus nepotistically protecting them from the testability prescribed

for the rest.(30) This again seems to be the case par excellence in the social sciences.

4 A fourth, more diffuse, objection is that the positivist view simply fails to do justice to the importance of description. Again, this point can be made quite plausibly in relation to science in general (for example, by a brief foray into the history of science) but again, it seems that social scientists are *peculiarly* concerned with adjudicating between rival descriptions of social phenomena. 'Expressive ritual' or misbegotten 'technology', 'late capitalism' or 'industrial society', 'fascism' or just 'right-wing dictatorship'? These may in some cases be merely verbal questions, in the sense that no importance whatever attaches to them, but these are, I think, the exception. More often, the decision about which of these terms to use involves substantive discussion about the structural feature of the phenomenon, just as in, say, moral or legal discourse.(31) Some descriptions are explanatory, as Winch, for example, has pointed out. And for the realist, at least, explanation has a great deal to do with the description of structural mechanisms. The positivistic covering-law model of explanation sets up an unduly extreme opposition between explanation and description.(32)

In sum, then, it is objected that the distinction between observational and theoretical language does not hold water, any more than the earlier positivists' reduction of the latter to the former. To this may be added a further set of objections to the positivists' prescriptions for the social sciences. These bear essentially on the reductionist programme associated with the unified science movement.(33)

The clearest formulation of a physicalist foundation for the social sciences can be found in Otto Neurath's 'Empirical Sociology'.(34) Neurath argues robustly for a materialist and behaviourist sociology or 'social behaviourism',(35) of which 'the living contemporary form ... is Marxism'.(36) 'Sociology is an empirical science like astronomy; the peoples can be compared to clusters of stars which are in closer contact with each other than with other star clusters.'(37) For Neurath, then, there is an essential unity of subject matter, as well as of method, among the sciences. '*All genuine science can only be physics* ... in a comprehensive physics there are spatio-temporal processes of the brain, nerves, throat, gestures, which replace "consciousness", a concept of pure Kantianism.'(38) 'Physicalism, unified science on a materialist foundation, brings us *the* order, that is the closed system of laws which one can control through observation.'(39)

Neurath's programme had little influence on sociology.
(40) Positivist influence was exercised, rather, on its
methodology(41) and its self-image. It was conceded that
the subject-matter of sociology was qualitatively different from that of the natural sciences.(42) However, this
did not affect the purpose of sociology, which was the
same as that of any other science: the construction of
theories and the formulation of empirically testable laws.
(43) Thus arose the somewhat curious situation in which
social scientists invoked a vulgarised positivist philosophy to support their own prescriptions, while philosophers of social science tended to present an account of
theory-construction which was utopian even in relation to
physics and then to note that the social sciences did not
really come very close to this ideal. The main criticisms
levelled at the positivist model are raised in the following alternative accounts.

2 HERMENEUTICS

This term is used here in the broad sense which it has
acquired under the impact of 'critical theory'. Besides
the writers traditionally understood as concerned with
hermeneutics, including the significantly different
'existential' version of Gadamer, I am including verstehende sociologists and analytic philosophers of the 'second' period, headed by the later Wittgenstein and by J.L.
Austin. What holds all these thinkers together, if anything does, is a common reaction against positivism. In
the verstehende tradition this is a clear thread running
from Droysen to ethnomethodology.(44) Within 'linguistic' philosophy, which developed in large part out of
logical positivism, this reaction only became clear in
retrospect, in a more careful reading of Wittgenstein and
in the work of Peter Winch.(45)
  Whereas the rationalists and realists discussed below
are concerned to attack the positivist account of science,
the tendency among hermeneutic theorists has been to
accept it as broadly true of natural science; the claim is
merely that another account is needed of the human sciences. It is clear, I think, that this partial acceptance
of positivist principles has prejudiced discussions of the
relation between the two groups of sciences.(46)
  It is not to be expected that such a broad current of
thought as the 'hermeneutic' one should show the same kind
of unity of purpose as did the logical positivists. The
core doctrine of this tradition with regard to concept
formation is, accordingly, less easy to pin down, though

it can be summarised very crudely in two theses:

(a) There are important differences of principle between the concepts appropriate to the natural sciences and those appropriate to the social or human sciences. This may be due to an essential difference in their subject matter (inanimate nature vs Geist) or in the different interests, resulting in different methods, with which we approach an essentially homogeneous subject matter.

(b) The concepts of social science are linked to those of everyday language more closely than positivists allow. There is no simple contrast between scientific and everyday concepts; the former are developed out of the latter in a variety of ways, but these involve modifications of the original notions rather than a clear break with them.

These two theses together yield the claim that social scientific concepts are parasitic in important ways on those used by actors in the 'Lebenswelt'. One version of this claim is that they must be reducible to, or at least compatible with, ordinary language concepts;(47) a weaker claim is that, while they may replace such concepts, they will always have originated in a world which is to some extent pre-interpreted. Moreover, 'pre-interpreted' in the social sciences means, at least in part, interpreted by the objects of inquiry themselves.(48)

What account, then, is given within this tradition of description and explanation? Clearly, hermeneutic theorists will reject the notion of physicalist reduction advanced by Neurath and the early Carnap. Moreover, they can scarcely be happy with a view which makes description an unproblematic activity and explanation a matter of derivability from covering laws. Hermeneuticians deny the explanatory significance of constant conjunctions; for them, a sociological explanation must be 'understandable' and will characteristically have as its object a single human action or a typical pattern of such actions and be cast in terms of 'purposes', 'motives', 'intentions', etc. As Weber put it,(49)

It is possible that future enquiry will bring to light non-meaningful laws underlying meaningful behaviour.... The recognition of the causal importance of such factors would not in the least, of course, alter the tasks of sociology and of the sciences of action generally. Their task would still be that of interpreting the meanings which men give to their actions and so understanding the actions themselves.

In other words, the hermeneutic account of explanation is intimately related to description, in a way that positivist accounts are not.(50) And though Weber sometimes takes a positivistic turn, followed by Theodore Abel, in characterising his account of Verstehen as a heuristic device, this is hardly adequate to the phenomena with which he is concerned.(51) If, however, one requires a stronger version of Verstehen, it is clear that one is in a realm where the adequacy of an explanation is no longer something which can be decided by pure logic or by tests of statistical significance. Zetterberg's language of verification and confirmation is replaced by the language of the 'hermeneutic circle'.

There thus arises the first of the two main problems which confront the hermeneutic programme: what criteria can be offered for the adequacy of interpretations? This question has generally been answered in one of two ways. The first answer seems manifestly wrong and the second may not be an answer. The first response will be discussed below:(52) what is required is a full participation in the 'meaningful reality' of (1) the (empirical) subject or (2) his/her culture. (The former is, crudely, the 'social phenomenological' variant; the latter, the 'Winchian' one.) If, as I would argue, neither of these alternatives allows an escape from relativism, we are left with the classic hermeneutic process which Gadamer calls the 'melting of horizons',(53) a process of mediation between our own interpretation and those of others, who may include the people being interpreted. Gadamer, like Ricoeur (who gives a less radical account of it), sees this situation as a fact of life.(54) Rationalists and realists, as we shall see, construe it as an inadequacy of hermeneutic theories and attempt a more ambitious response.

The second problem involves the picture of society which emerges from the hermeneutic tradition - a picture drawn in terms of meanings and interpretations which, it is argued, does not do justice to the real relations of power, exploitation, etc. which pervade social life. The attempt to construe such relations in terms of 'meanings' may give rise to a perverse and, moreover, ideological account of society. This was Karl Mannheim's charge at the 6th German Sociological Congress;(55) it is also one of Habermas's objections to Gadamer.(56) Again, realists, though not this time rationalists, share this anxiety.

3 RATIONALISM, REALISM AND MARXISM

I shall take two writers as exemplars of a rationalist philosophy of science, Martin Hollis and Deryck Beyleveld.

(57) My discussion of realism will focus on the strong version recently developed by Roy Bhaskar and which can also be found in some current discussions of sociological theory.(58) Finally, I shall ask how far Marxism can be assimilated to realism along these lines.

Rationalism and realism have a considerable affinity (though their divergences may ultimately be more significant for social theory). They oppose positivism in both its empiricist and conventionalist variants; their stress on the importance of theory goes beyond the simple antiempiricist denial of the existence of theory-neutral facts to argue for the importance of a priori theory,(59) the use of transcendental arguments, and the establishment of 'the right concepts' by means of 'real definitions'.(60) This means that they oppose the conventionalism of much verstehende sociology.

Rationalism, for Hollis and Beyleveld, involves two distinct theses: a general philosophical thesis that 'all sciences depend on necessary truths knowable *a priori*' and a special thesis that 'rationality assumptions are essential to social science'.(61) Hollis and Beyleveld bring out very clearly the attraction of the general thesis. Hollis writes: (62)

> I take recent philosophy of science to have shown that empirical judgements presuppose theoretical judgements but not to have abolished the need for truth in science ... the danger of a nominalist or conventionalist line on the choice of theoretical terms is thereby stark....

The rationalist response to this situation is to argue that:(63)

> there is a class of truths whose denial is impossible, with at least apparent examples in logic, mathematics, formal systems like kinship algebra or neo-classical micro-economic theory, and perhaps in epistemology or metaphysics and, arguably at any rate, in ethics and theology.

Some examples of this class will bring out the connection with the special thesis of social scientific rationalism. The most general example is one which Hollis discussed in a debate with Steven Lukes and others over the problem of understanding other cultures. Lukes argues that we can only understand 'alien' beliefs if their believers share with us some universal criteria of rationality, even if some of their other criteria of rationality diverge from ours.(64) Hollis (65) agrees, but insists that the assumption of rationality is not a hypothesis but a necessary assumption.

Whether synthetic a priori principles of this kind are

14 Chapter 1

merely the foundations of science or whether they stretch right into its sinews is perhaps still an open question for rationalism.(66) The latter claim seems plausible, at least, in the field of social science, where this is biased towards praxiology or the theory of rational action. Here, as in chess, it can be argued, if a move is the best move it is necessarily the best move.(67) I shall discuss realist criticisms of this position a little later. For the moment, it is sufficient to note that it seems prima facie to skew social theory towards the study of action and away from that of larger structures.(68)

Realism in the sense discussed here (69) must be distinguished from what Bhaskar calls 'empirical realism'. The latter he construes as a view which posits a correspondence between sense-experiences and the objects of those experiences and between constant conjunctions of such objects of experience (e.g. events) and natural laws. In so doing, it denies the active role of scientific theory in generating alternative descriptions of the world and rules out explanation in 'open systems' where, because of disturbing influences, one cannot identify constant conjunctions.(70) Transcendental realism, by contrast, insists on the active role of theory - a feature it shares with neo-Kantian and conventionalist views which Bhaskar includes under the term 'transcendental idealism'. It also, however, goes beyond transcendental idealism in insisting on systematic connections between science and the world, where both are seen as internally differentiated. We must distinguish between transitive objects - the concepts, theories, laws, etc. of science, and the intransitive objects to which these refer - the real structures and mechanisms of the universe. The universe, too, must be seen as stratified in its relation to our cognitive faculties.

The real, which includes mechanisms, events and experiences, must be distinguished from the actual (events and experiences) and the empirical (experiences alone). An event can occur without being experienced, e.g. a landslide on an unknown island, and a causal mechanism may still be active when it is counteracted by another and does not therefore produce a change at the level of events (and where there is therefore 'nothing' to experience). Empirical realism conflates these domains of the real, the actual and the empirical; it therefore 'works' as an adequate, if incomplete account, only under the special conditions of closure (e.g. by experimentation) and where events are 'correctly' perceived.(71)

Bhaskar argues that the need to recognise the stratification of science and the world follows by a transcendental argument from the nature of experimental activity; experimentation is only intelligible if it 'gives us ... access to structures that exist independently of us'.(72) It does not follow, however, that the nature of these structures is knowable in any unproblematic way. 'Things exist and act independently of our descriptions, but we can only know them under particular descriptions.'(73) This principle, which Bhaskar rather unfortunately calls 'epistemological relativism', does not, he insists,(74)

mean that it is impossible to communicate between different theoretical and conceptual schemes or that a scientist cannot know the same object under two or more different descriptions. To show the difference between say Newtonian and Einsteinian dynamics and that the latter is an advance on the former a scientist must be capable of doing so.

The way in which scientific argument and advance take place differs in the social sciences, to which I now turn. Here we are not likely to find any analogy to microscopy, which is so useful for realist accounts of the eventual 'discovery' of entities initially postulated for theoretical reasons. More generally, the possibility of experimental intervention is crucially restricted in the social sciences, for all kinds of reasons.

What then are the possibilities for scientific knowledge of the social? If we accept that positivism gives an inadequate account of description and explanation, both in science in general and a fortiori in social science, and if we agree that the hermeneutic tradition, too, does not provide adequate criteria of theory choice, there is a further possibility, offered by rationalism, of building up social theory on a priori foundations. But this, as we saw, involves an inevitable shift towards a focus on individual action as both explanans and explanandum. We seem to be left, pending the arrival of some new 'theory of emergence',(75) with an impoverished concept of social structures as the (intended or unintended) consequences of action.(76)

Moreover, it is not at all clear that rationalism provides an adequate account of agency. Is it really enough to say, with Hollis, that 'rational action is its own explanation'?(77) There may be a variety of equally rational choices in a given situation, and even if someone has only one good reason for acting in a certain way, that is not to say that he or she will act in this way or that, if he or she does act in this way, that it will be for this reason. As Alan Ryan has put it, 'The proposition that men act appropriately to their situation or that they act for good reasons, is such an obvious falsehood that it could only be defended as a conceptual truth.'(78)

Roy Bhaskar develops a more adequate alternative view of agency, based, it must be said, on the claim (which Hollis rejects(79)) that reasons are (potential) causes: (80)

> To suppose synthetic a priori that every belief or action has a rationale ... [as Bhaskar has done] is merely to suppose that for every belief or action there is a set of real reasons which, in conjunction with other causes, explains it. It is to suppose that the action is in part the result of a causally efficacious (real) reason, and hence (normally) of some causally efficacious reasoning process. It is neither to suppose (idealistically) that reasons completely explain every action; nor to suppose (rationalistically) that any reasoning process (whether implicit or explicit, unconscious or preconscious) occurring prior to (and in the case of neurotic and automatic actions perhaps long before) the action is valid. If such a reasoning process occurs or has occurred, it figures in an explanation of the action in virtue of its causal adequacy, *not* in virtue of its validity.

The stratification model seems to require that we allow for, at least, both agency and social structure, and that we do not identify the two. As Bhaskar points out, 'the properties possessed by social forms may be very different from those possessed by the individuals upon whose activity they depend'.(81) But if social structures can be said to be real, their properties are qualitatively different from those of natural structures. Bhaskar suggests three major differences:(82)

> (1) Social structures, unlike natural structures, do not exist independently of the activities they govern; (2) Social structures, unlike natural structures, do not exist independently of the agents' conceptions of what they are doing in their activity; (3) Social structures, unlike natural structures, may be only relatively enduring (so that the tendencies they ground may not be universal in the sense of space-time invariant).

I shall discuss Bhaskar's relational conception of the social in more detail in chapter 5. For the present, I shall move on to the epistemological implications of this conception. The chief limit on naturalism, the methodological unity of natural and social science, is not that social structures are not directly perceptible, but that they occur in open systems; theories about them cannot be decisively tested.(83) Second, possibility of measurement in the social sciences is limited by the irreversibility of some of the processes which they study and, more importantly, by the 'conceptual aspect' of their subject matter, which puts a premium on 'precision of meaning rather than accuracy of measurement as the a posteriori arbiter of theory'.(84)

On the other hand, though the social sciences are largely denied the benefits of experimental activity, they have the compensating advantage that 'they are *internal* with respect to their subject matter in a way in which tne natural sciences are not'.(85) Thus many social scientific phenomena are already identified under the descriptions of 'actors', the culture and so forth. The social scientist can build on this in(86)

an attempt at a real definition of a form of social life that has already been identified under a particular description. Note that in the absence of such a definition, and failing a closure, any hypothesis of a causal mechanism is bound to be more or less arbitrary.

Thus in social science attempts at real definitions will in general precede rather than follow successful causal hypotheses - though in both cases they can only be justified empirically, viz. by the revealed explanatory power of the hypotheses that can be deduced from them.

Real definitions of social structures can be generated in a non-arbitrary way by transcendental arguments from pre-scientific descriptions. Marx's 'Capital', for example, 'may most plausibly be viewed as an attempt to establish what must be the case for the experiences grasped by the phenomenal forms of capitalist life to be possible.'(87) Social scientific theories, then, are subject to various 'a priori controls'.(88) For example, neo-classical economic theory may be criticised a priori for failing to provide an adequate account of the reproduction and transformation of its objects.(89) Such an argument is in principle separable from any discussion about empirical testing of the two theories, although the concept of explanatory power should probably cover both. It can be shown, I think, that most intertheoretical conflict in the social sciences is fought out at a level which, if it has to be a priori or empirical, must be the former. It is argued, for example, that functionalism can only generate an impoverished account of social conflict and social change, that 'phenomenological' sociology cannot handle power, that Parsons's concept of power gives no adequate grip on the relation 'power over', and so on.(90)

What about the possibility of empirical testing, the 'measurement' of explanatory power? It is clear enough that in principle, even if we allow incommensurability, we

can rank theories in terms of their explanatory power. As Bhaskar puts it,(91)
> We can ... allow ... that theory Ta is preferable to theory Tb, even if in the terminology of Kuhn and Feyerabend it is 'incommensurable' with it, if theory Ta can explain under its descriptions almost all the phenomena pl ... pn that Tb can explain under its descriptions Bb1 ... Bpn plus some significant phenomena that Tb cannot explain.

The problem, though, is perhaps whether (a) social scientific theories can be formulated with sufficient precision to make comparison possible (the importance of descriptive considerations seems to complicate matters here), and (b) whether it is not more contentious in the social sciences, for these and other reasons, to decide whether something has been explained or not. The charge, for example, that functionalism cannot explain conflict and change is not answered merely by pointing to the work of Coser, Smelser, Parsons and others. The critic's claim is not that functionalists are condemned to silence on these topics, but that they cannot *really* explain them.

Are we forced, then, into abandoning empirical testability and left merely with a priori theory and the 'melting of horizons'? This is, I think, too pessimistic, just as the orthodox view of theory-testing is too sanguine. The following example may help both to bring out some of the difficulties of this question and to point to a guardedly optimistic answer. The example is sufficiently familiar to require only an outline presentation. It is Steven Lukes's concept of power (of which 'one-dimensional', 'two-dimensional' and 'three-dimensional' views are 'alternative interpretations and applications'), 'according to which A exercises power over B when A affects B in a manner contrary to B's interest.'(92) There is nothing in etymology or usage which requires one to define power with reference to interests rather than say, with reference to overt conflict; the claim is rather that this account extends the range of the concept 'further and deeper than others'. Hollis argues(93) that this should be seen as a real definition of power, or, more precisely, of 'power over', and that this account does justice to both of Lukes's claims:
(1) that power is an 'essentially contested concept' and
(2) that reasons can be adduced for choosing one concept rather than another.

This is, I think, an excellent example of the case for real definitions argued by Hollis and Bhaskar. But Lukes does not appear to accept this gloss and defines essential contestability with reference to conflicting values as

Chapter 1

well as conflicting theories.(94) The latter step, which Hollis rejects, is important for Lukes because he accepts a version of ethical relativism but not cognitive relativism.(95) Even so, Lukes argues, essential contestability does not imply relativism. Although unregenerate one- and two-dimensionalists can refuse to accept third-dimensional power, and its associated counterfactual reference to real interests, as an instance of power,(96)
they have to show why. Thus, for example, they have to show why they allow some counterfactual knowledge claims and not others, why they suppose that there must be a behavioural component to the exercise of power, why non-events can constitute neither the source nor the result of an exercise of power.
In an argument strikingly close to the type recommended above by Bhaskar, Lukes argues that the uniquely 'self-concealing tendency' of power implies that theories which restrict themselves to observable phenomena will be necessarily inadequate. He goes on:(97)
Considerations such as these are, I have found, capable of determining the intellects of some, if not of others. The only possible strategy in these circumstances is to bring out the full implications of failing to be thus persuaded. Such a strategy cannot 'substantiate the superiority' of one position against others in the manner of a knock-down proof. But why should we suppose such a proof to be available?
I have discussed this example in some detail because I think it helps to bring out what is often involved in intertheoretical conflict in the social sciences. The naively conceived project of 'measuring' political power in local communities turns out to involve crucial conceptual theoretical and perhaps moral choices. It may be objected that power is special in this respect, for the reason Lukes gives; I can only say here that I do not consider it particularly unusual.
It may be helpful at this point to sketch out a balance-sheet of the similarities and differences between rationalism and realism, both as philosophies of science and as legitimations of types of social theory. Rationalists and realists share Hollis's slogan that recent philosophy of science has 'shown that empirical judgements presuppose theoretical judgements but not ... abolished the need for truth in science'.(98) They diverge, however, on the ways in which truth is to be found; rationalists lay more weight on a priori theory, realists, perhaps, on 'explanatory power'. This divergence is continued into the sorts of social theory which they license: rationalists emphasise theories of rational (individual)

action, while realists may uphold naturalism and talk in terms of structures and mechanisms.(99) A useful indicator of these positions is whether a writer sees reasons as causes. Hollis denies this thesis;(100) Bhaskar affirms it,(101) as do Keat and Urry;(102) while Harré and Secord offer a qualified denial.(103) It is clear, I think, that the realist programme is the more ambitious one,(104) and has prima facie the greater appeal for social scientists.

Finally, it is necessary to ask how far realism in the form discussed here is compatible with Marxism. It is notoriously difficult to pin down Marx's philosophical and metatheoretical beliefs. What is most distinctive, however, about Marx and the tradition which he founded is probably the peculiarly intimate dialectical relationship which he postulates between the methods and concepts of science and the objects of inquiry. This is best illustrated by the notion of critique or criticism, which runs right through Marx's work from the 'Critique of Hegel's Philosophy of Right' to 'Capital', the critique of political economy.

Whatever the differences in style, method and subject matter between these two works, they share the underlying theme that the critique of social reality essentially (though by no means exclusively) involves the parallel critique of its theoretical representation, whether this be Hegel's theory of the state or classical political economy. As Marx wrote in the 'Grundrisse':

> In the succession of economic categories, as in any other historical, social science, it must not be forgotten that the subject, - here, modern bourgeois society - is always what is given, in the head as well as in reality, and that these categories therefore express the forms of being, the characteristics of existence, and often only individual sides of this specific society, this subject.(105)

> The exact development of the concept of capital is necessary ... just as capital itself, whose abstract, reflected image is its concept, is the foundation of bourgeois society. The sharp formulation of the basic presuppositions of this relation must bring out all the contradictions of bourgeois production, as well as the boundary where it drives beyond itself.(106)

There is thus an important sense in which Marx's explanandum in 'Capital' is a conceptual question (though one whose answer required detailed empirical as well as conceptual investigations): 'why labour presents itself in value and is measured via its duration by the value of the product of labour'.(107)

Taken together with his materialism, this strongly suggests that Marx is committed to some sort of realist philosophy of science which treats theoretical statements as being about real objects, structures and processes in the world,(108) since in the absence of some such relation between theory and reality it is difficult to see how these 'critiques' could have the explanatory power which Marx ascribes to them. But this is not, of course, an empirical realism; Marx makes great play of the distinction between essence and appearance, insisting that 'all science would be superfluous if the outward appearance and the essence of things directly coincided'.(109)

This realism may, however, be in tension with the more 'activist' position which Marx seems at times to adopt, in the 'Theses on Feuerbach' and elsewhere and which is pushed to an extreme point by Kolakowski in 'Karl Marx and the Classical Definition of Truth'.(110) Here the emphasis is on the constitution of 'the world' as an object of knowledge. However, one should not assume too readily that this is incompatible with realism, since realists themselves assert the possibility of alternative descriptions and levels of description.(111)

It is clear, however, that this tension is felt by Marxist writers as different as Jürgen Habermas, for whom reality is constituted as an object of knowledge via transcendental cognitive interests, and the authors of 'Marx's Capital and Capitalism Today', who stress the gap between discourse and the world and arrive at a position which seems to have affinities with pragmatism in both the epistemological and the political sense.(112) The most developed expression of this tension in discussions of concept formation occurs in Adorno's work, and especially in 'Negative Dialectics'. For Adorno, the realist postulate survives only as a utopian point of reference for a method of critique which compares phenomena with the implications embodied in their concepts.(113) In this philosophy of non-identity, 'the words we use will remain concepts. Their precision substitutes for the thing itself,without quite bringing its selfhood to mind; there is a gap between the words and the things they conjure.' (114)

The example of Marx raises again the general problem to which I referred at the beginning of this chapter, that of the relationship between philosophies of (social) science and social theories. The philosophies themselves, as we have seen, are clusters of views with a family resemblance rather than tightly structured, mutually exclusive positions. It is not to be expected that a particular social theorist will be unambiguously assignable to one or other

of these clusters. It is noticeable, in fact, that when
sociologists do label themselves as positivists or (social)
phenomenologists, they tend to over-conform to these positions and produce somewhat grotesque exaggerations of them.
  This does not mean, however, that the attempt to cate-
gorise social theorists in these terms is a waste of time.
We have seen that discussion of whether Marx was a 'realist' takes one to the heart of one of the most important
divides within Marxology and, more importantly, in subsequent Marxist theory. Similarly, I think it can be shown
that Durkheim's work is torn between realism and empiricism and that one's understanding of Durkheim's sociology
is enhanced if one pays attention to this conflict.(115)
Weber's work, likewise, is illuminated by Bhaskar's distinction between classical empiricism and transcendental
idealism, and his argument that both are committed to a
doctrine of empirical realism.(116)

4 CONCLUSION

In this extremely brief survey of what I take to be the
main alternative philosophical views one can take of science in general, and social science in particular, I have
tried to show that neither positivism nor hermeneutics
can offer rational criteria for the choice of concepts.
Positivism, at least in its later, holistic form, reform-
ulates the question as one of theory-choice and denies
the possibility of rational discussion at a less holistic
level than that of whole theories.(Realism, if it ties
itself to the notion of explanatory power, seems to be
taking the same direction, though its notion of explanation is significantly different.) The only variant of
positivism which escapes this problem is a radical empiricism which sets up at least a necessary condition for
successful concepts: that they be clearly related to
observables. But this position has its own problems which
led to its decisive rejection within the positivist tradition itself.
  The hermeneutic tradition leaves us with only a choice
between 'interpretations'. This might not be held to
matter, in the sense that we are not entirely unable to
say which interpretations of, say, a literary work are
more plausible than others, but it seems to imply a certain conservatism: we are trapped within the illusion of
the epoch without even the hope of making our escape by
bumping up against empirical data. As in the case of
positivism, there is a way out corresponding to radical
empiricism: this is the view that the actor's accounts are

Chapter 1

incorrigible, that the concepts of the social scientist must exactly match those of the actor. But this, too, seems to involve an intolerable relativism and would render any kind of social science redundant. Realism and rationalism, whatever their internal differences, share the promise of a more hopeful future, though it is not clear that their solutions are more than verbal ones. But these two birds in the bush are more appealing than the sorry mess of feathers and bones left by traditional positivistic and hermeneutic metatheories of social science. Some doubts are raised in this chapter and elsewhere in this book about the limits which the rationalist programme seems to impose on the social sciences. The rest of the book will therefore attempt to outline some possible advantages of adopting a realist perspective, by comparing it with other accounts.

2 Concepts in science

In this chapter I shall discuss the following three questions:
 (a) What concepts are (to be) used?
 (b) What definitions, etc. are (to be) given to them?
 (c) How are these concepts (to be) related to ordinary usage?

I shall also try to link the traditions identified at a very general level in the introduction with more specific theoretical currents within the social sciences. First, though, I shall briefly raise the general question of the relationship between language and science.

LANGUAGE AND SCIENCE

Science, especially social science, is expressed most of the time in natural languages.(1) Opinions vary as to whether this is an important feature of science and whether it is an advantage or a disadvantage. There is a widespread view, particularly strong among positivists, that it is not an essential feature of science that it be expressed in a natural language; this is as irrelevant to the content of scientific propositions as is the question of whether they are expressed in English or in French. In so far as natural languages are relevant to the context of discovery and the dissemination of science, it is as a potential source of confusion.

Pareto, for example, clearly saw ordinary language as a threat to scientific understanding:(2)

> To avoid in these volumes the danger, ever threatening to the social sciences, that meanings of words will be persistently sought not in the objective definitions supplied but in common usage and etymology, we would gladly have replaced word-labels with letters of the

alphabet - or with ordinal numbers .... We have refrained from doing so more often in fear lest our argument become altogether too tedious and obscure. The stronger a writer's commitment to positivism, the more likely he or she is to take this attitude to semantic questions.(3) George Lundberg, for example, enthusiastically upheld what has been called the Humpty-Dumpty theory of meaning: 'To the scientist ... words have whatever meaning is assigned to them.'(4) More sophisticated positivists, such as Lazarsfeld and Boudon, stress the need for terms, whether they are invented or taken from ordinary language, to be incorporated in formal systems which give them their meaning.(5)

Like other tenets of positivism, this robust view of the relationship between language and science is difficult to reconcile with the history of science, where the importance of language has long been recognised. The close relationship between Greek science and language to which Gadamer has alluded(6) was pointed out earlier by, for example, J.S. Mill(7) and F.A. Trendelenburg.(8) Ernst Cassirer, in an article on The Influence of Language upon the Development of Scientific Thought, defends Aristotle against their strictures.(9)

> He could scarcely distrust that general scheme of thought which was imposed upon him by the structure of Greek language. We must bear in mind the fact that the distinction between different types of languages is a very late attainment of philosophical and linguistic thought. Wilhelm von Humboldt was the first to give a systematic survey of the various types of language.

Maurice Crosland has shown that:(10)

> The importance of language in the history of chemistry is not merely a twentieth-century idea conceived under the influence of the philosophical school of linguistic analysis; it has always been insisted on by chemists themselves, men like Robert Boyle in the seventeenth century, Torbern Bergman in the eighteenth century and Berzelius in the nineteenth century.

Lavoisier, too, wholeheartedly accepted Condillac's assertion that 'the progress of the sciences depends entirely on the progress of their language'.(11) He soon found, however, that his project of producing a 'New System of Chemical Nomenclature' implied the resolution of substantive problems as well: 'While I proposed to myself nothing more than to improve the chemical language, my work transformed itself by degrees, without my being able to prevent it, into a treatise on the Elements of Chemistry.'(12)

In our social sciences, the case for paying attention

to language is perhaps even stronger. Baldamus argues that:(13)
> The only way in which we can fix our attention on changes in the qualitative content of theorising is to look at the history of the verbal-terminological substance of theoretical concepts. Here it is immediately clear that intractable discontinuities, in contrast to structural developments as in the history of mathematical logic, are the characteristic feature. Even the highest-level concepts, such as value, rationality, social constraint, society, social relations, social class, social norm, soziales Handeln, power, dominance, legitimacy, organisation etc. are contaminated by changing cultural connotations to such an extent that it is impossible to trace long-term continuities.... Moreover the development of sociology is riddled with verbal innovations of a very fast rate of *obsolescence*.

A magnificent example of the way in which attention to language can illuminate substantive studies is Stanislaw Ossowski's 'Class Structure in the Social Consciousness'. (14) In chapter XI, Semantic Conventions Considered as Social Facts, Ossowski makes the point, abundantly supported by the rest of the book, that 'in the humanities and the social sciences semantic conventions are not normally neutral in relation to material problems; semantic differences are usually a symptom of differences which reach into the core of the matter'.(15)

Ossowski goes on to draw a crucial distinction between 'terminological divergences' and 'conceptual differences': (16)
> Terminological differences occur when we are employing the same concepts but refer to them by means of different and translatable terms. For instance, Adam Smith called his three basic groups in the social structure 'orders', while Marx, when he accepted Adam Smith's division in the third volume of *Das Kapital*, called the same groups the three basic 'classes'. Here we are dealing with a difference of terminology only....
> A second and far more important category of the differences we are considering is to be found in situations where the same term refers to different concepts with similar but not identical extensions.

Ossowski's distinction is taken up in almost the same words by William E. Connolly, in 'Political Science and Ideology'.(17) Connolly goes on to discuss and reject a solution which is often proposed for conceptual disputes - in this case, over 'power'.(18)

An observer might suggest that the dispute be circumvented by applying a different term to each of the overlapping concepts now covered by the term 'power' and then deciding which concepts are applicable to given political situations. But such a suggestion misses a central problem. The conceptual dispute exists *because* we have found no adequate means of deciding which concepts best fit the decision-making process in contemporary politics.

Connolly also makes some interesting remarks about the subterranean influence of concepts which(19)

exert an impact on one's perceptions and interpretations but are not part of the individual's consciously articulated conceptual equipment. He may have implicit notions of what is properly part of 'the political', for example, and this underlying concept will guide his selections and definition of problems in ways he does not fully recognise.

Somewhat earlier, Connolly introduces the notion of alternative 'vocabularies':(20)

Concepts of class, conflict, manipulation, domination, alienation and mass are likely to be pivotal in a vocabulary of dissatisfaction: concepts of stratum, consensus, persuasion, authority, personal maladjustment and public are likely to form the corresponding pivots in a vocabulary of satisfaction.

From talking about 'vocabularies', there is an easy slide to talking about 'languages', as Feyerabend does in 'Against Method':(21)

I ... believe that scientific theories, such as Aristotle's theory of motion, the theory of relativity, the quantum theory, classical and modern cosmology are sufficiently general, sufficiently 'deep' and have developed in sufficiently complex ways to be considered along the same lines as natural languages.

It would not do to take this analogy too seriously; indeed it is not clear exactly what Feyerabend means by it, but is none the less a suggestive analogy. When one puts down a Marxist text and picks up a functionalist or ethnomethodological one, it is easy to believe that one has moved from one linguistic universe into another. Whether this is a helpful way of thinking about differences between sociological paradigms is, of course, another matter.(22) What is beyond question, I think, is the central and ineradicable role of language in scientific thought, something which is recognised in such diverse traditions as linguistic philosophy, the hermeneutics of Heidegger and Gadamer (23) and, in a rather different way, in Adorno's immanent method'.(24)

28 Chapter 2

(a) WHAT CONCEPTS ARE TO BE USED?

An answer to this question may take the form of prescribing certain concepts or kinds of concept, proscribing certain concepts or kinds of concept, or, perhaps most commonly, both. The prescriptions or proscriptions may be explicitly normative or may be presented in the indicative mood; this I take to be a relatively trivial rhetorical difference in this context. A more significant difference is between absolute prescriptions or, more often, proscriptions, and those which prescribe the 'reduction' or relativisation of a certain set of concepts to another set.

An example of an absolute proscription is Marx's rejection of the concept 'value of Labour' as 'an expression as imaginary as the value of the earth'(25) and 'price of labour' as 'just as irrational as a yellow logarithm'.(26) A relative proscription can be seen in Marx's more usual reformulation of bourgeois economic categories, in which the concept of capital, for example, is construed not as 'a thing, but rather a definite social production relation'.(27) Weber reduces the state, 'sociologically understood', to a complex of actions of a state-regarding kind, as part of his general reductionist approach to holistic concepts.(28) Durkheim, finally, places an absolute ban on the explanation of social phenomena in terms of psychological phenomena(29) and prescribes instead the use of terms denoting social facts. A relative prescription will often be merely the other side of a partial, reductionist proscription - for example Carnap's attempt to establish physical thing-language as the reduction basis of all scientific language.(30) 'Relative' here means relative to a particular level, that of the reduction-basis; a very different sort of relative prescription would be one which recommended the use of a concept on a purely heuristic basis. These distinctions, I should emphasise, are themselves merely introduced for purposes of clarification. Nothing important turns on their use at this stage of the discussion, though they do, of course, make oblique reference to substantive issues such as reductionism, emergence and so on.

Most prescriptions and proscriptions at the level of general theory, of course, are of classes of concepts rather than individual ones. The most dramatic involve the prescription of an entire language for one or more sciences. This may be a language in a strong sense, constructed ex nihilo (though not necessarily without making use of existing natural languages, mathematical and logical symbolism, etc.). Alternatively, it may just involve the purification of an existing set of terms. In an optional further step, some terms may be endowed with a transcendental status.

I shall now discuss briefly four views of these questions arising out of, respectively, logical positivism, linguistic philosophy, rationalism and Marxism.

Logical positivism was strongly in favour of linguistic innovation(31) and the construction of more adequate language systems. This attitude was based on admiration of the new 'language' of logic and mathematics developed by Frege, Russell and Whitehead, coupled with a classically empiricist mistrust of the contamination of experiential reports by the language in which they are expressed. The concept of protocol sentences was designed to avoid such contamination and achieve a bedrock of hard, purely descriptive data. We have already noted the positivists' relativisation of the philosophical 'languages' of materialism, idealism and so on; reducibility was to assure the descriptive foundation of all valid scientific propositions.

It was Neurath who pushed this idea to the extreme of urging the creation of a new, purified language for the sciences.(32) Carnap seems to have been content to rely on reducibility in principle.(33) And in time, as we saw in chapter 1, this iconoclastic approach was routinised to the distinction between 'theoretical' and 'observational' terms.(34)   Only Neurath, then, was committed to giving a substantive answer to the question 'what concepts?', and even he did not do so in practice. The orthodox positivist response to the question is a formal one; there are two classes of concept: observational and theoretical.

If logical positivism was sympathetic to linguistic innovation and reform, subject, of course, to the avoidance of metaphysics, there is a more conservative emphasis in linguistic philosophy and Gadamer's hermeneutics. J.L. Austin provides the following rationale for giving close attention to ordinary language:(35)

our common stock of words embodies all the distinctions men have found worth drawing, and the connexions they have found worth making, in the lifetimes of many generations: these surely are likely to be more numerous, more sound, since they have stood up to the long test of survival of the fittest, and more subtle, at least in all ordinary and reasonably practical matters than any that you or I are likely to think up in our armchairs of an afternoon - the most favoured alternative method.

Austin's demand for attention to ordinary usage was not unqualified: 'ordinary language is not the last word: in principle it can everywhere be supplemented and improved upon and superseded. Only remember, it *is* the *first* word. (36) He can, however, be seen as encouraging the idea that the social sciences can get a long way without straying far from the concepts and explanatory principles which are used in ordinary life. This approach was most significant in the UK in the late 1950s and early 1960s in philosophical psychology.(37) A rather more strident version was advanced by Harré and Secord.(38) Ordinary language, they wrote, 'is well adapted for explaining a pattern of social interaction in terms of reasons and rules .... The conceptual system embedded in ordinary language should provide the basis for the concepts employed in a realistic psychology.'(39)

Ethnomethodology, of which Harré and Secord broadly approve, adds a further dimension to this approach. Here, the social world is constituted by the interpretations or 'glossing practices' of its members.(40) There is a fundamental distinction between the social world and the natural world, and the important analogy,in this account at least, is not between natural science and social science but between (natural) science and everyday knowledge of the social:(41)

> Just as a scientific language assembles a corpus of scientific knowledge which provides the routine grounds for making scientific sense of the world, so natural language assembles a corpus of everyday commonsense knowledge which provides the routine grounds of inference and interpretation commonly available to lay members for making sense of the world.

This account therefore 'raises all members of the world to the status of sociological observers of it in which no one group can claim to have privileged access to an understanding of it'.(42)

A more strident conservatism can be found in the work of Gadamer, who, like Heidegger, rejects the instrumental use of language(43) and is suspicious of the very idea of scientific concept formation and 'the methodical alienation [Verfremdung] that comprises the very essence of modern science'.(44) Although he warns us not to understand 'truth' and 'method' as mutually exclusive, he is concerned with a form of truth 'that goes questioningly behind all knowledge [Wissenschaft] and anticipatingly before it'.(45)

Science is distinct from and ultimately subordinate to the broader, mundane consciousness with which hermeneutics is concerned. The two coexist in a sort of necessary tension which is mediated by language. Natural languages have their own way of describing the world:

The organisation of words and things, that is undertaken by each language in its own way, always constitutes a primary natural formation of concepts that is a long way from the system of the scientific formation of concepts. It follows entirely the human aspect of things, the system of man's needs and interests. What a linguistic community regards as important about a thing can be given a common name with other things that are perhaps of a quite different nature in other respects, so long as they all have the same quality that is important to the community. A nomenclature ... in no way corresponds to the concepts of science and its classificatory system of genus and species. Rather, compared with the latter, it is often accidental attributes from which the general meaning of a word is derived.(46)

There is a positive connection between the factuality of language and man's capacity for science. We can see this particularly clearly in the science of the ancient world, the specific merit and the specific weakness of which was that it originated in the linguistic experience of the world. In order to overcome this weakness, its naive anthropocentrism, modern science has also renounced its merit, namely its place in the natural attitude of man to the world. The concept of 'theory' can illustrate this very well.... Ancient theoria is not a means in the same [modern, RWO] sense, but the end itself, the highest manner of being human.(47)
This difference is exemplified in the nature of the concepts used:
in modern scientific usage a concept is more artificial and hence more fixed than in the ancient world, which did not have any foreign words and few artificial ones.(48)

What is a technical term? A word, the meaning of which is univocally defined, in as much as it signifies a defined concept. A technical term is always something artificial in so far as either the word itself is artificially formed or - as is more frequent - a word that is already in use has the variety and breadth of its meanings excised and is assigned only one particular conceptual meaning. In contrast with the living meaning of the words in spoken language, to which, as Wilhelm von Humboldt rightly showed, a certain range of variation is essential, the terminological use of the word is an act of violence against language.(49)

For Gadamer, then, scientific concept formation is a fundamentally ambiguous activity, which may be inevitable but must nevertheless be subordinated to hermeneutic awareness.

So far we have found not so much prescriptions or proscriptions of concepts, as general views about their construction. A further dimension is provided by the attempts to distinguish, within social scientific concepts in general, a restricted class of transcendental categories which are constitutive of the very possibility of social theory. The Austro-Marxists, in keeping with their Kantian inheritance, were sympathetic to this view. Max Adler, for example, claims, in an argument which I shall present in greater detail in chapter 3,(50) that 'sociality' is an a priori certainty for us, built into the categories of our thought in the same way as space and time.

Rene König has developed this idea within an otherwise orthodox positivist framework, arguing for the transcendental status of concepts such as 'social action, collective representations or normative expectations, the sociocultural person, role, group, etc., etc.'(51) In a later article,(52) König developed these ideas somewhat further. He stressed that categories in his sense had nothing to do with classificatory features ('Klassifikationsmerkmale'). Classification is always provisional and hypothetical,(53) whereas the main function of these categories is 'the systematic definition and transcendental description of the dimension of reality in which all possible objects of sociological investigation are located'.(54)

The sort of theoretical strategy König has in mind becomes clearer when he goes on to discuss Parsons. The introduction to 'The Social System', in which Parsons says that he is concerned with the 'exposition and illustration' of a 'conceptual scheme', 'for the analysis of social systems in terms of the action frame of reference' is, says König, exactly what he means by a 'soziologische Kategorienlehre'. Parsons, however, misunderstands his own enterprise by presenting this attempt 'as a "theoretical scheme" that subsequently needs to be empirically tested'. According to König, Parsons's system is not independent of substantive sociological theory and research - indeed its function is to unite and complete such work - but it is not itself testable. König refers here to Weber's quadripartite typology of action and to Parsons's own pattern variables; and indeed one is reminded of Weber's assertion that ideal types are not themselves hypotheses, but means to the construction of hypotheses. (55)

König's treatment of these issues is extremely brief.

One important ambiguity concerns the sort of concepts which are to be awarded this categorial status. 'Social action', of course; but what about 'role distance' or the 'trickle effect'? König merely hints at the sort of concepts which would *not* be acceptable as sociological categories: Parsons's 'Social System' was criticised by some contemporary reviewers(56) for not using concepts such as those of primary and secondary groups which were well established in empirical sociology. But Parsons was right not to incorporate them, since they were not generated and sustained by his own conceptual scheme. 'The incorporation of such concepts into a system of categories would have been ... mere "dogmatism"; a "critical" analysis has to go further than this.'(57) This suggests, though the reference is extremely brief, that what counts is not the level of generality of the concepts, but whether or not they are logically integrated into a conceptual system.

König's approach seems to have two main dangers. First, the problem which faces any transcendentalist approach, that particular concepts, once elevated to the status of categories, will be treated with excessive respect and resist attempts to transcend and relativise them. Second, he seems to be in danger of conducting the sort of reification of the 'sociological' perspective which Marxist critics, in particular, have perceived in much sociological work from Durkheim onwards. But whatever one's judgment about these problems and whether or not one can stomach the transcendental language which König uses, he has undoubtedly identified an important aspect of the way in which certain sociological concepts have frequently been used and in particular the kind of status which has been implicitly attributed to them. In other words, there is a recognition, which elsewhere is mainly confined to interpretative sociologists and Marxists (especially 'critical' theorists), of the importance of conceptual questions in social theory.

Rationalist social theories, as we have seen in chapter 1, tend to ascribe a similar transcendental status to, for example, the category of rationality. This, however, seems unfortunate, since it conflicts with the fact that we often want to find out if someone acted rationally or reasonably in a particular situation. If one restricts the claim to 'autonomous' actions(58) or, in the formulation suggested to me by Roy Edgley, makes the weaker claim that an action is simply something done for a reason (which may be a good or bad reason), this may not be enough to sustain a recognisably rationalist programme in social science. And if the rationalist tries to extend this status to other concepts of social science, this seems to make things worse. Roy Bhaskar offers a more limited and plausible account of the role of a priori theory.(59) This may be seen as according transcendental status to the concepts of social structure and of agency, in addition to those required by philosophical analysis of science in general.

In the works of Marx and Engels there is not, so far as I am aware, any systematic attempt to prescribe a set of concepts or to proscribe another set. There are, of course, frequent attacks on the speculative abstractions of Hegelian philosophy and classical political economy, where Marx urges that one should instead focus on 'real, active men', and the specific features of capitalist society. But the idea of starting one's investigation from some privileged set of concepts is not one which appealed to Marx, as is shown by his hostile comments on A. Wagner's gloss on his work:(60)

> In the first place [De prime abord], I do not start out from 'concepts'.... What I start out from is the simplest social form in which the labour-product is presented in contemporary society, and this is the 'commodity'. I analyse it, and right from the beginning, in the form in which it appears.

There is, however, something disingenuous about Marx's objection, since he is clearly starting from a concept of the commodity. The distinction he seems to have in mind is between abstract concepts, with no real relation to reality, and the phenomenal forms 'in which the phenomena of the external world 'represent themselves' in people's experience'.(61) Marx's characteristic mode of operation is to move from such forms to the essential relations 'whose existence explains why phenomena should take such forms'.(62) The distinction between the concepts of phenomenal forms and real relations corresponds in part to the positivist distinction between observational and theoretical terms, but with the proviso that Marx's distinction is not an abstract opposition of two sets of terms, but one which is grounded in the specific mechanisms of the reality under investigation. This does not mean that Marx's account of concept formation is unproblematic; we shall see later that he can be presented as giving a highly idiosyncratic reply to my second main question - the kind of specification that can be given to concepts. But there is a recent version of Marxism which does have a great deal to say about concepts: that centred on the work of Louis Althusser. Even if, as I think, this work is ultimately inadequate as an account of Marx and as an attempt to develop Marxist theory, it has a certain intrinsic interest.

The work of Althusser and his co-authors in 'Reading Capital'(63) is essentially a philosophical answer to the question 'How is Marxism possible?'.(64) Their answer, in outline, is this: by selecting the right concepts and articulating them within the right framework (problematic). This answer corresponds to (and perhaps derives from) their theory of knowledge: knowledge is not a relation between a knowing subject and a known object, but rather an effect produced by a set of concepts which make it possible to 'think' certain facts or states of affairs and not others. This is best illustrated by the heavy sarcasm which Althusser directs in the Preface ('From "Capital" to Marx's philosophy') at the idea that Marx simply 'saw' things which the classical economists had failed to see. (65)

Since a problematic consists of concepts and their articulations, it can be partially specified in terms of individual concepts; this is what Balibar does, for example, in part III of 'Reading Capital', in his essay on the fundamental concepts of historical materialism, centred on the concept of mode of production. But these concepts change their nature according to the different structures in which they are incorporated in the analysis of different modes of production. Concepts like labour-power or property, do not directly refer to(66)

> the elements of a construction, the atoms of a history. In reality ... these concepts designate the elements of the construction only mediately. What I have called the 'differential analysis of forms' is an essential intermediate step in the determination of the historical forms taken by labour-power, property, 'real appropriation', etc.

But with these qualifications about the complexity of the enterprise, it seems that Balibar sees the elucidation of the complete set of historical materialist concepts as a worthwhile aspiration.(67) This threatens to return Marxism to the sort of scholasticism to which Marx objected in Wagner and the rest of the German professoriat.

To round off this section, I should say something about Durkheim and Weber, whose approach to concept formation will be more systematically discussed elsewhere.

Neither of these writers prescribes a specific set of concepts,(68) though each of them has a preferred ontological frame of reference according to which such concepts should be constructed - 'social facts' for Durkheim, 'social action' for Weber. Just what ontological claims are involved in defining sociology as the study of social facts and action respectively, and how far these claims contradict one another, is a question to be discussed later.

36 Chapter 2

   Both Durkheim and Weber, as we shall see in a later
section, envisage the sociologist departing somewhat from
everyday usage in the construction of his or her concepts;
but whereas Weber sees this as a 'one-sided accentuation'
or 'idealisation' of certain features of empirical reality
so as to produce ideal-typical concepts,(69) Durkheim prescribes a more radical break with 'pre-scientific' concepts: 'We need, rather, to formulate entirely new concepts, appropriate to the requirements of science and
expressed in an appropriate terminology.'(70)

(b) WHAT DEFINITIONS OR OTHER SPECIFICATIONS ARE TO BE
     GIVEN TO OUR CONCEPTS?

This section is divided into four parts:
(1) A brief discussion of the types of definition identified by philosophers and their affinities with more general philosophical orientations.
(2) Positivist accounts of the place of definition in
science.
(3) Anti-positivist accounts, mainly arising from
        (a) post-Wittgensteinian analytic philosophy
        (b) hermeneutics
        (c) critical theory
        (d) rationalism and realism.
(4) A brief account of some sociological theorists not
discussed in earlier parts.

(1) Two concepts of definition

It is customary in philosophical logic to distinguish nominal definitions and real definitions. Nominal definitions may be 'lexical', i.e. statements of usage (a 'fau-
cet' is American usage for a 'tap') or stipulative, applying Humpty Dumpty's principle to things. ('Whatsoever
Adam called every living creature, that was the name
thereof.')(71) Real definitions, by contrast, claim to
do more than report linguistic usage (lexical) or announce
the speaker's intended usage (stipulative); they charact-
eristically(72) express some truth-functional claim about
the nature of something (e.g. 'a whale is a mammal').
They are in some sense about things rather than just about
words.
   This distinction is not entirely clear-cut, as Robinson
is at pains to emphasise (in perhaps a rather strained
way):(73)
     Words are immensely important to us ... [and second,]

... are essentially means by which *humans* deal with *things*, so that a sentence about words is necessarily also a sentence about humans and things.... The statement that 'hyle' means wood is as much about words as any statement can be, but it is also about the ancient Greeks and about wood.
Moreover, the two sorts of definition are not alternatives, since a real definition presupposes a nominal definition of the definiendum:(74)
If the sentence 'x is yz' expresses a significant real definition, then the word 'x' in this sentence must mean something, and not more than one thing, to the hearer apart from the predicate. For if the word 'x' does not mean anything to him before the sentence is uttered, it is not a real definition but a nominal definition of the word 'x', while if the word 'x' means more than one thing in this sentence, it is a muddle.
For Robinson, the term 'real definition' is itself a muddle:(75)
I conclude that the notion of a real definition is a confusion of at least the following twelve activities:
1) Searching for an identical meaning in all the applications of an ambiguous word
2) Searching for essences
3) Describing a form and giving it a name
4) Defining a word, while mistakenly thinking that one is not talking about words
5) Apprehending a tautology determined by a nominal definition
6) Searching for a cause
7) Searching for a key that will explain a mass of facts
8) Adopting and recommending ideals [76]
9) Abstracting, i.e. coming to recognise a form
10) Analysing, i.e. coming to realise that a certain form is a certain point of a certain complex of forms
11) Synthesising, i.e. coming to realise that a certain form is a certain part of a certain complex form
12) Improving one's concepts.
I conclude, secondly, that we had better drop the term 'real definition' and call each of the twelve different activities that 'real definition' has meant by a specific name, and confine the term 'definition' to nominal definitions.
Robinson seems to me excessively fastidious. We must, however, recognise that it is often not quite clear whether we are being offered a real definition or a nominal definition. Robinson cites Mill's definition of justice at

the end of 'Utilitarianism': 'It reads like a real definition; but Mill in his *Logic* denied the occurrence of real definition.'(77) Another example, which I shall discuss later, is Weber's definition of the 'basic concepts of sociology'. And a third example, which brings us close to the theme of the next part of this discussion, is Bertrand Russell.

Russell and Whitehead provide a classical account of stipulative definition: 'A definition is a declaration that a certain newly introduced symbol is to mean ... it is not true or false, being the expression of a volition, not of a proposition'.(78) But there also seems to be in Russell's concept of 'analysis' a theory of real definitions 'in which the properties of a given complex are enumerated'.(79) Now if a specialist like Russell can be so ambiguous about the accounts of definition which he offers, it is hardly surprising that social scientists should generate the same ambiguities. What is fairly clear, though, is that real definitions involve higher stakes than nominal definitions; as Robert Bierstedt put it, 'in order to arrive at real definitions it is necessary to leave the level of verbal or conceptual analysis and enter the field of social research'.(80) And this provides us with an important clue to what sort of definition a social scientist is likely to be appealing to: 'Those who hold the view that definition should come at the end have real definition much more in mind than nominal definition.'(81) The sciences in general, and the social sciences in particular, for reasons indicated in the first part of this chapter, are characteristically involved in terminological disputes which are more than merely terminological, and proposals to escape from these disputes by definitional fiat have been naively conceived and never successfully carried out.

Finally, I must draw attention to the connection, obscure though it often is, between nominal vs real definitions and the broader philosophical opposition between realism and nominalism (including phenomenalism and conventionalism). This, as Baldamus suggests, is a controversy which deserves more attention in its bearing on social theory.(82) Baldamus makes some suggestive comments about Tönnies, Marx and Parsons and suggests that a trend towards nominalism in late nineteenth-century sociology is paralleled by one in probability theory. Max Scheler, in 'Die Wissensformen und die Gesellschaft', had adumbrated a sociology of nominalism, 'the nominalistic way of thinking which is linked to every intellectual revolution against an old and ossified intellectual world'. (83) In an unpublished manuscript appended to the book, he applies this to Weber.(84)

Many positivist philosophers of science, as we shall see in the next section, considered that they had transcended such traditional antitheses as that between realism and nominalism. Their inclinations are generally nominalistic, at least at the level of definitions; indeed some commentators would claim that nominalism is a definitional characteristic of positivism.(85) But there was an anti-positivist current within American sociology between the wars making a rather inexplicit, but none the less powerful claim for a less nominalist approach to definitional questions.(86) This was strengthened after the war in the 'second phase' of analytic philosophy(87) and the revival of rationalist and realist approaches finally provided a clear philosophical rationale for anti-nominalist themes.(88)

(2) Positivism and definitions

We have already noted the positivists' characteristic suspicion of 'bewitchment' by language and their strongly instrumental attitude to language; this sustains not only the ability to switch at will between materialistic and idealistic 'language', as one might switch from German to English, but also the freedom to perform analytic 'reductions'. (By way of contrast, no one who attaches great significance to the linguistic structuring of the Lebenswelt is going to be happy with the idea that social predicates could be reduced to physical thing-language.)

Positivists have taken different views about the question of definition - the main question being whether they can usefully be laid down by fiat (as Lundberg argued(89)) or whether the clear and precise concepts which were generally agreed to be desirable could emerge only from a more long-winded process of formalisation in a deductive system.(90) There was also general agreement that what one wanted to avoid was a scholastic exchange of purely verbal definitions and assertions - one way to do this was to leave aside all questions of definition until the theoretical principles of the science in question were thoroughly established. Walter Eucken adopted this position in opposition to what he called 'conceptual' or 'formal' economics (Begriffsnationalökonomie).(91) Freud, too, defended himself against the charge that it was(92)

> impossible to take a science seriously whose most general concepts are as lacking in precision as those of libido and of instinct in psycho-analysis....
> The fundamental concepts or most general ideas in any of the disciplines of science are always left

indeterminate at first and are only explicated to begin with by reference to the realm of phenomena from which they were derived; it is only by means of a progressive analysis of the material of observation that they can be made clear and can find a significant consistent meaning.

Turning now to more classically positivist writers, it is important not to suggest that they line up solidly in favour of nominal definitions and against real definitions. Hempel, for example, discusses both even-handedly,(93) and recommends Carnap's 'explications' as a species of real definition:(94)

An explication sentence does not simply exhibit the commonly accepted meaning of the expression under study but rather proposes a specified new and precise meaning of it.

Explications, having the nature of proposals, cannot be qualified as being either true or false. Yet they are by no means a matter of arbitrary convention, for they have to satisfy two major requirements: first, the explicative reinterpretations of a term, or - as is often the case - of a set of related terms, must permit us to reformulate, in sentences of a syntactically precise form, at least a large part of what is customarily expressed[95] by means of the terms under construction. Second, it should be possible to develop, in terms of the restricted concepts, a comprehensive, rigorous, and sound theoretical system.

One should note the characterisation of explications as 'proposals' without a truth-value and the extensionalist concept of meaning. But men like Carnap, Hempel and Nagel were remarkably undogmatic in their treatment of definition, probably because of their scientific knowledge.

Their views on definition, then, have to be looked at in a broader context of the distinction between theoretical and empirical terms and the connection between them. (96) It may, however, be suggested that classical positivism provided a favourable environment for vulgar positivists like Lundberg to simplify these questions into the mere injunction to define one's concept ab initio; (97) a view which found expression in rather quaint attempts to achieve a consensus on definitions among sociologists, historians, etc.(98) A full account of this whole orientation would have to discuss the reception of Bridgeman's operationalism, Ogden and Richards's 'Meaning of Meaning' and in a more eccentric vein, Korzybski's 'non-Aristotelian semantics'.(99) It would not, however, be particularly fruitful.

41 Chapter 2

(3) Non-positivist views of definition

'Who can define a dog?' (Whewell)
I referred earlier (100) to the more or less visceral
opposition of Blumer to Lundberg. Blumer raised doubts
of a basically hermeneutic sort which have a long history.
(101) One can plausibly argue that social reality is not
such that it can be precisely captured by exact concepts
with agreed definitions or formal theoretical schemes and/
or that agreed definitions, even if desirable in theory,
presuppose a degree of agreement among social researchers
which, for good reasons, does not exist. As Natanson put
it in a passage quoted earlier:(102)
> The reason that the vocabularies of social scientists
> cannot be cleared up in some concerted operation and
> rendered uniform is that terminology is most often the
> reflection of an implicit Weltanschauung. Furthermore,
> the reluctance of many theoreticians and methodologists
> with regard to adopting a kind of theoretical Esperanto
> is rooted in the fact that among them there are serious
> philosophical differences. Language can reflect under-
> lying consensus; it cannot create it.

For those taking this sort of view, the Committee on
Conceptual Integration had its equivalent in the more descriptive lexicographic undertakings of Waxweiler, von
Wiese and Eubank.(103) In the Anglo-Saxon world, a non-
positivist approach to definition gained a powerful stim-
ulus from Wittgenstein's critique of definitions and from
other anti-positivist currents in European thought.

(a) Analytic philosophy

Michael Scriven and Steven Toulmin have developed, within
the philosophy of science, some of the insights of the
analytical tradition of conceptual analysis or, as Scriven
calls it, 'content analysis':
> Content analysis is undertaken in the belief that the
> meaning of terms or concepts or logical problems can
> only be thoroughly understood if we include a meticu-
> lous examination of the circumstances in which they
> occur, rather than relying on a relatively rapidly
> extracted formalisation of their apparent internal
> logical features. The content analyst's viewpoint as
> thus stated has two important corollaries. First, it
> regards the rigour of symbolic logic as partly spurious;
> for the problems of analysis with which we are faced
> concern already existing concepts and problems, and
> experience makes very clear that these are not governed

42 Chapter 2

> by rigorous rules and definitions.... Second, it views
> the utility of symbolic logic as partly illusory; the
> chief claim for symbolic logic - that it provides a
> means of *avoiding* as well as solving problems - is held
> to rest on the mistaken belief that a language can in
> general be rich enough to perform the tasks required of
> it without containing the traps which produce the con-
> fusion or puzzlement.... The content analyst employs a
> different tool; instead of formalisation, he uses com-
> parison. The purpose of these comparisons is to elicit
> the less apparent significance of the concept (etc.)
> which is under analysis. It is thought that the pro-
> cess of exhaustive comparison with cases in which the
> meaning of the concepts is clear is the best way of
> discovering the function of the expression(s) being
> considered. The function is not itself the meaning
> but is a guide to the meaning.(104)

> The essential point to be made is that 'definitions'
> are usually mnemonic devices, rough approximations
> which serve usefully as a first analysis of a term's
> meaning but require - in any important case - almost
> unending supplementation via examination of paradigm-
> atic examples of the term's use.(105)

Scriven argues that his own approach is convergent with that of more recent positivism:(106)

> It is no accident that, on the one hand, Carnap's
> school has had to abandon the long search for precise
> definitions of theoretical terms in science in terms
> of the observation language[107] and, on the other
> hand, the contextual analysts have eschewed the great
> tradition of systematic philosophy with its deductions
> and definitions of the important concepts.
>
> Even more significant is the fact that in both
> cases the successor to the definition has been exem-
> plification. The 'definition by postulate' and the
> 'correspondence rule' of the semiotician and the
> 'appeal to ordinary language' of the Oxford analysts
> are two sides of the same coin. For the postulates
> of an interpreted theory are the paradigm cases of the
> use of the theoretical terms, just as the standard
> cases of the use of a term are those which exemplify
> its meaning *if anything can*.

It is not entirely clear, however, that the approach recommended by Scriven and Toulmin can perform more than a hermeneutic task of bringing out the presuppositions of a given usage. The only way in which conceptual analysis could generate prescriptions is in the vulgarised form which privileges ordinary usage.(108) Gadamer, for exam-

ple, does not invoke 'ordinary language' in so many words, but his strictures on definition within philosophy seem to involve some such claim:(109)
Language and concept are obviously so closely bound to each other that to think we can 'apply' concepts - as for instance, when we say 'I call it so-and-so' - damages the binding force of philosophising. Individual consciousness has no such freedom when it wishes to philosophise. It is bound to language - not only the language of the speakers, but also the language of the dialogue that things carry on with us. Today science and the human experience of world encounter each other in the philosophical problem of language.

Adorno's critique of definition superficially resembles those which can be found in analytic philosophy and in Gadamer's hermeneutics. It is based, however, on very different premises. I would suggest, somewhat hesitantly, that it helps to understand Adorno if one sees him as upholding a realist ontology but denying, except as a utopian reference point, a realist epistemology which would license our knowledge of reality.(110) Instead, we are forced back on dialectics.

As Adorno puts it in his major philosophical work, 'Negative Dialectics':
The name of dialectics says no more, to begin with, than that objects do not go into their concepts without leaving a remainder, that they come to contradict the traditional norm of adequacy.(111)

things are not simply so and not otherwise, ... they have come to be under certain conditions. Their becoming fades and dwells within the things; it can no more be stabilised in their concepts than it can be split off from its own results and forgotten.(112)

Thus Adorno agrees with Gadamer and Husserl, though from very different premises, that the objectification intrinsic to scientific definition does not satisfy the philosophical ideal of cognition:(113)
To yield to the object means to do justice to the object's qualitative moments. Scientific objectification, in line with the quantifying tendency of all science since Descartes, tends to eliminate qualities and to transform them into measurable definitions. Increasingly, rationality itself is equated *more mathematico* with the faculty of quantification.

The same constraints apply to philosophical thought:(114)
Whenever we try by a merely posited, 'operational' definition to strip the concept of freedom of what

philosophical terminology used to call its idea, we are
arbitrarily diminishing the concept for utility's sake,
in comparison with what it means in itself.
   In a series of introductory lectures in sociology,
Adorno returned to these themes with a critique of 'the
attempt ... really to ... get rid of the concept in sociology, i.e. to reduce concepts to mere counters which serve
as abbreviations for the states of affairs which they
embrace, but without having any independent significance
[Selbständigkeit].'(115) Constrained by the needs of his
audience to give some sort of definitions of sociological
terms, Adorno insistently qualifies them:(116)

> When I use concepts like capitalism or class, these
> should not be understood as conceptual definitions. I
> don't want it to be said that class is this and that,
> as is the case for example with Weber. What is really
> posited at the same time is a complex of propositions
> and judgements - basically a theoretical complex which
> transcends them and from which even individual concepts
> or individual entities cannot be abstracted in isola-
> tion.

   There seems to be a disjunction between what Adorno
implies would count as adequate knowledge and the best
that he feels able to offer with his immanent method.
Reification is so pervasive that the only way to obtain
genuine knowledge of the social structure is by exploring
the antinomies contained in non-dialectical philosophies
and sociologies. But this 'immanent method' is in the
end little more than a radicalised and historically
informed version of linguistic analysis - a critique of
social theory, but not, except in gestural form, a social
theory itself.
   Rationalist and realist philosophies claim that science
and philosophy need to make more ambitious claims, cast in
terms of real definitions. In a passage already quoted in
part, Martin Hollis gives the following rationale:(117)

> The case for real definitions applies in any science
> where theory regulates descriptions of experience and
> does not just record and file them. It starts by not-
> ing that facts cannot be regarded as the referents of
> theory-free observation statements and that the para-
> digmatic theoretical statements, used to introduce
> primitive concepts, serve to rule out counter-examples
> to the theory in advance. But then there is a large
> snag, when we demand that the statements of a sound
> theory be both defeasible and true. Newton's laws of
> motion or the neo-Classical laws of supply and demand
> are not disconfirmable, since their regulative func-
> tion is to ensure that disconfirming instances have

been wrongly classified. Their truth, if they are
true, results from their being devices for introducing
the right concepts, rightly specified. So they are
defeasible only if there are objective criteria for the
choice and specification of the right concepts. In
other words I take recent philosophy of science to have
shown that empirical judgements presuppose theoretical
judgements but not to have abolished the need for truth
in science. Although the danger of a nominalist or
conventionalist line on the choice of theoretical terms
is thereby stark, it is not clear how a conceptualist
line avoids it. It can do so, I submit, only by making
old-fashioned claims for the possibility of real definitions.
Roy Bhaskar construes real definitions in science as
'fallible attempts to capture in words the real essences
of things ...',(118) i.e. 'their intrinsic structures,
atomic constitutions and so on which constitute the real
basis of their natural tendencies and causal powers'.(119)
In natural science, real definitions are characteristically based on empirical discoveries about the properties
of things. 'We may discover, quite empirically, that the
most important explanatory property or real essence of
hydrogen, identified as the lightest gas, is its atomic
structure; and then attempt to express this discovery in
a real definition of hydrogen.'(120) In social science,
given the concept-dependent nature of social activities
and the activity-dependent nature of social structures,
'attempts at real definitions will in general precede
rather than follow successful causal hypotheses.'(121)
I shall say more about this approach later; for the present, I suggest that it offers, prima facie, the most promising way of doing justice to the importance of conceptual questions in science in general and the social sciences in particular, without reducing questions of truth
to a conventionalist as-if or a hermeneutic 'melting of
horizons'.

(4) I shall now examine the theories of Marx, Tönnies,
Durkheim and Max Weber in terms of the oppositions sketched out above.
Marx has very little in explicit terms to say about
definition; an account of his likely views has to be read
into the corpus of his work, and this has given rise to
accounts as different as those of Bertell Ollman and
Louis Althusser. Althusser and his co-authors attribute
to Marx a fairly conventional view about the place of
definitions:(122)

Marx undoubtedly regarded as a theoretical requirement
of the first order the need to constitute an adequate
scientific terminology, i.e. a consistent system of
defined terms in which not only would the words already
used be concepts but in which the new words would also
be concepts and moreover ones which define a new object.
As we noted earlier, both Althusser and Balibar see
their role as the clarification and definition of the
terms used in Marx's scientific discourse. Ollman's Marx,
by contrast, is committed to a philosophy of 'internal
relations' and hence, presumably, to the use of real definitions:
> 'Identity', 'abstract', 'essence' and 'concrete' ...
> are all used by Marx, as they were by Hegel, to mark
> some aspect of the whole in the part, to refer to an
> ontological and not a logical relation.(123)

When Marx says 'division of labour and private property
are ... identical expressions', he is not offering an
empty tautology but directing us to the internal ties
he sees between these two in real life.(124)

For Marx, concepts are 'forms' or 'manifestations' of
their own subject matter ... they come into existence
as part of the conditions to which they apply ...
their meanings alter with changes in these conditions
and ... as a result, they invariably express more of
this structured whole than is evident in their core
notions.(125)

Ollman's account seems better able to do justice to
Marx's characteristic turn of phrase and to the continuing
influence of Hegel on his thought.(126) Althusser is
probably right, however, that one should not attribute to
Marx the radical hostility to definition which Engels
evinces in the foreword to vol.III of Capital:
> [Fireman's observations rest on] ... the mistaken
> assumption that Marx wishes to define where he is only
> analysing, or that one may look in Marx's work at all
> for fixed and universally applicable definitions. It
> is a matter of course that when things and their mutual
> interactions are conceived, not as fixed, but as
> changing, that their mental images, the ideas concern-
> ing them, are likewise subject to change and transfor-
> mation; that they cannot be sealed up in rigid defini-
> tions, but must be developed in the historical or
> logical process of their formation.

Engels's account seems to rest on a rather grossly
simplified notion of the dialectic as the more or less
mechanical reproduction in changing concepts of a changing
reality.

Chapter 2

Marx, of course, was cheerfully sarcastic about the scholastic treatment of economic concepts, in a passage quoted earlier.(127) And in 'Theories of Surplus Value' he wrote in a similar vein that he was not concerned with concepts but with functional relations between things. (128) But at the same time, he clearly believed that a radical nominalism was inadequate to deal with important features of economic reality; for example, although 'the money-form is merely the reflection thrown upon a single commodity by the relations between all other commodities', it is not 'itself a mere symbol'.(129) The most plausible account of Marx's position seems to be that he was basically a realist, and one who saw no problem of principle in the relations between concepts and their objects, between language and the world.(130) What counts for Marx, as suggested above, is the distinction between two sorts of object, phenomenal forms and real relations.

After the complexities of Marx, Tönnies's position is refreshingly transparent. He is worth a mention here, both because of his intrinsic importance as a (neglected) classical sociologist and because of his interest in terminological questions, to which he devoted a short monograph.(131) Tönnies allows the scientist complete freedom to adopt stipulative definitions, quoting with approval Pascal's assertion: 'Rien n'est plus libre que les définitions.'(132) He recognises the danger that a plurality of terminological conventions may inhibit scientific intercourse between groups which adopt different conventions,(133) but he seems to believe that this problem can be mitigated by a healthy nominalism.

Durkheim's views on definition, like his more general epistemological views, are not easy to establish. He seems to believe that scientists should provide clear nominal definitions at the beginning of their investigations, but he gives this prescription a 'realist' gloss: (134)

> Every scientific investigation is directed toward a limited class of phenomena, included in the same definition [qui répondent à une même définition]. The first step of the sociologist, then, ought to be to define the things he treats, in order that his subject matter may be known. This is the first and most indispensable condition of all proofs and verifications. A theory, indeed, can be checked only if we know how to recognise the facts of which it is intended to give an account. Moreover, since this initial definition determines the very subject matter of science, [constitue l'objet même de la science] this subject matter will or will not be a thing, depending on the

nature of the definition.
   In order to be objective, the definition must obviously deal with phenomena not as ideas but in terms of their inherent properties. It must characterise them by elements essential to their nature, not by their conformity to an intellectual ideal. Now, at the very beginning of research, when the facts have not yet been analysed, the only ascertainable characteristics are those external enough to be immediately perceived....
[Thus] ... *the subject matter of every sociological study should comprise a group of phenomena defined in advance by certain common external characteristics, and all phenomena so defined should be included within this group.*
   Durkheim's position seems then to be a realist one; moreover, it is not an empirical realism, since he clearly countenances the existence of properties which are not immediately observable. The initial definition of an object of inquiry in terms of 'external characteristics' is merely provisional:(135)
   it will be said that, in defining phenomena by their apparent characteristics, we are allowing to certain superficial properties a significance greater than that of more fundamental attributes.... This reproach rests on a confusion. Since the definition in question is placed at the beginnings of the science, it cannot possibly aim at a statement concerning the essence of reality; that must be attained subsequently.
   Durkheim goes on to claim, more contentiously, that these 'external characteristics' are not 'accidental' but 'bound up with the fundamental properties of things':(136) 'if the principle of causality is valid, when certain characteristics are found identically and without exceptions in all the phenomena of a certain order, one may be assured that they are closely connected with the nature of the latter and bound up with it'.(137)
   It is not clear just what Durkheim is claiming here. One could hardly object if he is merely saying that the external characteristics of things are often a useful indication of their natures; but Paul Hirst understands him to be making the more radical claim that: 'experiential knowledge can be a knowledge of the *essence* of things (and not merely of their appearances) because the external forms of phenomena are deterministic expressions of the essence; the essence is present in the given phenomena'.(138)
   Hirst does not provide evidence that Durkheim actually did mean this; one could argue, however, that some such view is implicit in the use which Durkheim makes of

Chapter 2

definition in his substantive works.(139) Hirst's broader argument is in any case independent of this particular interpretation; it is that Durkheim does not provide an adequate account of the constitution of scientific data; in this case, 'social facts':(140)

the 'givenness' of these facts ... is quite spurious. These facticities are given to us by a definite theoretical system.

Durkheim maintains in his general theory that we define a particular facticity by common external characteristics and that we work back by successive approximations to the reality which these characteristics embody and of which they are the phenomena. But, contrary to Durkheim's claim, this deeper reality must already be given for the immediate and visible 'facts' to be defined. It is given by the heurism of the definition of the field of the given. The definition of 'ascertainable characteristics ... external enough to be perceived' is not a product of pure perception but a product of theory. The definition specifies which phenomena are perceivable and it depends on an already given characterisation of the deeper reality of which they are the phenomena.

There are, then, three possible arguments against Durkheim's account of definition. First, it may presuppose an implausible and unargued relation between 'essence' and 'appearance'. Second, and more generally, it certainly presupposes an account of the constitution of data; this is not adequately developed. Third, it may be claimed that the way in which Durkheim uses his definitions is out of keeping with his statements in the 'Rules' about their provisional character. I shall return to the last two objections in chapter 3.

Weber, like Durkheim, will receive more detailed treatment in later chapters, but it is appropriate here to say something about his account of definition. As we have seen, Weber adopts an instrumental view of concepts as 'means of thought for the intellectual mastery of empirical data'.(141) There is nothing illegitimate about the precise definition of social scientific concepts in ideal-typical form since 'every concept which is not purely classificatory diverges from reality'.(142) The sociologist, in particular, is distinguished from the historian by a divergence of interest which leads to a difference in the nature of their concepts:(143)

As in the case of every generalising science the abstract character of the concepts of sociology is responsible for the fact that, compared with actual historical reality, they are relatively lacking in fullness of concrete content. To compensate for this disadvantage, sociological analysis can offer a greater precision of concepts.

It is not, therefore, surprising that Weber presents his definitions of 'basic sociological concepts' at the beginning of 'Economy and Society' as a set of stipulations, to be followed just so long as they are 'useful' in concrete research. Hence the recurrent formulation 'x is here defined as', 'soll heissen'.

But Weber also insisted that a definition of religion could only come at the end of an investigation of religious phenomena.(144) If we adopt Bierstedt's principle of interpretation (above, p.38), this suggests that he may have had real definitions in mind. So too does his claim in the prefatory note to 'Economy and Society' to be attempting 'only to formulate what all empirical sociology really means when it deals with the same problem'. And it is clear that his definitions are not only categories to aid further research, but also the condensation of a vast amount of historical scholarship and also, in many cases, of conceptual reflection within specialist sciences such as administrative science, law and economics and the contemporary European reality with which they dealt.(145)

Thomas Burger, one of the most impressive recent commentators on Weber, argues that he does introduce his ideal typical concepts by means of real definitions. The notion of real definition which Burger attributes to Weber is a more empiricist one than mine; he associates Weber with Rickert's view that the definition of a concept is a set of one or more empirical statements giving the extension of the concept:(146)

> [General concepts] ... are summary representations of common aspects of many phenomena. Their definitions, i.e. the sets of statements equivalent to the concepts, must therefore be interpreted as constituting descriptions of the features which many or all known phenomena have in common. [Similarly] ... laws must be interpreted as *descriptions* of certain aspects of many known concrete cause-effect relationships, as summaries of such facts past, present and future.

This is quite a plausible account of what Weber was actually doing in enunciating his definitions. It should be noted, however, that the view (which fits naturally with this account) that concepts are not so much means as ends of social scientific research is not very prominent in Weber's thought, though he occasionally seems to be asserting it.(147) Second, Burger's does not seem a good account of what Weber, in his later works, at least, thought he was doing; by then, his nominalistic assumptions were deeply entrenched, though, as we have seen, certain ambiguous formulations seem to gesture towards the notion of real definition. I shall argue in chapter 4 that this would have provided Weber with a more adequate account of his own practice.

(c) SOCIAL SCIENCE AND ORDINARY LANGUAGE

Every metatheory of science (whether of science in general, of social science as distinct from natural science, or of particular natural or social sciences) involves some conception of the relation between the discourse of that science and non-scientific discourse. These theories can be roughly assigned to places on a continuum between those which stress the separation of science from everyday life and those which stress continuities between the two and the former's ultimate dependence on the latter. There are two different ways of expressing this idea, the first in terms of the distance between the two discourses: the second in terms of the nature of the division - whether it is seen as continuous or discontinuous. Logically these are distinct: one can have a continuous series of shades between black and white or a discontinuous jump between two shades of green. In practice, however, the two ideas get run together in the philosophy of science, and in what follows I shall talk simply of 'continuists' and 'separatists', dealing with the nuances of different positions as they arise. I shall contrast Durkheim's radical separatism with the continuist tendencies of the verstehende tradition. After pausing to note a partial volte-face by separatists in economic theory, I shall discuss the attempts of Husserl, Schutz and recent critical theory to resolve the dilemma.

The term 'continuist' is of course borrowed from the controversy in French philosophy and history of science between Emile Meyerson, who argued, for example, that the theory of relativity was implicit in Newton's 'Principia', (148) and Gaston Bachelard, who stressed the discontinuities in the development of science, of which a striking example was the rise of 'non'-classical theories: 'non-Newtonian' mechanics, 'non-Euclidian' geometry, etc.(149) The idea of a break ('rupture') between pre-scientific and scientific thought, or between successive scientific theories, has been popularised in the English-speaking world in the Althusserian distinction between ideology and science. It can be traced back at least as far as Bacon, though in the philosophy of social science it seems to be particularly congenial to French thinkers - one thinks immediately of the positivist and Durkheimian traditions. In German-speaking countries, by contrast, there seems to have prevailed a 'softer' view of science, less abrasive and sure of itself, more anguished about keeping links with other modes of awareness and with the Lebenswelt in general.(150) On this (somewhat caricatural) view of European thought, Marburg neo-Kantianism, Mach and the Vienna Circle appear as part of a subordinate tradition, just as Bergson and the phenomenologists do in France.

Durkheim argued that social science is something radically different from, and develops in opposition to, 'all lay notions and the terms expressing them'.(151)

The concepts of ordinary language are(152) necessarily crude, since they are formed day after day, in the course of daily experience, unmethodically and uncritically. They express things exactly as our sensibility presents them to us, as we find it useful to represent them to ourselves so that we can adapt ourselves painlessly to them: but not as they are.

By adopting these everyday representations too uncritically, 'sociology has dealt more or less exclusively with concepts and not with things'.(153)

Sociological concept formation, then, cannot rely on ordinary language to yield more than a point of departure, an indication 'of the existence, somewhere, of an aggregation of phenomena which, bearing the same name, must, in consequence, probably have certain characteristics in common'.(154) In a footnote to this passage, Durkheim elucidates this relation:(155)

In actual practice one always starts with the lay concept and the lay term. One inquires whether, among the things which this word confusedly connotes, there are some which present common external characteristics. If this is the case, and if the concept formed by the grouping of the facts thus brought together coincides, if not totally (which is rare), at least to a large extent, with the lay concept, it will be possible to continue to designate the former by the same term as the latter, that is, to retain in science the expression used in everyday language. But if the gap is too considerable, if the common notion confuses a plurality of distinct ideas, the creation of new and distinctive terms becomes necessary.

By way of illustration of the prevalence of this attitude in French social science, I shall briefly mention three leading post-war writers: Claude Lévi-Strauss, Alain Touraine and Pierre Bourdieu.

Lévi-Strauss writes in 'Tristes Tropiques'(156) that he found phenomenology objectionable

in that it postulated a kind of continuity between
experience [le vécu] and reality. I agreed that the
latter encompasses and explains the former, but I had
learnt from my three sources of inspiration[157] that
the transition between one order and the other is discontinuous, that ... to reach reality, one has first
to reject experience and then subsequently to reintegrate it into an objective synthesis devoid of any
sentimentality.
 This orientation can be seen to underlie Lévi-Strauss's
concept of social structure, which 'has nothing to do with
empirical reality but with models which are built up after
it'.(158)
 For Alain Touraine, too, sociological analysis only
begins 'when the historical given, whether individual or
collective, is split up [décomposé]'.(159) Touraine takes
a characteristically separatist view of the contribution
of common-sense understanding.(160)

> The first task of a sociology of action is systematically to reject the use of any notion borrowed directly
> from social reality and above all from the interpretation which individuals or collectives give of their
> own action.... The level of a salary, the size of an
> enterprise, the ideology of a trade union, the content
> of a film are nothing but observational data which
> cannot have a place in sociological analysis until
> they have been transformed. This break with concrete
> reality, which is common to all scientific methods,
> is particularly important in sociology, which has
> defined itself for so long as the knowledge of *social
> reality* - whereas it cannot be anything but the study
> of *social action*. This implies the splitting up of
> reality into a number of fields of analysis; even the
> combination of these fields of analysis does not exhaust a reality which also requires a descriptive
> analysis (événementielle).

Bourdieu, Passeron and Chamboredon agree:

> Familiarity with the social universe constitutes for
> the sociologist the epistemological obstacle par excellence, because it continually produces illusory
> (fictives) conceptions and systematisations and at the
> same time renders them credible.(161)

> Sociology would be less vulnerable to the temptations
> of empiricism if it was sufficient to remind it, with
> Poincaré, that 'the facts do not speak'. It is perhaps the curse of the sciences of man to have to do
> with an *object which speaks*.(162)

Bourdieu makes the same points in Structuralism and the

Theory of Sociological Knowledge:(163) structuralism follows Marx, Durkheim and others who divest 'individual consciousness of the gnoseological privilege granted to it by the spontaneous theory of the social'. The anthropologist(164)

> gives no credit to the representation the subjects form of their situation but, rather, tries to explain it. However, anthropological science would not perhaps deserve any consideration if it were not its task to restore the agents to the sense of their practice by unifying, against the appearances of their irreducible opposition, the truth of the lived-through significance of conduct and the truth of the objective conditions that make such conduct and the experience of it possible and probable.

It would be easy to find similar views expressed by positivistically inclined Anglo-Saxon writers. I have deliberately chosen theorists who are clearly not positivists in any conventional sense - they are probably best described as conventionalists(165) - to make the point that the opposition is not a clear-cut one between nominalistic positivism and a hermeneutic approach.

The contrary view, which stresses the closeness and mutual interaction between science and everyday thought has characteristically been expressed in terms of some version of methodological dualism: the thesis that there is some qualitative difference between the methods appropriate to the natural sciences and those appropriate to the 'social', 'human', 'moral' or 'cultural' sciences. Thus the simple opposition 'Lebenswelt'/'science' becomes Lebenswelt/$\frac{\text{natural science}}{\text{social science}}$ and it becomes possible to argue that the relation of everyday knowledge of the social world to social theory/science is different from the relation of everyday knowledge of the natural world to natural science. This argument generally relies on some notion of what in the language of hermeneutics is called 'Vorverständnis' or 'pre-understanding' - the claim being that we have some more immediate or intimate access to social reality than to natural reality. This may be combined with the view that despite this head start, the social or human sciences cannot attain the level of formalisation, precision, predictive certainty, or whatever, that is possible in the more 'advanced' natural sciences. And this may lead in turn to the further argument that this is not what we want anyway in the human sciences, that they are governed by other purposes and interests.

The first writer who must be mentioned in this context is Vico and his relativisation of Cartesian method. Vico

neatly turned the tables on Descartes by arguing that the a priori knowledge obtained by, for example, mathematical reasoning(166)
is not, as Descartes supposed, discovery of an objective structure, the eternal and most general characteristics of the real world but rather invention: invention of a symbolic system which men can logically guarantee only because men have made it themselves, irrefutable only because it is a figment of man's own creative intellect.

Having 'broken the spell of Cartesianism'(167) at this point, Vico became gradually more hostile to geometrical method and more enthusiastic about the possibilities of history (which Descartes had despised). There then emerged the idea that 'we' can understand our past because we have made it: we can imaginatively reconstruct the process of its creation - a kind of knowledge which we cannot have of natural entities, though God can because he made them. As Berlin puts it, Vico 'uncovered a species of knowing not previously clearly discriminated, the embryo that later grew into the ambitious and luxuriant plant of German historist *Verstehen*'.(168)

I shall not discuss the verstehende tradition in detail here, but I think it is clear that the work of Droysen, Dilthey and Rickert upholds, with varying emphases, an alternative ideal of knowledge to the one which they identify in the natural sciences: a form of knowledge which, whatever the possibilities for its theoretical systematisation, remains intimately linked to everyday modes of thought and understanding.(169) It is worth noting, however, that even Durkheim accepts a degree of 'pre-understanding' of society, though he sees it as not so much a resource for the social scientist (see the faint praise expressed in his footnote to the 'Rules' (170)) but rather as a source of misunderstandings which caused sociology, more than the other sciences, to linger in a prescientific, ideological stage.(171)

Not only did sociology have to pass through this initial phase, but it had, by its very nature, to linger there much longer than the other sciences. Social facts are indeed human creations [réalisations]: they are a product of human intelligence and will. It does not seem at first sight that they can be anything other than the expression [exposition] of the ideas, innate or not, which we carry in ourselves, and their application to the different cases of life. The organisation of the family, of contract, of the state and of religion appears as a simple extension [prolongement] of the idea we make for ourselves of religion, the state, the family, etc.

Once again, what continuists see as a resource, separatists see as an obstacle. It is, of course, possible for a writer to adopt a position between the two extremes. Marx, for example, was passionately committed to the ideals of science, in the broad sense of Wissenschaft, and in particular to the idea that science uncovers connections between things which are not immediately apparent: 'All science would be superfluous if the outward appearance and the essence of things directly coincided.' (172) For all his criticisms of the excessive 'abstraction' of Hegelian philosophy and classical economics, he in no way questioned the need for abstraction in science: 'in the analysis of economic forms neither microscopes nor chemical reagents are of assistance. The power of abstraction must replace both.'(173) But Marx also rejected the idea of the sharp separation of science and everyday life: 'The idea of *one* basis for life and another for science is from the very outset a lie.'(174)

Marx's simultaneous adherence to these three claims - the ideal of science, the potential unity of science, and the unity of science and life - makes his views particularly interesting in this connection. This is not the place to discuss his approach in detail, but it can perhaps be summed up as follows: whereas Durkheim recommends that we should sweep aside 'prenotions' (whether they come from initial appearances, everyday actions or previous theoretical formulations) to get at 'the facts themselves', Marx attempts to operate at three levels at once: that of 'the facts', that of phenomenal appearances and that of earlier theories. The question he asks in 'Capital' neatly illustrates the three levels: 'why labour is expressed in value, and why the measurement of labour by its duration is expressed in the magnitude of the value of the product'.(175)

The history of neo-classical economics is also interesting in this connection. Attacked by the 'Historical School' for excessive abstraction and remoteness from reality, Carl Menger introduced a distinction between a 'realistic-empirical' and an 'exact' approach to science. The former, inductive, approach can only yield approximate regularities; phenomena cannot be ordered into 'strict types' and laws, but only into 'real types and empirical laws'.(176) But there is another, 'exact' mode of investigation which(177)

> seeks to ascertain the simplest elements of everything real. It strives for the establishment of these elements by way of an only partially empirical-realistic analysis, i.e. without considering whether these in reality are present as *independent* phenomena.... In

this manner theoretical research arrives at ...
results ... which, to be sure, must not be tested by
full empirical reality (for the empirical forms here
under discussion, e.g. absolutely pure oxygen, pure
alcohol, pure gold, a person pursuing only economic
aims etc. exist in part only in our ideas).
One of the central themes of the controversy between
Menger and Schmoller was the analysis of economic motivation. Schmoller criticised the 'psychological' assumptions of the classical economists, while Menger replied
that to take self-interest as a basic motivational postulate was merely a convenient simplification: economics
did not deny the existence of other motives, any more than
pure mechanics denied the existence of air-filled spaces.
(178)
Partly because of Menger's own substantive work, these
questions of motivation came to predominate in subsequent
discussions of the relationship between 'pure' economic
theory and some broader approach to economic phenomena.
Alfred Schutz, for example, accepted the need for abstract
economic theory and merely pointed out the danger that
economists may forget about the connection between their
theoretical formulations and the world of everyday life:
'in economics, as in all the other social sciences, we
always can - and for certain purposes must - go back to
the activity of the subjects within the social world: to
their ends, motives, choices, and preferences'.(179)
What was more paradoxical, in the light of Menger's
caveats, was the tendency of liberal economic theory,
from about the end of the nineteenth century, to present
itself as a broadly common-sense theory of rational individual motivation. In other words, one can find a characteristic fusion of Verstehen, common-sense, rational
action theory and individualism.
As examples of this 'verstehende economics', Göran
Therborn(180) mentions Ludwig von Mises, Lionel Robbins,
Fritz Machlup, and in particular Philip Wicksteed's
instructively named 'The Common Sense of Political Economy' (1910), which aimed to lead the reader 'directly and
inevitably, from the facts and observations of his own
daily experience to an intimate comprehension of the
machinery of the commercial and industrial world'.(181)
As Therborn shows, a verstehende theory may easily (he
would say must) be ideological in its implications; for
example, 'the theory of profit has tried to understand it
as a recompense for something, for labour and diligence,
for abstinence or risk-taking'. In other words, 'bourgeois and petty-bourgeois "common sense" has left its
ideological finger-prints on the scientific analyses and

intelligible predictions of market regularities'.(182)

I have discussed these economic developments at some length since they shed an interesting light on certain parallel developments in sociological theory. I have already drawn attention to the affinities between
    (1)   the positive value placed on common sense
    (2)   verstehen
    (3)   rational action analysis
    (4)   individualism
This does not mean that these four elements may not, in some circumstances drift apart; (it is easy enough, for example, for a deductive theory of rational action to move away from common sense understanding and from verstehen seen as the grasp of concrete motives). But, by and large, we may expect to find traces of these affinities.

There is, however, a second feature of economic theory which recurs in sociology (most strikingly, as I shall argue later, in the work of Alfred Schutz). This is the 'peaceful coexistence', of a theory oriented around these four elements and giving an important place, at least in its self-presentation, to 'meaningful adequacy' and to Anschaulichkeit, or intuitive comprehensibility, at the level of motivation, and a classically positivist and pre-dictivist analysis of explanation. The theory is legitimated, in other words, at its two extremes: first, by the 'meaningful adequacy' of its motivational assumptions, and second, by its ability to make successful predictions. The latter is, of course, the more important, but one should not ignore the ideological significance of the former in reassuring practitioners about the value of their theories and providing a means of justifying them in the eyes of the lay audience.(183)

In later sections of this book I hope to display various instances of this 'couple'. My objections to it, very briefly, and elliptically, are two-fold:

    (1) It 'ties down' a theory to empirical reality at the two ends - the 'meaningful adequacy' of its conceptualisation and the success of its predictions - without providing any possibility of rational evaluation of the body of a theory. The impoverished positivistic conception of theory as a machine for generating predictions is given an illusory grounding, which for classical positivism was anyway unnecessary.

    (2) The two 'points of attachment' are themselves inappropriate for the job they are intended to do. A good theory is not necessarily one whose concepts and explanations have some immediate plausibility and attachment to the Lebenswelt, though it must be able to say something about the relations between its own concepts and those of

ordinary language (and those of earlier theories), if only
that ordinary language and earlier theories are utterly
inadequate. Nor, as has been generally agreed in the
philosophical literature, is predictive success a good
criterion of the adequacy of a theory or the explanations
which it affords.
Max Weber's conception of the relation between science
and pre-scientific thought is basically a separatist one,
though the place which he attributes to values, or more
accurately Wertbeziehung in scientific concept formation
makes his separatism much less strident than Durkheim's.
Weber broadly accepts Menger's distinction between history and theory, or between an 'empirical-realistic' and
an 'exact' approach, but he differs from Menger in the
account he gives of the difference. First, the difference between the two approaches is grounded not so much
in differences in the reality with which they deal (the
socio-historical totality vs a distinct aspect or side of
reality) as in differences in the cognitive interests
with which we approach the phenomena. The 'economic'
('sozialökonomisch') character of a phenomenon is not an
objective property of it, but merely a function of our
cognitive interest. However, it should be noted that
Weber goes on to distinguish between strictly 'economic'
phenomena, those which are 'economically relevant' (e.g.
certain aspects of religion) and those which are 'economically conditioned', such as the social stratification
of the artistic public.(184) Second, underlying this
difference between a 'systematic' and a 'historical'
approach is a more important difference between the kind
of knowledge which is desirable and possible in the natural sciences and that which is appropriate to a science
like economics. To expect to deduce concrete, quantitative predictions from economic 'laws' is a 'naturalistic
prejudice';(185) economic 'laws' can only have an ideal-typical form. Their failure to apply in individual
cases does not impugn their heuristic value.(186) The
concepts of the cultural scientist are constructed with
reference to values; thus the ground is cut away from any
attempt such as Durkheim's to distinguish between 'normal'
and 'pathological'; such judgments can only be made relatively to a set of values, which may be those of the
sociologist or of the people whose activities are being
examined or may be drawn by the sociologist from some
entirely different source.
But with all these qualifications, science is still
something significantly different from common sense:(187)
> The 'daily experience' from which our theory starts is
> naturally the common starting-point of *all* empirical

specialisms. Each of them wants to go beyond this
experience and must want to do so - for this is precisely the basis of its right to exist as a 'science'.
The phenomenologist Edmund Husserl sees separatism as
a problem. The sharp distinction between positive science
and the Lebenswelt which he identifies in the practice of
science since at least the time of Galileo is, he believes,
part of the pathology of the sciences. In 'The Crisis of
the European Sciences'(188) he traces the withdrawal of
post-Galilean(189) science from contact with the life-
world (in which, of course, it nevertheless remains
grounded): 'the surreptitious substitution of the mathe-
matically substructed world of idealities for the only
real world, the one that is actually given through perception, that is ever experienced and experienceable - our
everyday life-world'.(190) This withdrawal does not vitiate the very real discoveries of the sciences, but it
does constitute a severe limitation on their 'rationality'
(191) and consequently on their 'meaning' for humanity.
   The remedy for this harmful separation is not the
demolition of science, but rather a phenomenological
analysis, itself scientific, of the life-world: 'the
proper return to the naïveté of life - but in a reflection which rises above this naïveté - is the only possible
way to overcome the philosophical naïveté which lies in the
"scientific" character of traditional objectivistic philosophy'.(192) Husserl does not deny the superiority of
science to prescientific thinking(193) or to what in the
Vienna Lecture he calls the 'religious-mythical attitude'.
(194) But the distinction between positive science and
non-scientific thought is complemented by a third term,
philosophy, which affords a deeper perspective from which
both 'common sense' and positive science reveal their
inadequacy. Philosophy must set itself higher standards
of clarity and self-awareness than the positive sciences,
'which settle down on the basis of an experience of the
world which is assumed to possess unquestioned existence'.
(195)
   Husserl's problematisation of the relations between
science and the life-world recurs, as I shall show in a
moment, in such different contemporary movements as
ethnomethodology, existential hermeneutics and recent
critical theory (especially Habermas).(196) But it is
worth spelling out here that Husserl's notion of the constitution of scientific and other objects in the Lebenswelt is based on an ideal, transcendental subject and has
nothing necessarily to do with the contingent acts of
empirical human subjects such as their 'definitions of
the situation', 'accounting procedures', etc. This dis-

tinction has been frequently overlooked in loose contemporary discussion of 'phenomenological sociology'.(197)
In view of the extent to which Schutz uses a Husserlian vocabulary and adopts Husserlian assumptions, it is important to note the formal differences between their approaches. 'The Phenomenology of the Social World'(198) can perhaps be understood as asking a transcendental question - how is verstehende sociology of a Weberian kind possible? - but Schutz's answer is in empirical terms, drawing attention to analogues of Weber's typifications in the typifications which we all practise in the life-world and within the limits of the 'natural attitude'.(199) All this means that, in Gorman's words,(200)
Schutz's concept of science is significantly different from Husserl's own. Husserl held that the transcendental reduction allows us to perceive apodictic knowledge, essentially independent of empirical subjects but constituted subjectively. Facts, meaningfully perceived in the empirical world, are reflections of this transcendental body of knowledge. Schutz, on the contrary, contends that the 'eidos' is directly concerned with facticity in the form of empirical types.
How then does social scientific knowledge, for Schutz, differ from everyday knowledge in the life-world? The difference between them is basically grounded in the different attitudes, the different systems of 'relevances' of the social scientist and the ordinary actor in the life-world.
To become a social scientist the observer must make up his mind to step out of the social world, to drop any practical interest in it, and to restrict his in-order-to motives to the honest description and explanation of the social world which he observes.(201)

What ... is the specific attitude of social science to its object, the social world? Fundamentally, it is the same as the attitude of the indirect social observer toward his contemporaries. It is different, however, in one respect: no directly experienced social reality is pre-given to social science as such. The world of social science is simply not identical with the world of the social scientist, who is also a man living in the social world. But the world of predecessors is indeed pre-given to social science, and only this is pre-given to history. The whole context of knowledge of social science is therefore necessarily different from that of the indirect observer of social life.(202)
Schutz is, of course, a methodological dualist. Although

62 Chapter 2

the social scientist's attitude to the social world 'is
that of systematising scrutiny rather than that of living
experience, ... his data ... are the already constituted
meanings of active participants in the social world'.(203)
The social scientist provides a second-order interpretation
of an object-domain which is already pre-interpreted by
its members, 'objective meaning-contexts of subjective
meaning-contexts'.(204)
   This is an advantage which the social scientist has
over the natural scientist: 'the data of the social sciences have, while still in the prescientific stage, those
elements of meaning and intelligible structure which later
appear in more or less explicit form with a claim to categorical validity in the interpretive science itself.'(205)
It is therefore particularly paradoxical for the social
sciences to imitate the natural sciences in their 'objectivistic' orientation:(204)

> As soon as they grant to the natural sciences their
> objectivity as their own independent attribute, the
> social sciences themselves fall into objectivism, for
> only mind [Geist] has being in itself and is independ-
> ent. To regard nature as something in itself alien to
> mind and then to found the cultural sciences on the
> natural sciences, and thus supposedly to make them
> exact, is an absurdity.

But for all this, there are certain postulates which
any science must satisfy:

> There is the postulate of consistency and compatibility
> of all propositions not only within the field of that
> special branch of science but also with all the other
> scientific propositions and even with the experiences
> of the natural attitude of everyday life in so far as
> they are safeguarded, although modified, within the
> finite province of theoretical contemplation; more-
> over, the postulate that all scientific thought has
> to be derived, directly or indirectly, from tested
> observation, that is, from originary immediate exper-
> iences of facts within the world; the postulate of
> highest possible clarity and distinctness of all
> terms and notions used, especially requiring the
> transformation of confused prescientific thought into
> distinctness of explicating its hidden implications;
> and many more.(207)

> All scientific knowledge presupposes concepts and
> judgements, both of which have to be formed with an
> optimum of clarity, distinctness, and exactitude.
> None of these qualities is peculiar to everyday, com-
> mon-sense thought. Its concepts, bound to the neces-

Chapter 2

sities of a concrete and therefore very determined situation, are clear only in so far as the interest of the actor requires that the situation be elucidated in several of its complications. The actor in his everyday activities is not guided by the intention of finding out the real nature of facts or the real essence of causal sequences and natural laws. He is, as James calls him, 'a rule-of-thumb thinker'.(208)
And in a passage that could have come from Durkheim's 'Rules', Schutz warns that:(209)
When common-sense assumptions are uncritically admitted into the apparatus of a science, they have a way of taking their revenge. This may appear through equivocations creeping into its basic concepts and thereby working an adverse effect on research. Or it may occur through a failure to see that apparently diverse phenomena are really of the same type, a failure generated by not having penetrated beyond the appearance to the roots of the phenomena in question. If this danger hangs over every science, its threat to sociology is especially acute. For sociology's task is to make a scientific study of social phenomena. Now, if social phenomena are constituted in part by common-sense concepts, it is clear that it will not do for sociology to abstain from a scientific examination of these 'self-evident' ideas.

Before leaving Schutz, it is necessary to say something about his concept or postulate of 'adequacy'. The main source for this (though only one of several) is his paper Common Sense and Scientific Interpretation of Human Action. Here Schutz sets up three 'postulates' for scientific model constructs of the social world:
(1) logical consistency
(2) subjective interpretation
(3) adequacy:(210)
Each term in a scientific model of human action must be constructed in such a way that a human act performed within the life-world by an individual actor in the way indicated by the typical construct would be understandable for the actor himself as well as for his fellow-men in terms of common-sense interpretations of everyday life. Compliance with this postulate warrants consistency of the constructs of the social scientist with the constructs of common-sense experience of the social reality.

How satisfactory is this postulate of adequacy as a guide to concept formation? Schutz does not offer much in the way of argument for it, but then perhaps it is unreasonable to expect an argument for what is really an expression of support for a certain way of studying reality. Perhaps it should be understood not as a logical requirement, but simply as a practical desideratum 'if one wants to keep social theory free from abstract metaphysics'.(211) But this sounds rather feeble.

If one tries to give it a strong formulation, as a necessary condition for any social theory to be acceptable, there seem to be at least four objections:

(1) It is not clear how the criterion is to be applied: is the suggestion that the actor must accept the proffered account as correct (rather as one might say that a necessary condition for the success of a psychoanalytic interpretation is its acceptance by the analysand) or merely as an intelligible and possible account? How seriously are we meant to take the reference to the actor and his fellow-men? (If it is merely a thought-experiment in the mind of the social scientist, then Schutz's postulate of adequacy collapses into Weber's 'meaningful adequacy' and again looks suspiciously weak.)

(2) If we revert to a strong formulation of the postulate, what about the familiar problems of false consciousness, ideology, etc.? (A radical Schutzian could no doubt reject such questions, but the price seems rather steep.(212))

(3) Schutz himself has argued that the 'relevance structures' of the social scientist (in which presumably the discussion of adequacy is grounded) are systematically different from those of everyday actors in the lifeworld, being relatively isolated from concrete social life and having a disinterested, theoretical focus. This seems to threaten any strong claim to consistency between the constructs of the social scientist and those of common-sense experience of social reality.

(4) On the other hand, the life-world itself is not 'semantically homogeneous'; it is itself the arena of a whole range of typifications at different levels of abstraction (the levels being a function of different relevance structures). Schutz can accurately refer to his dog, Rover, as 'Rover', 'a setter', 'a dog', 'an animal', etc., depending on the context of the reference. This seems to weaken the contrast between 'life-world' and 'science' and threaten any notion of 'pure description'.

Schutz's own practice seems to indicate that he took a fairly casual attitude to the postulate of adequacy. His own substantive essays, such as The Stranger, tend to be relatively untheoretical descriptions of social situations, rather in the manner of Simmel, which seem to rely on evoking a feeling of plausibility or descriptive adequacy in the mind of the reader. It is difficult to imagine him writing, say, 'The Social System', yet he seems to view Parsons's earlier work with considerable respect, as is indicated by his correspondence with Parsons during the War.(213)

Even more significant, perhaps, is Schutz's enthusiasm for economics, 'the social science that has achieved the highest degree of unification of its conceptual scheme', (214) and for 'the utilitarian theory of choice and decision, upon which is founded, admittedly or not, the model used by practically all social scientists for explaining human action'.(215) Schutz does not deny the value of abstract economic theory, in which it sometimes seems that 'notions like "saving", "spending", "capital", "unemployment", "profit" and "wages" are used as if they were entirely detached from any relationship to the activities of economic subjects'. The only danger is that economists may forget all about the connection between their theoretical formulations and the world of ordinary life: 'in economics, as in all the other social sciences, we always can - and for certain purposes must - go back to the activity of the subjects within the social world: to their ends, motives, choices and preferences'.(216) Schutz's own preference, both here and in relation to Weber and Parsons, is clearly for examining the 'interface' between 'theory' and the 'life-world'. His instincts are continuist, and he flirts with an almost absurdly strong version of continuism, only to abandon it when confronted with the apparently impressive structures of micro-economic theory. Parsons, indeed, who himself upholds an inverted continuism by assimilating, in effect, the rest of life to science, charges Schutz with separatism:(217)

> It seems to me that Dr. Schutz poses an altogether unrealistically sharp contrast between the point of view of the actor and the point of view of the scientific observer and analyst, virtually dissociating them from each other. Quite the contrary it seems to me that they are closely connected and that 'doing' science is an extreme type of action.

Finally, I should like to make some very brief remarks about the way in which the relationship between science and pre-scientific thought is conceived in the 'critical theory' of the 'Frankfurt school'. There is considerable continuity in this respect from Adorno and Horkheimer, who dominated the early period of critical theory, to Habermas and Apel who have been most prominent in the last fifteen years. They combine a conviction that science is a distinctive form of knowledge with an intense interest in the relationship between science and the social totality, both at an epistemological level and at the level of the relationships between theory and practice (and these two levels are, in their view, also intimately related).

Horkheimer's concern with the relationships between theory and practice can be seen in an early essay: 'What decides the value of a theory is not only the formal criterion of truth, [but rather] its connection with the tasks which are undertaken by progressive social forces at a particular historical moment.'(218) Adorno, in a lecture given in 1968, expressed a similar hostility to the rigid separation of science from non-science: 'If one does not bring into every scientific investigation pre-scientific interests or extrascientific concepts, the scientific ones also are no longer present.'(219) Or as Habermas put it in an early essay: 'The positivistically cleansed demarcation set between knowledge and evaluation of course represents less a result than a problem.'(220)

Habermas, unlike Adorno and Horkheimer, explicitly draws on Husserl's concept of the Lebenswelt, while rejecting Husserl's tendency to argue for a pure theory freed from contamination by interest.(221) For Habermas, it is precisely by means of interests, not the contingent interests of scientists but the 'quasi-transcendental' (222) interests which guide cognition, that the connection between science and the Lebenswelt is preserved. (223) But just as one must criticise the objectivistic pretensions of positivist science, one must also reject Gadamer's notion of the 'universality of hermeneutics'; (224) scientific criticism (or critical science) is required to uncover the causal impediments to the kind of awareness (Selbstverständigung) which Gadamer envisages.

Habermas's notion of cognitive interests replaces the traditional versions of methodological dualism(225) with a trichotomy between empirical-analytic science, based on an interest in technical control; hermeneutics, based on an interest in understanding; and 'critical science' exemplified by psychoanalysis and Ideologiekritik and governed by an interest in emancipation. These three interests have a transcendental function in that they govern the constitution of the object domains of the respective scientific approaches.

Science, therefore, reveals a unity of reasoning and a 'differential meaning-constitution of object domains'. (226) The social sciences may be governed by any one, or by more than one, of the three cognitive interests.(227) I shall return to this theme in discussing the concept of constitution, but it is worth noting in the present context

that Habermas now stresses the distinction between
'action' and (scientific) 'discourse' and between genesis
and validity, in such a way as to play down the importance
of the continuity between 'the constitution of *scientific*
object domains' and 'the objectivations that are going on
in practical life'.(228) A more positive, and also more
'continuist' approach is, however, hinted at in the following passage:(229)
> Concept formation in sociology is obviously linked up
> with the everyday concepts in which members of social
> groups construct the normative reality of their social
> environment. This suggests developing sociological
> action theory as a theory that attempts to reconstruct
> the universal components of the relevant pre-theoretical
> knowledge of sociological laymen.

This section has been largely expository in its purpose.
The questions it raises about the appropriate relationship
between social scientific discourse and ordinary language
in the life-world cannot, I think, be answered at this
level but require a more systematic discussion of concept
and theory formation.(230) It seems to me clear, however,
that these questions cannot be brushed aside, as the positivist tradition tended to do, once one accepts the
importance of linguistic issues for science in general
and for the social sciences in particular.(231) It is
true that this recognition of the constitutive role of
language in social theory has been mixed up with the
traditional shibboleths of methodological dualism and,
to compound confusion, with a misunderstood 'social'
phenomenology and that it has often led to what Giddens
has called a 'paralysis of the critical will'.(232) But
it is no less clear that the hermeneutic tradition has
pointed to important and neglected aspects of the linguistically mediated relations between the social sciences and the 'life-world'.

One can accept all this without abandoning the naturalist aspiration that social relations can still be elucidated in a way which deserves to be called scientific
(in the English and French sense of the term). It does
require some qualification of the 'revelatory'(233) pretensions of the social sciences, but not the abandonment
of a critical attitude to 'ordinary usage', 'common sense'
and 'members' practices'. One way of putting this would
be to say that the concept-dependent, language-bound,
undetermined and incomplete character of the natural sciences, which has now been generally recognised, is also a
feature of the social sciences, only more so.(234)

3 Constitution

1 INTRODUCTION

The concept of theoretical constitution or 'object-constitution', the establishing of an object of scientific inquiry, has been used, since the time of Kant, in a wide variety of senses, but has also received little systematic examination.(1) It has found its way into social theory via phenomenology (Husserl and Schutz) and critical theory (Habermas and Apel), though I shall argue that some account of constitution is present implicitly in the work of most social theorists and is, in fact, essential to any adequate social theory. I shall also argue that although the concept of constitution has been most fully elaborated in the broadly idealist frameworks of neo-Kantian and phenomenological philosophies, it is not incompatible with the realist theory of science upheld by Roy Bhaskar; indeed the concept of constitution represents one way of marking the difference between Bhaskar's transcendental realism and what he calls empirical realism.

In my view, one can distinguish an epistemic or theoretical sense of constitution, which is opposed to empiricism, and a somewhat less common ontological or practical sense, the sense in which Marxism claims that 'we make our own history' (or society), and various 'idealist' theories, such as those of Simmel, Schutz and subsequent 'phenomenological' sociologists, claim that 'society' is made up of meanings and interpretations which are negotiated in interaction. This distinction is, however, primarily an analytical one; while some theories appear to be concerned solely with one or the other sense of constitution, the majority make reference to both senses. Marxist theories of knowledge, for example, aim to situate epistemic constitution within a broader process of practical constitution in which society is produced by human practice.

Conversely, for the idealist theories, the interpretative 'work' which constitutes society in an ontological or practical sense is partly or wholly a matter of acts of epistemic or theoretical constitution.

The concept of theoretical constitution has its source in Kant, and is central to the broad and influential tradition which Thelma Lavine called interpretationism:(2)

The distinguishing feature of interpretationism, from the German Enlightenment through American pragmatism to mid-twentieth century *Wissenssoziologie* is an affirmation of the activity of mind as a constitutive element in the object of knowledge. Common to all of these philosophical movements, although they are unequally aware of it, is the epistemological principle that mind does not apprehend an object which is given to it in completed form, but that through its activity of providing interpretation or conferring meaning or imposing structure, mind in some measure constitutes or 'creates' the object known.

The second, ontological, variant can be found in the Marxist tradition and is pithily expressed in Marx's 'Theses on Feuerbach' - in particular, in the following passages of the first and third theses:(3)

The chief defect of all hitherto existing materialism ... is that the thing, reality, sensuousness, is conceived only in the form of the *object* or of *contemplation*, but not as *human sensuous activity, practice*, not subjectively. Hence it happened that the *active side*, in contradistinction to materialism, was developed by idealism - but only abstractly....

The materialist doctrine of the changing of conditions and of education forgets that it is people who change circumstances and that the educator must himself be educated.

As Marx put it somewhat later, 'Men make their own history, but ... under circumstances directly encountered, given and transmitted from the past.'(4)

It must be admitted that the epistemic and the ontological senses of constitution(5) are not easily separable in the works of particular writers. There are essentially two ways in which they may be assimilated to one another. The first is an idealist thesis that the social world is constructed and sustained (constituted$_o$) by means of interpretations of social reality produced by human beings (constitution$_e$). Something approaching this view can be found in Simmel's essay How is Society Possible?(6) and in much symbolic interactionist and 'phenomenological' sociology. As W.I. Thomas put it, 'If men define situa-

tions as real they are real in their consequences.'(7)
The second way in which the two variants of constitution can be assimilated is hinted at in Marx and in Marxist writers such as Lukács. In this tradition, the emphasis is on acts of practical constitution$_o$, which may include constitution$_e$ as a subordinate activity. Cognition, and theoretical activity in general, lose the privileged place which they enjoy in most philosophical systems. Instead, they are understood as aspects of human practice as a whole, and may, further, be judged by their contribution to this practice.(8)

> The question whether objective truth can be attributed to human thinking is not a question of theory but is a *practical* question....
>
> All social life is essentially *practical*. All mysteries which lead theory to mysticism find their rational solution in human practice and in the comprehension of this practice.

I shall argue that neither of these alternatives is satisfactory. The idealist version is radically inadequate, while the 'Marxist' version, though broadly right about the place of thinking in human life, does not take sufficient account of the specificity of constitution$_e$. It is more helpful, I shall argue, to see the two processes as separate and thus recognise the specific importance of each.

Before looking in more detail at the ways in which the term 'constitution' has been used, it is necessary to say a bit more about what this alleged process involves. When Marx asserted a version of constitution$_o$, that 'men make their own history', he immediately qualified it: 'but ... under circumstances ... transmitted from the past'. This is a familiar theme of Marxism which does not require elaboration here; all I wish to point out is that similar qualifications are made in the case of constitution$_e$. One can construct a crude sort of continuum between a strong and a weak thesis of constitution. Both ends of the continuum share an emphasis on the creative activity of the knowing subject, but whereas the strong version holds that the subject is entirely free to construct its own 'world', weak versions hold that this creative activity of the subject is guided, either by the nature of the object known(9) or by the transcendental conditions of any (human) perception.

The strong extreme is represented by a solipsistic view that the external world is my own invention, or that even if there is an external world, no true knowledge of it is possible; all we have are our individual independent views of it. Nietzsche seems to have held some such view, as

Chapter 3

shown in such works as 'The Gay Science' and the sections of his 'Nachlass' devoted to the critique of philosophy and science. It is not appropriate here to enter the deep waters of Nietzschean exegesis,(10) but the following quotations are sufficient, I think, to establish that Nietzsche's relativistic conception of knowledge as an outgrowth of the 'will to power' involves a strong constitution thesis.

We have arranged for ourselves a world in which we can live - by positing bodies, lines, planes, causes and effects, motion and rest, form and content; without these articles of faith nobody now could endure life. But that does not prove them. Life is no argument. The conditions of life might include error.(11)

In opposition to Positivism, which halts at phenomena and says, 'These are only *facts* and nothing more', I would say: No, facts are precisely what is lacking, all that exists consists of *interpretations*. We cannot establish any fact 'in itself': it may even be nonsense to desire to do such a thing. 'Everything is subjective', ye say: but that in itself is *interpretation*. The 'subject' is nothing given, but something superimposed by fancy, something introduced behind. - Is it necessary to set an interpreter behind the interpretation already to hand? Even that would be fantasy, hypothesis.

To the extent to which knowledge has any sense at all, the world is knowable: but it may be interpreted *differently*, it has not one sense behind it, but hundreds of senses. - 'Perspectivity'.

It is our needs that *interpret the world*....(12)

The will to truth is a process of *establishing things;* it is a process of *making* things true and lasting, a total elimination of that false character, a transvaluation of it into *being*. Thus, 'truth' is not something which is present and which has to be found and discovered; it is something which has to be *created* and which gives its name *to a process*, or, better still, to the Will to overpower, which in itself has no purpose: to introduce truth is a *processus in infinitum,* an *active determining* - it is not a process of becoming conscious of something, which in itself is fixed and determined. It is merely a word for 'The Will to Power'.(13)

A similarly strong version of constitution can be found in an informal paper by Harold Garfinkel, based on his PhD thesis.(14) In this paper, Garfinkel follows Felix

Kaufmann in distinguishing between a 'correspondence theory' and a 'coherence theory' of reality.

A person is said to entertain a correspondence theory of reality if it can be shown that the person's theorising about the world employs the view that there is a difference between the perceived object of the 'outer world' and the concrete object (exemplified in the metaphorical admonition that the cake of the universe may be cut in diverse ways, or that the objects of the outer world are indubitably out there but they may be variously invested with meaning). The concreteness of the object in this view is a property of the object; such concreteness being independent of the various modes of attending of an experience.

The correspondence theory makes a separation between the real world and the subjective interpretation of the real world....

The leading premise of the 'congruence' theory of reality is that the perceived object of the 'outer world' is the concrete object, and that the two terms, 'perceived object' and 'concrete object' are synonymous and interchangeable terms. Rather than there being a world of concrete objects which a theory cuts this way and that, the view holds that the cake is constituted in the very act of cutting. No cutting, no cake, there being no reality out there that is approximated since the world in this view is just as it appears.(15)

David Walsh, a disciple of Garfinkel, makes the same argument more briefly in relation to social reality: sociological phenomenology 'would deny the existence of the social world independently of the social meanings that its members use to account it and, hence, constitute it'.(16)

Later in this article, he draws the moral for the analysis of 'social structure': this 'cannot refer to anything more than members' everyday sense of social structure since it has no identity which is independent of that sense'.(17)

David Silverman makes the same point in his Introductory Comments in chapter 1 of the book: 'our argument is that social phenomena are constituted (that is, made into objects, into "real" things) by the interpretive work of members'.(18)

These examples have been chosen to illustrate a strong version of constitution$_e$. There can be no question of providing illustrations of the 'weak' extreme of the spectrum since, as I suggested above, it fades away into empiricism. As a result, this chapter does not continue the pattern of contrasting positivism, interpretivism, rationalism, realism, etc. The discussion of constitution$_e$ is fought out among non-positivists (though not necessarily, I shall argue, non-naturalists).

Two final remarks of an introductory kind remain to be made. First, I shall have very little to say about the constitution of the 'subject', a question which has received considerable attention in recent French work drawing on Marxism and psycho-analytic theory. A more important problem is exactly what is claimed to be constituted: is it things, the 'meanings' of things, phenomena, etc.?

If we return for a moment to Lavine's formulation, in which 'the activity of mind ... [is] ... a constitutive element in the object of knowledge', we must ask what 'the object of knowledge' actually means. Does it mean something like our concept of an object, an object-as-we-conceive-it, or does it mean the real object, to which our knowledge is an approximation? Realists and Kantians agree in selecting the first answer, however much they diverge in their subsequent elaboration of it.(19) The objects are, in Bhaskar's sense, transitive objects of science, or, in Kant's sense, phenomena. The 'object' in 'object-constitution' is usually to be taken with a grain of salt. This is not to say that some writers do not slide from objects of knowledge to objects tout court; many neo-Kantians seem to equivocate on this issue and Nietzsche, of course, robustly denied any distinction between the real world and the apparent world: 'the "true world" is a "lying addition"'. Husserl's formulations, cited below on pp. 91 ff. are similarly ambiguous. Often it seems that the question of what is alleged to be constituted merges with the continuum between strong and weak versions of constitution; only in the case of materialist versions of constitution$_o$ is it clear that what is constituted by human practice is the real world, whether or not we know it correctly.

The uses of the concept of constitution can be represented as a family tree descending from Kant, with intermarriage between the various branches beginning with the second or third generation. Very schematically, one can put the position thus. Kant's stupendous but unstable synthesis was not taken over in toto by his successors. The Marburg neo-Kantians, Hermann Cohen, Paul Natorp and others, were perhaps the closest to the master. This was not, however, their intention, if Paul Natorp is to be believed: they wanted, rather, to reculer pour mieux sauter, to go back to Kant as a prelude to advancing in directions more compatible with contemporary natural science.(20) The 'South-Western', 'Baden' or 'Heidelberg' school of neo-Kantians (Windelband, Rickert, later Emil Lask and to some extent Max Weber) were even more selective in their appropriation of Kant.

If neo-Kantianism is taken as one line of descent from Kant, another is that of Hegel and subsequently Marx. Here the emphasis shifts, if I may anticipate my argument, from constitution$_e$ to constitution$_o$, first in a rather ambiguous form with Hegel, and then more explicitly, with Marx, under the heading of praxis or practice. The third major component is the phenomenology of Husserl. This is not, of course, a 'Kantian' philosophy, any more than Hegel's was, but Kant's work and not least his concept of constitution played a crucial role in setting the conditions for these later developments.(21)

These three traditions then became entangled with each other in highly complex ways; the following connections seem to be the most important. First, neo-Kantianism and phenomenology developed in parallel - united by their opposition to psychologism, divided in the accounts they gave of subjective experience.(22) Second, there are the influential Kantian and neo-Kantian interpretations of Marxism, ranging from Max Adler's important work in the early decades of this century to Alfred Schmidt's more recent contributions.(23) These interpretations of Marxism are distinguished by their emphasis on epistemological questions. There is a similar emphasis, more generally, in the 'second generation' of critical theory, in particular in the work of Habermas and Apel. The third set of connections is between Marxism and phenomenology, and in particular existential phenomenology. Here again, what is involved is a conception of constitution$_o$ which gives an important place to constitution$_e$ and aims at a synthesis of the two.(24)

In the rest of this chapter, I shall try to trace the most important variants of constitution theory in these traditions and to bring out the connections between them. I can do this, of course, only in outline, since a full account would require an intellectual history of the greater part of post-Enlightenment European philosophy and social theory. In particular, the connections between philosophy and social theory, such as those between neo-Kantianism and Weber's sociology, can only be drawn in a sketchy and tentative manner. I hope, however, that this will be enough to make the point of the chapter, that these diverse accounts of constitution indicate the need for a synthesis which takes the concept of constitution seriously in both its 'epistemic' and its 'ontological' variants. This, it seems to me, can best be done within the framework of a realist theory of science.

2 KANT AND NEO-KANTIANISM

Kant, having inaugurated the 'Copernican turn' in the theory of knowledge of 'suppos[ing] that objects must conform to our knowledge',(25) offers an account of constitution which can be placed towards the 'weak' end of the continuum. For one thing, it is objects of experience, not things in themselves, which are constituted.(26) Second, he does not often use the term 'constitution' except in the sense of 'structure' or 'make-up'.(27) The significant use of the term is in its adjectival form, in the antithesis 'constitutive'/'regulative', applied to the principles or rules for the employment of the categories. Thus the axioms of intuition and the anticipations of perception, which establish, respectively, extensive and intensive magnitude, 'may ... be called constitutive', (28) while an analogy of experience is(29)
> only a rule according to which a unity of experience may arise from a perception. It does not tell us how mere perception or empirical intuition in general itself comes about. It is not a principle *constitutive* of the objects, that is, of the appearances, but only *regulative*. The same can be asserted of the postulates of empirical thought in general ... They are merely regulative principles, and are distinguished from the mathematical, which are constitutive, not indeed in certainty - both have certainty *a priori* - but in the nature of their evidence.

It is important to note that, contrary to widespread belief, Kant does not see the categories themselves as constitutive; rather, it is the rules of their objective use which have a constitutive role.(30) In general, there seems to be something of a paradox in that while in one sense the concept of constitution is central to Kant's whole project, it appears in a rather muted form. Husserl, whose own account will be discussed later, raised precisely this objection in a manuscript fragment which also sheds an interesting light on his own philosophical priorities. According to Husserl, Kant's accounts of the constitution of nature for science(31)
> obviously presuppose a phenomenology and an insight into the constitution of the lower levels of experience - a task which Kant did not take in hand. Even where he touched on it, he had no idea of its importance. As a result he fails even to formulate the

problem correctly. The problem of constitution altogether: its stages, the need to carry out the systematic descriptions appropriate to each stage, to elicit the fundamental connections and to evaluate the various a priori possibilities which are open possibilities within the sphere of what is fixed, i.e. of the pure ego and pure consciousness, and then to construct these in such a way as to fulfil the idea of 'objective' knowledge - all this is alien to Kant, however much his critique of reason tends towards this problematic and occasionally comes very close to it.

The criticisms of Kant which Husserl raises in this passage cannot usefully be discussed within the limits of this chapter, since they would involve a systematic comparison of the work of both thinkers. It is clear, however, that Husserl is arguing for much closer attention to the details of the 'subject's' constituting activity than Kant is interested in providing. There seem to be, crudely, two reasons for this divergence. First, Husserl was simply much more interested in such matters; it is generally agreed, moreover, that his later work shows a distinct tendency towards the preoccupations of Lebensphilosophie.(32) Second, and more interestingly, we can ask what reasons Kant had for dealing fairly schematically with such matters. The answer, I think, is clear. Kant was concerned to provide transcendental arguments about the nature of the human faculties. The conclusions of these arguments are binding on all human beings and, more importantly, they are not based, in principle at least, on detailed claims about the way in which the process of knowledge actually takes place.

This opposition between Kant and Husserl must not be over-stated. Both thinkers declared their opposition to what Husserl called psychologism, and neither, perhaps, was able to avoid it. The general point, however, is this: where an account is given in terms of transcendental arguments, the processes of constitution run along rails; at worst, there is the possibility of derailment if, for example, the categories are extended beyond their effective limits. It is when the transcendental constraints are relaxed, as they are to a limited extent in Kant's 'Critique of Judgement' and more boldly in neo-Kantianism and, I would argue, in part at least of Husserl's work, that interesting questions arise about alternative possibilities in constituting theoretical objects and about what kinds of principles, if any, one can adduce to decide between these alternatives.

There is, in fact, a rather stronger emphasis on the notion of constitution in Kant's 'Critique of Judgement'.

Chapter 3

The faculty of judgment has the task of mediating between the understanding, which has its own sphere ... in the faculty of knowledge, in so far as it contains a priori constitutive principles of knowledge',(33) and reason, which provided constitutive principles a priori in relation to the faculty of desire, as described in the 'Critique of Practical Reason'. Theoretical and practical philosophy, the spheres of nature and freedom, must somehow be linked.(34)

Albeit, then, between the realm of the natural concept, as the sensible, and the realm of the concept of freedom, as the super-sensible, there is a great gulf fixed, so that it is not possible to pass from the former to the latter (by means of the theoretical employment of reason), just as if they were so many separate worlds, the first of which is powerless to exercise influence on the second: still the latter is *meant* to influence the former - that is to say, the concept of freedom is meant to actualize in the sensible world the end proposed by its laws; and nature must consequently also be capable of being regarded in such a way that in the conformity to law of its form it at least harmonizes with the possibility of the ends to be effectuated in it according to the laws of freedom. - There must, therefore, be a ground of the *unity* of the supersensible that lies at the basis of nature, with what the concept of freedom contains in a practical way, and although the concept of this ground neither theoretically nor practically attains to a knowledge of it, and so has no peculiar realm of its own, still it renders possible the transition from the mode of thought according to the principles of the one to that according to the principles of the other.

Cassirer's commentary(35) gives a useful gloss on this change of emphasis in Kant's philosophy.

The problem of which the *Critique of Pure Reason* took no account is that, while we must demand the systematic unity of experience even as regards the particular laws, we cannot establish this unity. For, as far as the understanding and its *a priori* knowledge of nature is concerned, we cannot exclude the possibility that actual experience might show us such a variety and heterogeneity of empirical laws as would make it impossible for us to relate them to one another in a system. The variety of empirical laws and of natural objects might be endlessly great, so that nature would present us with a chaotic aggregate and would reveal not the slightest trace of a system.

78 Chapter 3

We can quite clearly see what Kant's problem is. The understanding presents us with a world which is determined by the objective laws of the understanding. But if we are to have real experience, we must also presuppose that nature as regards its empirical laws will be intelligible to the human mind. If nature showed us only laws which were totally different from one another, we should be unable to apprehend it. Experience depends upon two *a priori* presuppositions: (a) that nature is determined by universal laws, and (b) that the empirical laws of nature are intelligible to the human mind.

That we are entitled to make the first of these presuppositions Kant has shown in the *Critique of Pure Reason*, by establishing the objective validity of transcendental laws. The second we may call a subjectively necessary transcendental presupposition; for we presuppose it, not because there are any objective reasons why we should believe it to be the case, but because without it experience would be impossible. 'Thus it is a subjectively necessary transcendental *presupposition* that this unlimited diversity of empirical laws and heterogeneity of natural forms, of which otherwise we might be afraid, actually does not occur in nature. We must presuppose, on the contrary, that nature, through the affinity of particular laws which stand under more general laws, provides itself with the qualities necessary for it to become experience as an empirical system.

Two points can be made, in very general terms, about this direction of Kant's thought. First, the distinction between things in themselves and phenomena appears to come under further strain, in addition to the internal difficulties raised by generations of readers of the 'Critique of Pure Reason'.

> the principle of Judgement which assumes an empirical system of nature, although only a system of our concepts of empirical objects, rests upon a transcendental *a priori* principle, i.e. a principle which is not merely concerned with our concepts of natural objects, but also with the objects themselves. We presuppose that the natural objects are of such a kind as to make it possible for our Judgement (a) to arrive at empirical concepts (which would be impossible if natural objects were totally different from each other), and (b) to compare these concepts with each other and to arrange them in a system.(36)

The second point is that in the very attempt to introduce order into an area of possible uncertainty and subjectivism, the 'unlimited diversity of empirical laws and heterogeneity of natural forms', Kant has to allow a greater role to human subjectivity. As Cassirer puts it,

> The principle of Judgement is of an entirely different kind from the objective principles of the understanding, which are necessary conditions of experience as such. It is a subjectively necessary principle, a necessary maxim of scientific enquiry....
> The principle of Judgement may be called an objective principle in so far as in enquiring into nature we must employ it, and cannot but assume that nature will adapt itself to our faculty of Judgement. But we may also call it subjective; for it is quite different from the objective principles of the understanding, and we are quite incapable of knowing prior to actual experience to what extent nature will comply with our desire to bring about the systematic unity of empirical laws.(37)

All Kant's thought is of course characterised by this involution of subjective and objective. The crucial distinction here, however, is that 'the understanding provides us with definite rules, whereas Judgement can do no more than provide us with a guiding principle, a principle which enables us to look for empirical concepts'.(38) To put it metaphorically, the transcendental guidelines have become less like tramlines and more like a radio beacon.

The Marburg neo-Kantian movement carried forward this shift of emphasis away from transcendental principles (and the distinction between phenomena and noumena) towards a greater emphasis on subjective construction. Their primary interest was in scientific cognition rather than general epistemology,(39) and it was one of the central tenets of this school that the objects of science are not simply 'given' but are constructed by the human understanding. Paul Natorp, who shared with Hermann Cohen the 'leadership' of this direction of neo-Kantianism, put it sharply at the beginning of his 'Allgemeine Psychologie': (40)

> All naive reflecting on basic problems of knowledge is initially directed quite unscrupulously at the *object* as though it were something given. One knows perhaps quite well, without yet being aroused thereby to any doubts, that in fact objects are in every case perceived, visualised, thought by us, the *subjects*. They are objects of consciousness.

Ernst Cassirer made the same point somewhat more fully at the beginning of volume II of 'The Philosophy of Symbolic Forms':(41)

> It is one of the first essential insights of critical

philosophy that objects are not 'given' to consciousness in a rigid, finished state, in their naked 'as suchness', but that the relation of representation to object presupposes an independent, spontaneous act of consciousness. The object does not exist prior to and outside of synthetic unity but is constituted only by this synthetic unity; it is no fixed form that imprints itself on consciousness but is the product of a formative operation effected by the basic instrumentality of consciousness, by intuition and pure thought.

As Fritz Kaufmann has pointed out, this is a considerable departure from Kant. 'Whereas to Kant knowledge is essentially intuition, the strict imperceptibility [Unanschaulichkeit] of the object of knowledge is proclaimed (from Cohen to Cassirer) as the true corner-stone of the "critical" theory of knowledge.'(42) While retaining in a sense a subject-object theory of knowledge, the neo-Kantians dissolved both subject and object into mere terminal points of the laws of thought, 'the immanent laws according to which thought does not accept its object as simply given, but constructs it in conformity with thought's own way of looking at things'.(43) The unity of the perceiving subject was likewise not given but constructed, by reversing the processes by which spirit had been objectified in science, art and morals.(44)

What one finds in Marburg neo-Kantianism, then, is a rather strong constitution$_e$ thesis, which leads to a kind of conventionalism. It would not be difficult, I think, to fill out the lines of influence from Cohen, via F.A. Lange, to Vaihinger.(45) At the same time, neo-Kantianism was a powerful resource in the early development of positivism.(46)

It is within the other school of neo-Kantianism that one finds a systematic discussion of problems of social theory.(47) Here, significantly, there seems to be a shift from an exclusive emphasis on constition$_e$ to an account of social and historical life which raises questions of constitution$_o$.

I shall confine myself to Rickert, Simmel and Max Weber. Here, constitution appears as essentially a matter of selection, not from a Kantian manifold,(48) but from a reality which, without some selective mechanism, would be too complex to be known. In the works to be discussed here,(49) Rickert takes for granted the purely epistemological questions concerning the initial constitution by a transcendental ego.(50) He starts with an empirical ego, exemplified by the natural or cultural scientist, confronted by a reality which is already formed in the Kantian sense, but not yet organised systematically in the manner of science. To do this, the subject requires a further set of conceptual forms which are methodological rather than constitutive in the strong sense.(51)

Rickert starts from the common neo-Kantian view of knowledge:
> Empirical reality proves to be for us an immense manifold, which seems to become even greater, the deeper we delve into it and analyse it into its individual parts. For even the 'smallest' part contains more than any finite man is able to describe....
> If we had, then, to *copy* [abbilden] reality in concepts, we should be confronted as knowing subjects [als Erkennde] by a task which was in principle impossible. Hence if anything which has so far been achieved may in any way claim to be knowledge it will have to be the case that cognition is not a process of copying by means of a description of 'phenomena', but one of *reconstruction* [Umbilden]. We may add, moreover, that this always involves a *simplification* by comparison with reality itself.(52)

There are, according to Rickert, two ways in which this simplifying reconstruction can be carried out. Empirical reality can be treated as 'nature', in which case we are interested in the general laws which it instantiates, or as 'history', in which case we are interested in individual(53) events as manifestations of values.(54)

Out of the enormous abundance of individual, i.e. discriminable, objects, the historian first considers only those which either themselves, in their individual peculiarity as bearers of complexes of meaning, actually embody cultural values or stand in some relationship to them. And out of the enormous abundance of differentiable components constituting the singularity of every object, he then selects, in turn, those on which its significance for cultural development depends and in which historical individuality, as distinguished from mere discriminable differentness, consists.

The concept of culture thus provides for historical concept formation the *principle for the selection of the essential* aspects of reality, just as the concept of nature as reality considered in relation to the universal does for the natural sciences. The concept of an historical individuality that can be represented as a real expression of complexes of meaning is first *constituted* [konstituiert] by means of the values that attach to culture and through reference to these values.

Rickert, like Max Weber after him, distinguished between reference to values (Wertbeziehung) and value-judgments:(55)
> The science of history must ... avoid making practical

judgements on its objects and evaluating them as good
or bad, but it can never lose from sight the relations
of the object to values in general, since it would
then be unable to separate historically important from
historically unimportant processes in empirical reality.
   Rickert, however, gives a less 'existentialist' account
of the origins of these values than does Weber; they are
what he calls 'general (or universal) cultural values'
(allgemeine Kulturwerte):(56)

> The values which guide and determine historical concept
> formation by reference to values ... [are] ... entirely
> taken from cultural life....

   What internally determined values guide historical
presentation, and in what the internally determined
concept of culture consists, can never be said by
logic, but only by historical science itself and an
overall philosophy or theory of Weltanschauungen
oriented to historical science.
   There is a considerable ambiguity in Rickert's model
of historical analysis about exactly where these values
are located, or at least which of the various possible
locations of them has logical priority over the others.
The most plausible interpretation seems to be something
like this. First, there must be values present in the
historical subject matter itself; we cannot write history
in terms of the concept of art or morality unless the
people whose history we are writing have these concepts
themselves. To say this, however, is also to say that
there must be some link between the 'native' concepts
and the general cultural values which the historian
shares with his or her culture. 'We only have an historical interest in a given reality when it is bound up with
real psychic entities who themselves take up a position
in relation to universal human values.'(57)
   The ultimate status of these values is a matter which
cannot be decided within an empirical science such as
history: we simply have to assume their universal status.
(58)

> if history is to compete with the kind of universal
> validity which natural science claims when it establishes laws of nature, we have to assume that certain
> values are not only factually valid for all members
> of certain communities, but that the recognition of
> values universally can be demanded as necessary and
> inevitable from every scientific investigator.

The historian cannot but start with the values of his
own community.(59)

> If the historian constructs his concepts according to
> the values of the community to which he himself belongs,

the objectivity of his account will seem to depend entirely upon the accuracy of his factual material, and the question whether this or that event of the past is important [wesentlich] cannot arise. He is immune from the charge of arbitrariness if he relates, for example, the development of art to the aesthetic values of his culture and the development of the state to its political values. He thus creates a narrative which, so far as it avoids unhistorical value *judgements*, is valid for everyone who accepts aesthetic or political values as normative for the members of his community. If on the other hand the historian has first to 'work his way into' ['hineinleben'] alien cultural values, in order to be able to give an objective account even of cultural developments which are remote from his own from the standpoint of their own historical centres,[60] this work too can be performed in principle by a purely empirical registration [Konstatierung] of facts. The historian asks what values are valued by the historical centres, or in what meaning-structures they really live. Only if a 'world history' is to be written can doubts remain whether the guiding value orientations used in this operation can count on empirically observable recognition in all the cultural communities embraced by this account. But this last situation does not affect the empirical objectivity of the individual accounts.

We are not concerned here with the inadequacies of Rickert's account of historical concept formation,(61) but with the concept of constitution that is involved in his account. It can easily be seen that there is an ambiguity about whose values are involved in the constitution of historical reality and what their status is. Andrew Arato states Rickert's problem neatly in his very stimulating article on neo-Kantianism:(62)

> given the implicit problem that historical reality is constituted not only by historians but by historical actors, he was forced to adopt a non-transcendental point of view here ...(63)

[but he] ... tried to hold onto the point of view of the transcendental constitution of culture, even as he began to assign value-realisation to empirical subjects.(64)

Rickert's problem is therefore one of 'distinguishing between the constitutive activity of the historian and the creative activity of the historical actor'.(65) A similar problem pervades the work of Georg Simmel.

Simmel insists, perhaps even more strongly than Rickert,

84 Chapter 3

on the concept of constitution. This comes out most clearly in 'The Problems of the Philosophy of History',(66) which is explicitly presented as 'a critique of historical realism: the view according to which historical science is simply a mirror image of the event "as it really happened"'.(67) Simmel claims:(68)

> The constitutive power of the intellect in relation to nature is generally acknowledged. However the point that the intellect has the same constitutive power in relation to history is obviously more difficult to grasp. This is because mind is the material of history.

Simmel's aim is (69)

> to establish that the sovereign intellect also forms the construct of *mental existence* which we call history only by means of its own special categories. Man as an object of knowledge is a product of nature and history. But man as a knowing subject produces both nature and history.

Simmel defends an orthodox neo-Kantian view of knowledge:

> A science of the total event is not only impossible for reasons of unmanageable quantity: it is also impossible because it would lack a *point of view* or *problematic*. Such a problematic is necessary in order to produce a construct that would satisfy our criteria for knowledge. A science of the total event would lack the category that is necessary for the identification and coherence of the elements of the event. There is no knowledge as such: knowledge is possible only in so far as it is produced and structured by constitutive concepts that are qualitatively determined.(70)

> ... historical knowledge represents a transformation of experienced reality. Like the natural sciences, history is dependent upon the formative purposes of knowledge and the a priori categories which constitute the form or nature of knowledge as a product of our synthetic activities.(71)

> There is absolutely no mechanical correspondence between knowledge and its object. Instead, a complex and dialectical process of mediation can be identified, a process in which knowledge stands in a variety of different relationships to its object; this holds true whether or not the object of knowledge is the mind itself [as is the case, according to Simmel, with history].(72)

History, like natural science, has to constitute its own material, with the difference that:(73)

History as science encounters this material as a kind of half-formed or proto-product. It is already constituted by a priori forms of comprehension. The categories which constitute this material as history are already present in the material itself, at least in an embryonic or modified form. They cannot be distinguished from this material so absolutely or definitely as we can distinguish the category of causality from the idea of mere temporal succession.
The historian therefore starts from an already partially interpreted life-world, reinterpreting it so as to make it into something which can count as history. 'From raw material constituted by reality that is grasped in its concrete immediacy, history produces a structure with different dimensions and another style.'(74)
Simmel makes a similar argument about sociology, which is, however, even more remote than history from immediate experience. Sociology is a second order science, making eclectic use of the products of other sciences which are themselves syntheses.(75)
it does not apply itself directly to the primitive material which other sciences work on. Instead, as a so to speak second order science, it creates new syntheses out of what for the other sciences is already a synthesis. In its current state it provides merely a new standpoint for observing known facts.
Sociology does not have a real object, 'society', any more than astronomy studies 'the cosmos' tout court (rather than the movements of individual stars).(76) What 'pure sociology' does is to abstract from phenomena(77)
the mere element of sociation. It isolates it inductively and psychologically from the heterogeneity of its contents and purposes, which, in themselves, are not societal. It thus proceeds like grammar, which isolates the pure forms of language from their contents through which these forms, nevertheless, come to life. In a comparable manner, social groups which are the most diverse imaginable in purpose and general significance, may nevertheless show identical forms of behaviour toward one another on the part of their individual members. We find superiority and subordination, competition, division of labour, formation of parties, representation, inner solidarity coupled with exclusiveness toward the outside, and innumerable similar features in the state, in a religious community, in a band of conspirators, in an economic association, in an art school, in the family. However diverse the interests are that give rise to these sociations, the *forms* in which the interests are realised may yet be identical.

It is clear that what Simmel is talking about here are empirical forms of interaction, rather than forms in which reality is transcendentally constituted. This can be illustrated even in Simmel's famous excursus, How is Society Possible?(78) Here, Simmel draws an explicit parallel, and contrast, with Kant's account of nature: 'the unity of society needs no observer. It is directly realised by its own elements because these elements are themselves conscious and synthesising units ... the consciousness of constituting with the others a unity is actually all there is to this unity.'(79)

In this highly ambiguous essay, Simmel seems to be describing an epistemic process with, so to speak, an ontological upshot. Society is constituted$_o$ by individual acts of constitution$_e$; thus 'particular, concrete processes of the individual consciousness' achieve 'the production of a societal unit out of individuals'.(80) It may be that Simmel's use of epistemological language(81) is somewhat misleading. But if, as a number of critics have suggested,(82) he is offering an ontological and perhaps in part a psychological answer to the question he poses, this answer comes out in a highly idealist form. Against this, one must surely recognise that society is made up of more than conscious processes and that these conscious processes themselves are not reducible to the consciousness which we have of them. Simmel's substantive sociology seems implicitly to accept this,(83) in which case the 'Kantian' excursus becomes an embarrassing irrelevance.

An alternative reading of Simmel's excursus, ingeniously advanced by Karin Schrader-Klebert,(84) attempts to avoid these undesirable ontological consequences by reformulating his question as one about the possibility of sociology, rather than society. Simmel's concept of society functions as a regulative idea in the Kantian sense: a *'projected* unity' which aims 'to bring unity into the body of our detailed knowledge, and thereby to *approximate* the rule to reality'.(85)

I shall discuss this idea in more detail in chapter 5. Shrader-Klebert's interpretation is partially supported by Simmel's frequent references to sociology as a method. (86) On the other hand, there is also considerable evidence of a shift of emphasis in Simmel's thought from a transcendental conception to an empirical one, this being reflected (as well as to some extent obscured) in his concept of form.(87) Perhaps the most that can be said is that Simmel never resolved this ambiguity, never provided a stable account of the relationship between the theoretical constitution$_e$ of history by the historian and the constitution$_o$ of history by human actors.(88) This crucial problem, as we have seen, preoccupied Rickert; it can be found, somewhat less starkly, in Max Weber, and it is again central in existential phenomenology and Marxism. Max Weber's account of constitution is one of the aspects in which his work is closest to that of Rickert. (89) Like Rickert, Weber gave a central place to Wertbeziehung as a principle of selection.(90) He applies a similar principle to the construction of concepts, which is a matter of appropriateness to the task in hand, a 'Zweckmässigkeitsfrage'(91) and the investigation of causal relationships, where what determines how far these should be pursued is 'the value ideas which dominate the scientist and his age'.(92) 'The concept of culture', he claims, 'is a value-concept'(93) and the 'socio-economic' quality of an event is a function of our cognitive interests, rather than its objective property.(94)

I think that Weber's formulation of these principles is emphatic enough to make it reasonable to talk about a theory of constitution in his work. At the same time, however, we must remember that this is not a constitution ex nihilo, out of a mere chaotic flux of sensations, but rather a matter of selecting certain facts and relationships which are relevant from a particular point of view. In other words, the problem is not that there are no real causal connections between things in reality, but rather that there are so many of them that we can only make sense of them from particular points of view. As Deryck Beyleveld puts it, with exemplary clarity:(95)

> We can attribute to Weber a two-tier conception of the constitution of our knowledge of empirical reality. At the first and more abstract level there are theoretical presuppositions or categories which constitute our knowledge in the Kantian sense. *Within* non-relativistic and universal frameworks so constituted there are points of view which are constituted by cognitive interests which are relative. The non-relative categories underlie a fixed reality which the relative ones give us different perspectives on.

What becomes of historical or social-scientific objectivity, on Weber's account? Without going into interpretative details of the sort alluded to in the previous note, we can set up two scenarios in abstract terms, using Beyleveld's dichotomy. In the first, the 'relative' side is confined to the selection and evaluation of problems: what we choose to study and what interest, if any, our work has for others. Both these questions are of course independent of the truth or validity of the results. There is considerable textual evidence that this is Weber's position; in the 'Objectivity' essay, for example, he emphatically denies

> that the investigations in the cultural sciences can only ... have *results* which are 'subjective' in the sense that they are *valid* for one person and not valid for another. What changes is rather the degree to which they *interest* one and not the other. In other words: *whatever* becomes the object of investigation ... is determined by the value-ideas dominating the scientist and his time; but as to the 'How?', the method of investigation ... the scientist, of course, here as everywhere is bound to the norms of our thinking.(96)

This position of Weber's can only be occupied without discomfort if one accepts his restriction of constitution to the selection of what is '*worth* knowing' from the empirically given.(97) This seems, however, to presuppose an ontology of atomic facts which are selected and given 'cognitive value' by value-related frameworks. A stronger constitution thesis, which he should perhaps have taken more seriously than he did, is that the value-conditioned (98) selection of aspects of social reality to be investigated may tend also in all interesting cases, to make the results of the investigation irremediably subjective.(99)

In the end, I suggest, Weber retained a deep-seated empiricism, the empiricism of a brilliant historian; it is an unstated premise of his methodology that theories, wherever they come from must 'bump up against' reality and be judged by it. This reality consists of discrete facts which are knowable directly. We may disagree over whether a particular fact is properly characterised as 'economic', as part of 'culture', or whatever, but our knowledge of it is independent of these disagreements. Hence the emphasis on selection in the way Weber poses the problem, even in passages such as this: 'There is no absolutely "objective" scientific analysis of culture - or ... - of "social phenomena" *independent* of special and "one-sided" viewpoints according to which - expressly or tacitly, consciously or unconsciously, - they are selected, analysed and organised for expository purposes.' (100)

Weber offers, then, a very weak account of constitutione, though he occasionally flirts with what seems like a stronger version. His more speculative reflections bear not so much on cognitive relativism of the sort which might seem to follow from his position, but on the fact that the pursuit of science and truth itself rests on a choice.(101)

So far we have looked only at constitution as the act of the social scientist. It could, however, be argued that Weber also has a theory of the way in which social reality is constituted by individual action, and furthermore, the way in which actions are themselves constituted by the meanings which actors attach to them - their projects. This is, of course, the aspect of Weber's work which Schutz draws out and elaborates. There is also textual evidence that Weber was committed to these views, especially in the opening chapter of 'Economy and Society', with its starting point in action, defined in terms of the subjective meaning which the actor 'attaches' to it and his insistence that the sociologist must view social collectivities such as 'states' as '*solely* the resultants and modes of organisation of the particular acts of individual persons'.(102)

Some commentators have suggested that all this stress on action is no more than a bow in the direction of current theoretical fashions and is of no importance in his substantive work.(103) This is a grotesque exaggeration; Weber frequently, even characteristically, discusses social structures such as bureaucracy or the priesthood in terms of the 'typical actions' of incumbents of these roles. What must be admitted, however, is that Weber pays little more than lip service to the idea of 'subjective meaning' as an object of empirical inquiry; he retreats very rapidly to the level of ideal-typical characterisation of actions and intentions. And though he is certainly interested in the unintended consequences of action, and to this extent in the relation between actors' and observers' categories, he is not concerned with the 'social construction of reality' in the manner of Schutz or Simmel.(104)

These two senses of constitution can be brought into relation with each other if we return to the transcendental/empirical polarity which was mentioned in connection with Rickert and Simmel. As I suggested above, Weber gives an existentialist twist to Rickert's concept of Wertbeziehung. Where Rickert stressed the generality of cultural values, Weber stresses their diversity and the likelihood of fundamental and irresoluble conflicts between them.(105) This Nietzschean theme is one which is conventionally and rightly associated with Weber's later work, and in particular with the essays on science and politics as vocations. It seems, however, that at the same time as Weber lays greater weight on the conflict between values in the world, the methodological significance of values is played down. In 'Economy and Society', as I noted above, the emphasis is on what verstehende sociology is concerned with, in the sense of interested in. It is only indirectly interested in 'non-meaningful events' such as plagues or physiological reactions, or in juridical concepts of the state or the limited company, or in individual events. What is involved here is a kind of 'scientific' evaluation,(106) relatively remote from actual value conflicts. In fact, of course, this is very close to Rickert's original conception. What seems to happen in Weber's work is a certain divergence between his growing stress on existential combat between rival values in the world and his account of social scientific concept formation.(107) In the latter case, Wertbeziehung does come close to collapsing, as Runciman wants it to, into a matter of theoretical presuppositions.(108)

What account does Weber offer of the status of values in these two senses? The first sense can be dealt with easily: there is a constant conflict between rival value-conceptions, such as that between the ethic of the Sermon on the Mount and the requirements of political action. This conflict cannot be resolved by rational means, least of all the means of science. To attempt to do this would be not only to stretch science beyond its limits, but also to adopt an existentially inauthentic position as a moral actor.(109)

Wertbeziehung in the context of scientific concept formation is a very different matter. Here we may distinguish three sets of presuppositions. The first concerns the ultimate value of science, truth, etc., überhaupt. One may choose to adopt or not to adopt this value.(110) If one does accept scientific truth as a value, one is then committed to a further set of presuppositions concerning such matters as scholarship and respect for evidence. Third, there are the presuppositions of a particular discipline or specialty such as verstehende sociology, some of whose principles were indicated above. These are all empirical rather than transcendental presuppositions; they are satisfied to varying degrees by different scientists. Nevertheless, it can be argued that they are constitutive of the activities to which they refer, at least where these activities are understood in an ideal-typical sense.

In conclusion, then, I suggest that Weber's account of the constitution$_o$ of human social life (including such activities as science) gives a central place to meaningfully oriented human action. The constitution$_e$ of social reality is essentially a matter of selection from all the infinitely complex connections and interrelations which may be observed in empirical reality; this selection is governed by some combination of general cultural values, the individual values of the scientist, the values which he or she hypothetically adopts as an organising device (e.g. to present the world-view of a particular social

Chapter 3

group), and the theoretical presuppositions of the relevant scientific discipline.

3 HUSSERL, SCHUTZ AND 'PHENOMENOLOGICAL' SOCIOLOGY

Husserl almost certainly took the term 'constitution' from the Marburg neo-Kantians, whose work he increasingly appreciated as he himself moved from an empirical to a transcendental framework.(111) Earlier, his slogan 'Back to the things themselves' was at least an implicit criticism of the contemporary vogue in neo-Kantian and positivist philosophies for dissolving things into thought-constructs or sense-impressions. Husserl's philosophy can be plausibly represented as a search for certainty which leads him, paradoxically, to a bizarre form of transcendental idealism.(112) A full account of Husserl's concept of constitution would have to be grounded in the development of his thought as a whole. The basic themes of this development are still hotly contested among Husserlian scholars; all I can do here is to outline some salient features of Husserl's very ambiguous concept of constitution.

One way into Husserl's account of constitution is via his distinction between phenomenology and ontology.(113)

The ontological approach ... takes entities in their identity and for the sake of their identity as something fixed. The phenomenological-constitutive approach takes the entity in flow, namely as the unity of a constituting stream.[114] It follows the movements, the offshoots, in which such an entity and every component, side and real property of such an entity is the correlate of identity. This approach is to some extent kinetic, or 'genetic': a genesis which belongs to a 'transcendental' world which is totally different from that of natural and natural scientific genesis.

As we have seen, Husserl complained that Kant did not do justice to the complexity of these transcendental-psychological processes. Fritz Kaufmann presents Husserl's differences with neo-Kantianism in much the same terms:(115)

The abstraction of the ... [phenomenological] ... constitutive process ... is not so remote as to make it a mere dialectical construction. Even when intentional experience [intentionales Erlebnis] is not a matter of personal activity, it is still borne and animated by living consciousness. And, whereas Natorp speaks of a quasi-automatic and utopian 'movement of the categories' as such, taken to enjoy a sort of mythical super-being, Husserl deals not only with the categories but with the *kategorein* itself, the very acts of determining things.

How radical is Husserl's account of constitution in terms of the continuum referred to at the beginning of this chapter? Current Husserl scholarship does not offer a unanimous answer to this question. Eugen Fink who, with Ludwig Landgrebe, was one of Husserl's closest collaborators, interprets him in the most radical way: 'In Husserl, the meaning of "transcendental constitution" fluctuates between formation of sense and creation.'(116) Most other commentators seem to agree that Husserl always meant something much less than 'creation'.

One point at least is fairly clear: Husserl takes some trouble to rule out a Kantian reading which would distinguish between reality 'for us', constituted by consciousness, and reality 'in itself': 'We should not let ourselves be misled by talk about the transcendence of a thing with respect to consciousness or about its "being in itself". The genuine concept of the transcendence of the thing ... can be drawn only from the essential content proper to perception.'(117)

As Sokolowski puts it, glossing an earlier passage, 'The world that we perceive, the world that we "constitute", is the real world. The world of phenomena is not a veil between us and reality; it is reality itself'.(118) And yet, Husserl insists, 'between consciousness and reality there yawns a true abyss of meaning'.(119) To quote Sokolowski again, 'What reality is in itself can only be reached by consciousness even though it must remain, in principle, radically distinct from and transcendent to consciousness. This is the mystery of intentionality, the mystery of consciousness.'(120)

We must therefore look rather more closely at Husserl's account of the role of subjectivity. His reference to an abyss between consciousness and reality, and his rejection of a Kantian account of the abyss, point towards a weak formulation of constitution.(121) Second, it is also significant that 'Husserl's analyses of constitution always possess a certain formalism. They leave room for a facticity in what is constituted, and do not explain away, by means of subjectivity, the content of what is the object of intentionality.'(122) Subjectivity provides the necessary but not the sufficient conditions for objects to have meaning.(123) It is in this sense, perhaps, that we should understand the formulation in the Encyclopedia Britannica article: 'Not the world or any part of it appears, but the "sense" of the world.'(124)

It is not easy to decide how to take this claim. Formally, it seems to mark out the phenomenological concept of constitution as something very different from the neo-Kantian one. In practice, however, it may not make very

much difference. The feeling that this may be in part a verbal solution to a tension within Husserl's thought is strengthened if one looks at the way in which he sets up the transcendental situation. As Kolakowski puts it, constitution(125)
> is not a creation ex nihilo; rather it is an act of endowing the world with meaning. In transcendentally reduced consciousness, however, each act of reaching the object *is* an act of supplying it with meaning; any sense is the product of constitution, including, in particular, the sense of an object as an *existing* one.

In other words, we are simply returned to face the fundamental contrast between empirical and transcendental. As we saw earlier, Husserl is concerned with the transcendental grounding of knowledge in general and the sciences in particular.(126) Phenomenology, as Beyleveld puts it, confronts two imperatives in this role: it must be true to the phenomena, showing what is given to pure or transcendental consciousness, and it must show how these phenomena are grounded in the constituting acts of the transcendental ego.(127) Transcendental constitution in this sense retains a limited popularity,(128) but Husserl's programme is generally recognised to be impracticable in anything like its original form. Kolakowski neatly states the central problem:(129)
> we have no universally valid criteria to catch meaningful structures ... everyone has a different insight which itself proves that we are far from apodictic certitude. It would be fair to say that the destiny of Husserl's project was similar to that of Descartes: his *pars destruens* turned out to be stronger and more convincing than his belief to have discovered an original well of certitude. This seems to be the common lot of philosophers.

Husserl's project having led to an apparent dead end, most writers who have tried to apply a phenomenological approach to social theory have abandoned his transcendental framework. Constitution becomes an empirical act by an empirical subject. This is the case with Alfred Schutz, the leading representative of this tradition.

We have already noted Schutz's remark that 'the phenomenologist ... does not have to do with the objects themselves; he is interested in their *meaning*, as it is constituted by the activities of our mind'.(130) A few pages earlier in the same article, he writes:(131)
> our knowledge of an object, at a certain given moment, is nothing else than the sediment of previous mental processes by which it has been constituted. It has its own history, and this history of its constitution

can be found by questioning it. This is done by turning back from the seemingly ready-made object of our thought to the different activities of our mind in which and by which it has been constituted step by step.

In a more seminal article, Commonsense and Scientific Interpretation of Human Action, Schutz introduces the same ideas via a discussion of Whitehead, and refers to James and Dewey as well as to Bergson and Husserl. 'Facts' are abstractions, 'selected from a universal context by the activities of our mind. They are, therefore, always interpreted facts.'(132) (And in particular):(133)

> The thought objects constructed by the social scientists refer to and are founded upon the thought objects constructed by the common-sense thought of man living his everyday life among his fellow-men. Thus, the constructs used by the social scientist are, so to speak, constructs of the second degree, namely constructs of the constructs made by the actors on the social scene, whose behaviour the scientist observes and tries to explain in accordance with the procedural rules of his science.

Schutz's account of constitution can be specified by saying that it is (1) empirical,(134) (2) radical, and (3) at least in intention, methodological or epistemic rather than ontological. I shall discuss these three claims in turn.(135)

(1) Husserl's account of constitution, as we have seen, is almost always a transcendental one. Schutz, after believing for a time that intersubjectivity had to be grounded in a transcendental reduction, came to see it, as, in Gorman's words, 'not a problem of constitution to be solved in the transcendental sphere, but a basic attribute of our life-world, adequately described only by phenomenologically analysing that life-world'.(136) As Schutz puts it in 'The Phenomenology of the Social World':

> The purpose of this work, which is to analyse the phenomenon of meaning in ordinary [mundanen] social life, does not require the achievement of a transcendental knowledge that goes beyond that sphere.... In ordinary social life we are no longer concerned with the constituting phenomena as these are studied within the sphere of the phenomenological reduction. We are concerned only with the phenomena corresponding to them within the natural attitude.(137)

> [In other words] the level at which the social world is constituted in acts of everyday life with others - Acts, that is, in which meanings are established and interpreted.(138)

Now if Husserl's phenomenology, by confining its attention to consciousness, runs the risk of becoming wholly solipsistic,(139) Schutz is in danger of arriving at a somewhat similar position by the opposite route. If constitution is the act of an empirical ego, it is no longer, as it is for Husserl, wholly separate and sui generis; it becomes what Beyleveld calls an 'ordinary activity'.(140) Thus on the one hand, 'knowledge' becomes a matter of convention, and on the other, arguably, the empirical ego can change the world merely by constituting it in a different way.(141) Schutz can escape these consequences only if his notion of constitution is sufficiently limited or if it can be shown to have no more than methodological significance.

(2) It should, however, be fairly clear from the preceding discussion of Schutz that his account of constitution is closer to the radical end of the spectrum.(142) Meaning is not something discovered 'tel quel' in reality; it is 'lived experiences which give meaning to an action'. (143) *'Meaning is a certain way of directing one's gaze at an item of one's own experience.'*(144) This interpretation must not be exaggerated; Schutz strongly implies in the same passage that there are differences in the potential meaningfulness of objects:(145)

what we call behaviour is already meaningful in a more primitive sense of the term. Behaviour as a lived experience is different from all other lived experiences in that it presupposes an activity of the Ego. Its meaning is therefore constituted in Acts wherein the Ego takes up one attitude or position after another.

And there seems little doubt that Schutz subscribed to Weber's principle that 'the course of human action and human expressions of every sort are open to an interpretation in terms of meaning [sinnvolle Deutung] which in the case of other objects would have an analogy only on the level of metaphysics'.(146) But for all that, Schutz remains firmly in the phenomenological tradition of the analysis of meaning in terms of acts of Sinngebung, as 'an operation of intentionality'.(147)

It might be argued that Schutz's famous 'postulates' for what he calls 'scientific model constructs of the social world' represent some sort of limit on the social scientist's freedom of theoretical constitution. But as I argued in the previous chapter, the low-key way in which Schutz presents the postulates suggests that they are not intended to do much in this regard.(148)

(3) In Burke Thomason's ingenious interpretation, Schutz holds a radical version of the constitution thesis

but only as an epoché, i.e. in a non-ontological form.
(149) Thus:
> For Schutz, no ontological claims about the *real* status
> of social reality are involved. His view that men 'con-
> struct' [aufbauen] the world in the process of consti-
> tuting its meaningful [sinnhafte] character is adopted
> purely for the purpose of disclosing the sense men make
> and then act upon in daily life ... he makes no claim
> that social reality *is* only a complex of humanly con-
> stituted objectivations and typifications....(150)
>
> Only by keeping carefully in mind the methodological
> character of Schutz' constructionist orientation can
> one possibly account for such things as his tolerance
> of Parsons' action framework and his rejection of
> Garfinkel's 'congruence theory'.(151)

This is a plausible interpretation of Schutz's intentions.
All he requires us to do is, as Deryck Beyleveld puts it,
'to see the objects of the natural attitude as having
their nature constituted, as not being given'.(152)
Indeed, Schutz implies at one point that this epoché
might be understood as an epoché of an epoché:(153)

> The suggestion may be ventured that man within the
> natural attitude also uses a specific epoché, of
> course quite another one than the phenomenologist.
> He does not suspend belief in the outer world and its
> objects, but on the contrary, he suspends doubt in
> its existence. What he puts in brackets is the doubt
> that the world and its objects might be otherwise
> than it appears to him.[154] We propose to call this
> *epoché* the *epoché of the natural attitude*.

At the end of 'The Phenomenology of the Social World'
Schutz puts his own project in context with a distinction
between two classes of social science:(155)

> First, they can be *pure theories of the form* of the
> social world, which deal with the constitution of
> social relationships and social patterns, the act-
> objectivities and artefacts in the conscious processes
> of individuals who live in the social world, meanwhile
> comprehending all these things by a purely descriptive
> method. However, the social sciences can also take as
> their subject matter the *real-ontological content* of
> the social world as already constituted and study the
> relationships and patterns in themselves - the already
> given historical or social acts and the artefacts as
> objects independent of the subjective experiences in
> which they were constituted.

Schutz is proposing, so to speak, a division of labour
within which he and Parsons can continue to get on with

Chapter 3

their respective projects without treading on each other's toes.(156) In a sense, Schutz transferred to his own project the principle which, he argued, held for phenomenology in general:(157)
the results of phenomenological research cannot and must not clash with the tested results of the mundane sciences, or even with the proved doctrines of the so-called philosophies of the sciences ... phenomenology has its field of research in its own right, and hopes to end where the others begin.
What style of theorising one adopts, whether one writes 'The Social System' or The Stranger, is a matter of personal decision.(158)

I have dwelt on this aspect of Schutz's project at some length because this notion of an intellectual division of labour between separate sciences, each making heuristic assumptions within its own province of meaning but avoiding any claims about reality in general, radically threatens the realist view of social science for which I have been arguing in this book. Schutz is evading his responsibilities in presenting his work as he does. First, there is a question of pragmatics; in presenting the social world under the aspect of its constitution, Schutz inevitably makes it appear flimsier, less substantial than it is conventionally thought to be. This is, of course, a perfectly reasonable view to uphold, but it generates an obligation to say something to one's readers about how one views its implications. Whether or not Schutz is committed to a substantive ontology of the social, his work clearly insinuates one, and this requires discussion.(159) Second, to the extent that there is more to social reality than the process of its constitution, Schutz is needlessly restricting the explanatory possibilities of his social theory. It is a pleasant irony that sociology, which cut its teeth analysing the division of labour, should increasingly exemplify it in the division between structuralist macrosociology and interactionist or phenomenological microsociology; but the latter division is not, perhaps, a necessary one.(160)

These inadequacies of Schutz's magnificent attempt to synthesise subjectivist philosophy and social theory also seem to threaten subsequent attempts in this direction. (161) Many recent formulations are so loosely expressed that it is impossible to know how to evaluate them even as programmes.(162) There seems to be a tendency within ethnomethodology to push the concept of constitution to its limit,(163) while relying on some notion of social/ linguistic intersubjectivity to mitigate the irrationalist implications of this step. So far there is no sign of a satisfactory solution to these problems; on the contrary, most writers in this tradition appear not to take them at all seriously.(164)

So far in this chapter we have been dealing with epistemic accounts of constitution, and indicating the points at which they touch on ontological questions. Within the Marxist tradition, as we shall see, this emphasis is reversed. The dominant theme is the ontological self-constitution of (socialised) human beings, with some writers also stressing the specificity of epistemic questions.

4 THE MARXIST TRADITION

Having jumped in section 2 from Kant to turn-of-the-century neo-Kantianism, we must now trace the other line of descent to Hegel and Marx. Hegel's opposition to Kant is neatly indicated in his 'Lectures on the History of Philosophy': (165)

> the Kantian philosophy no doubt leads reality back to self-consciousness, but it can supply no reality to this essence of self-consciousness, or to this pure self-consciousness, nor can it demonstrate Being in the same. It apprehends simple thought as having difference in itself, but does not yet apprehend that all reality rests on this difference.

Hegel quotes the introduction to the 'Critique of Judgement', in which Kant writes that 'the faculty of judgement must assume as a principle for its own use that what is contingent for us contains a unity, which for us indeed is not knowable, and yet thinkable, in the connection of the manifold with an implicitly possible experience'. Hegel comments:

> This principle hereby at once falls back again into the subjectivity of a thought, and is only a maxim of our reflection, by which nothing is to be expressed regarding the objective nature of the object, because Being-in-itself is once for all fixed outside of self-consciousness, and the Understanding is conceived only in the form of the self-conscious, not in its becoming another.(166)

From his discussion of Kant one can extract the two central aspects of Hegel's thought which are relevant to the question of constitution.(167) First, there is something he shares with Kant: his denial of unmediated knowledge.(168) Second, his critique of epistemology, where 'it is assumed that the material of knowledge is present in and for itself in the shape of a finished world apart from Thinking, that Thinking is in itself empty, and comes to that world from outside as Form to Matter'.(169) Despite the throwaway formulation, this passage actually points to the positive side of Hegel's critique of epistemology: the claim that reality in itself, and not just in the cognitive relation, is conceptually mediated. Partially independent of this substantive claim is the criticism of epistemology which Hegel puts forward in the Introduction to the 'Phenomenology'(170) in justification of his own alternative, The exposition of knowledge as a phenomenon (Die Darstellung des erscheinenden Wissens). (171)

What Hegel's philosophy offers, under the name of absolute knowledge, is the unity of thought and reality. If one looks at the world rationally, it will look rationally back.(172) For Marx, however, reality is not a product of thought; it is therefore a contingent question whether, and if so how, reality can be rationally comprehended. Marx agrees with Kant and Hegel that there is no immediate knowledge; it requires an effort of conceptual abstraction. With this proviso, there can be a partial identity of thought and reality sufficient to sustain the operation which Marx calls 'critique'.(173) Whether Marx is committed to, or able to sustain, a stronger or more precise view than this is not at all clear; the question is hotly disputed between defenders and opponents of identity theory (Identitätsphilosophie).(174) The question with which we are primarily concerned in this chapter is, however, the partially independent one of the role of constitution$_e$ and of epistemological questions generally, in Marx's thought and in that of later Marxists.

It may be best to set out the relationships between these questions in abstract terms before relating them to concrete formulations. If identity theory is right, there may or may not be a 'problem of knowledge' and a role for constitution$_e$. In other words, there are two alternatives. Either absolute knowledge is guaranteed simply by human practice, rationally comprehended (a materalist version of Hegel), or it is obtained only with the aid of a specific theoretical operation (whatever may also need to be done in reality to render that reality knowable). If identity theory is wrong, and there is no 'absolute knowledge', then the problem becomes one of explaining how we approximate to some such knowledge. It may be purely a matter of practical activity, rationally comprehended, or there may be an additional 'problem of knowledge', involving questions of constitution$_e$. In either case, there is a material process of constitution$_o$, the production of the human world, including human beings themselves.

Chapter 3

Let us now attach some names to these views. I have already cited, in the introductory section of this chapter,(175) some utterances of Marx which suggest that he is denying the existence of a separable 'problem of knowledge'. Marx is undoubtedly concerned to deny any special dignity to the knowledge-process; it becomes an aspect of social humanity's practical activity in the world.(176) Just as repellent is the idea of any universal method, applicable to any subject matter at all: a correct method is one which enables us to penetrate the real relations in a given slice of reality. The relations between method and content and between real relations and the phenomenal forms in which they appear are the central themes of Marx's account of scientific knowledge.(177) Like Hegel, though on a very different basis, Marx insists on the links between these concepts.(178) Science must start from and do justice to (though not reproduce uncritically) the phenomenal forms, such as the wage-form, which we find in social reality.

Marx clearly says enough about these matters to show that he does believe that the knowledge-process has a certain specific quality of its own. No less clearly, he is committed to some ontological claims about reality - at least to the possibility of being able to distinguish between phenomenal forms and real relations. And this movement from phenomenal forms to real relations must surely involve the initial positing of real relations which, if they existed, would explain the phenomena.(179)

Is it legitimate, then, to talk about a problem of knowledge in Marx (and by extension a problem of constitution$_e$)? I think it is, with the proviso that his is a relatively weak version of constitution, involving the postulation of hypothetical mechanisms which are then checked out to see if they are indeed operative. It does not seem illegitimate to call this a theory of constitution. In many ways it recalls the Kantian version, according to which our knowledge of the world is rationally secured via reflection on the constituting activity of the subject.(180)

In discussing Marx's work in these terms, it is necessary to explain away some passages which seem to suggest a more empiricist view, in which knowledge of visible forms is presented as entirely unmediated and unproblematic. 'The German Ideology' is a prime source of such insinuations, with its contrast between philosophical premises and 'real premises from which abstraction can be made only in the imagination ... real individuals',(181) the former premises being merely 'the distorted language of the real world'.(182)

These statements must not be taken too literally, any more than Marx's related claim in the 'Notes on Wagner' that he does not begin with concepts but with the social form of the commodity (as though the concept of the commodity were not itself a concept).(183) Derek Sayer, who rightly stresses that Marx saw himself as starting from empirically given premises rather than philosophically deduced ones, provides a penetrating account of Marx's intention.(184)

Phenomenal forms are most simply defined as those forms in which the phenomena of the external world 'represent themselves' in people's experience. This does not imply either that human activity plays no role in constructing the world that thus presents itself, or that what is presented is not already conceptually mediated. It merely supposes that at any given point there exists a constituted world whose phenomena have achieved what Marx calls 'the stability of natural, self-understood forms of social life' and which in the first instance confronts its participants as a simple datum.

Having indicated a minimal sense in which there seems to be an implicit theory of constitution in Marx's work, I shall now briefly discuss some other writers in the (broadly defined) Marxist tradition. Besides their intrinsic interest, these contributions should help to make clear the terms of the discussion. In particular, it seems that the tension in Marx-interpretation between 'realist' and 'dialectical' or 'activist' emphases(185) can be better understood, though not dispelled, by looking at the problem as one of constitution.

The influence of Kant lies heavily over much of this discussion, from Max Adler through to Habermas and Apel. (186) Adler traces the slow growth of interest in the relationship between Kant and Marx.(187) The initial attempts to confront Kant and Marx took place chiefly within ethical theory.(188) Max Adler rejected 'the fashionable desire to "supplement" Marx by Kant and, as it were, to provide a philosophical justification of socialism'.(189) Rather, he argued for a kind of convergence between the two thinkers, especially on epistemological questions. On the one hand, he claims that Marx's thought 'comes to meet the critical consequences of epistemology in the decisive point of the basically entirely intellectual nature of the concept of "thing" grounded in the regularity of consciousness'.(190) On the other, the concept (which he attempts to extract from Marx's work) 'of the socialised consciousness as a transcendental-social consciousness is the real meaning of

the epistemological critique of Kant, Fichte and Hegel'.
(191) Adler believed that Marxism, like any other sociological theory, required a transcendental foundation: 'It must be possible to demonstrate *in the observation of the object itself*, i.e. in our theoretical orientation, a ... transcendental principle which *brings the objects of science themselves, variously organised, before the cognitive faculty.*'(192)

Max Adler does not often refer to 'constitution', but the idea is fairly clearly present in his work. As we have seen, he stresses the need for a transcendental foundation of sociology;(193) this must, moreover, be found in a specifically social a priori which is the basis not only of social theory,(194) but also of intersubjectively valid knowledge of natural objects.(195) This is not just an a priori certainty which one can have of our own sociality, a certainty that, as Adler put it, 'Robinson [Crusoe] is not only an economic myth but also an epistemological impossibility'.(196) Adler is also asserting that what we call 'sociality' is 'a relation of human existence which is grounded in a form of the human cognitive faculty'.(197)

In other words, far from social science needing to be grounded in 'practical' philosophy, the transcendental basis of social being is grounded in theoretical reason. (198) It is because sociality, like space and time, is built into the categories of our thought that we are able to be sociable at all. There is an obvious parallel between Adler's position and Simmel's answer to the question 'How is society possible?'(199) And lest one should think that Adler's epistemological formulation of the basis of the social is to be taken metaphorically, he objects that Simmel, having raised the crucial epistemological question, does no more than reveal the 'psychological preconditions of social interaction'.(200)

Georg Lukács attempted, in the last years of his life, to formulate a historical materialist 'ontology of social being'.(201) Lukacs was not afraid of using the unfashionable terminology of ontology, but he insisted on the difference between Marxism and other ontological theories: (202)

> what is involved [in Marx's economics] is ... a scientificity which never loses its connection with the spontaneous ontological orientation of everyday life, but on the contrary continuously purifies this critically and develops it to a higher level; and which consciously elaborates the ontological determinations that necessarily lie at the basis of every science. It is precisely here that it clearly sets itself in opposition

to any kind of constructive philosophy, whether logical or otherwise. But a critical defence against the false ontologies that arise in philosophy in no way means that this scientificity takes up an ultimately anti-philosophical position. On the contrary. What is involved is rather a consciously critical collaboration between the spontaneous ontology of everyday life and scientific and philosophical correctness.

Within Marxism, ontology is prior to epistemology; (203) Lukacs criticises any rationalism which ascribes to a conceptual apparatus 'a general significance that is independent of the facts of the real world, and even lays down the law to them'.(204) What is crucial is the real, ontological constitution of social being - a historical process which is both a qualitative jump, from organic to social being 'and at the same time a laborious process, taking thousands of years ... until the new categories of being increase both extensively and intensively to a point where the new level of being can constitute itself as something fully formed and autonomous [auf sich beruhend]'.(205) The changing functions of production and consumption which Marx describes in the 'Grundrisse' (206) mark out 'a stage at which the genuine harmonisation of man, the tendency for the autonomous constitution of the categories of social being, is proclaimed'.(207)

Social being is, however, something in which consciousness is crucially involved:(208)

it is a specific characteristic of social being that consciousness is not simply a consciousness of something that ontologically remains completely indifferent towards its being known, but rather itself forms, in its presence or absence, correctness or falsity, a component of being; thus consciousness in the ontological sense is no mere epiphenomenon, irrespective of whether its concrete role in the given case is important or vanishingly small.

This is brought out concretely if one examines the concept of labour.(209) Labour is a teleological process, and it is part of the essence of teleology that it can only function in a real sense if it is posited. If a process is to be legitimately characterised as teleological when its being is outlined in concrete ontological terms, one must also prove ontologically beyond any doubt the being of the positing subject.(210)

Whereas ... causality is a principle of a self-motion ... dependent on itself, ... teleology is essentially a posited category. Every teleological process contains an object in view [Zielsetzung] and thereby a

consciousness which posits that object. Positing
therefore means in this connection no mere raising-
into-consciousness, as with other categories, above
all in the case of causality. Rather, consciousness
initiates with the act of positing a real process -
the teleological process. Positing therefore has here
an ineradicably teleological character.(211)
For labour to be successful, we must have an accurate
knowledge of causal connections in reality. Here Lukács
introduces a distinction between an ontological and an
epistemological sense of positing.(212)

If these [causal connections] are misidentified in the
process of investigation, they cannot be posited - in
an ontological sense - at all. They remain effective
in their natural way, and the teleological positing is
abolished, in the sense that it is reduced, as something which cannot be realised, to a mere fact of consciousness which is necessarily impotent in relation to
nature. Here the distinction between the ontological
and the epistemological sense of positing is immediately graspable. Epistemologically, an act of positing
which misses its object is still an act of positing ...
But the ontological positing of causality in the complex of a teleological positing process must grasp its
object correctly, or else it is - in this connection -
no positing process at all.

Lukács claims, quite unconvincingly, that the combination of causal and teleological processes which is involved in labour resolves traditional ontological questions
about the relation between causality and teleology.(213)
His ontology of social being is nevertheless an impressive
attempt to restate what is sometimes disparagingly called
the 'metaphysics of labour' contained in Marx's philosophical anthropology. And his claim that consciousness
is crucial to social being may be read as providing the
outlines of a more adequate and more recognisably materialistic formulation of Adler's very obscure assertions.
Lukács, like Marx, provides an account of ontological
constitution in which epistemic constitution has a place.

Lukács's very general discussion of labour forms an
interesting contrast with Alfred Sohn-Rethel's attempt to
locate the roots of epistemology and of 'Western' science
in general in the growth of an exchange economy and the
separation of intellectual and manual labour. I have
already referred(214) to Sohn-Rethel's concept of 'the
social synthesis: the network of relations by which society forms a coherent whole'.(215) When these relations
are mediated primarily by way of the 'exchange abstraction', the way is open to abstract thought in general.

'Commodity exchange, when attaining the level of a monetary economy, gives rise to the historical formation of abstract cognitive concepts able to implement an understanding of primary nature from sources other than manual labour.'(216)
Science, to put it bluntly, is grounded in the reification of relations of production and exchange.(217) This does not, however, vitiate it as an intellectual and practical activity, though it does mean that its operations are biased in certain directions; the most important example of this bias is the isolation of 'objects of study from the context in which they occur'.(218) Furthermore, scientists do not know what Sohn-Rethel has set out to tell them and are 'steeped in false consciousness about their function and the nature of science itself'.(219) Science does not need to be changed, in the ways canvassed by Marcuse and others, to an activity which is somehow less manipulative in its approach to nature.(220) With socialist relations of production, and a socialist consciousness among scientists, we will be guaranteed the awareness of the natural and social totality which (apart from the misuses to which science is put) is the only serious lacuna in contemporary science.
It is impossible here to discuss all the implications of Sohn-Rethel's imaginative sketch. It is clear, however, that his is an important attempt to identify some links between the two senses of constitution which are discussed in this chapter. In outline, the ontological constitution of exchange relations makes possible the constitutione of nature as an object of scientific study.
For another view of the place of constitution in Marx's philosophy, I turn to Alfred Schmidt. Schmidt has no sympathy for approaches like that of Adler, in which Marx's 'critical theory has been ransacked again and again in search of an epistemological "foundation", which Marx neither wished nor needed to give.'(221) Marx does, however, have an epistemology; Schmidt summarises his interpretation of this in the preface to the English edition of his book. Marx adopted an 'intermediate position' between Kant and Hegel; this

> was a consequence of the fact that, like Hegel, he refused to make epistemological reflections *before* the investigation of the concrete content of knowledge, but that at the same time, as a materialist, he could not accept the conclusion Hegel drew from his rejection of epistemology, namely the speculative identity of Subject and Object. Kant's problem of the 'constituents' of the objects of knowledge was thus (objectively) restored for Marx, but not in the sense of a simple

return to transcendental philosophy, but on the basis definitively attained by Hegel in his critique of Kant. (222)

In Marx, what 'constitutes' the 'normal' world of everyday experience, and what establishes intersubjectivity, is not an aggregate of purely intellectual ordering functions performed by a supra-individual 'consciousness in general', but collective, 'objective activity', i.e. practice.(223)

We have already seen Schmidt ascribe to Marx 'the ... view ... that Subject and Object entered into changing configurations'; he goes on to draw an analogy with the variable proportions of raw material and labour embodied in different products of labour. Furthermore, there is a clear historical shift to the predominance of the Subject: (224)

under pre-industrial conditions the objective, natural moment is dominant, whilst in industrial society the moment of subjective intervention asserts itself in increasing measure over the material provided by nature....

With the ever-increasing reduction of nature in modern times to the level of a moment in social action, the determinations of objectivity entered progressively and increasingly into the Subject. This displacement of emphasis within the labour relationship towards the subjective side was conceptually expressed by the principle that only what was 'made' by the Subjects was in a strict sense knowable. This principle was at first understood in an abstractly logical manner, from Descartes up to the German idealists but was given a radically historical interpretation by Vico and Marx.

Schmidt presents a measured account of Marx's epistemology, which recognises the active, constitutive role of human practice without obliterating what Marx and Engels called the unassailable 'priority of external nature'. (225) 'The problem of the constitution of the world returned in a materialised form in Marx's theory, since Marx was attempting, by means of the concept of practice, to preserve both the idealist moment of creation and the moment of the independence of consciousness from external being.'(226) Practice, Schmidt suggests a few pages later, 'can only be the criterion of truth because - as a historical whole - it *constitutes* the objects of normal human experience, i.e. plays an essential part in their internal composition'.(227) This, then, is an ontological use of constitution, but on the next page Schmidt sets it

alongside the epistemological sense:
In so far as objectivity falls into the historically expanding realm of human intervention, it is the result of a process of composition; in so far as it falls outside this realm, it is at least mentally preformed.... Like the use-value, objectivity is constituted from two elements, a 'material substratum' which 'is furnished by nature without the help of man', and formative labour.(228)

Schmidt has established, I think, that there is an important place for the notion of constitution, understood in an epistemological as well as an ontological sense, in the interpretation of Marx. Further, he has implied that this does not push one into a subjectivistic interpretation. (229) However, Schmidt skates over the problem that most of the structures and mechanisms of nature exist and operate in the absence of any human intervention. It is clear that this tension between 'subjectivistic' and 'objectivistic' interpretations of Marxism remains alive.(230)

In turning to 'Althusserian'(231) Marxism, we are abruptly returned to an epistemological problematic and to an epistemological account of constitution.(232) This tradition has been largely concerned, as Raymond Aron pointed out, with the question, 'How is Marxism possible?' (233) It is, therefore, not surprising that the problems of constitution are taken seriously. The most sustained account is in Althusser's The Object of Capital.(234) We have already noted(235) Althusser's stress on the need for Marx 'to constitute an adequate scientific terminology, i.e. a consistent system of defined terms in which not only would the words already used be concepts but in which the new words would also be concepts and moreover ones which define a new object.'(236) For example:(237)
> there is no *immediate* grasp of the economic, there is no raw economic 'given', any more than there is any immediately 'given' effectivity in any of the levels. In all these cases, the identification of the economic is achieved by *the construction of its concept*, which presupposes a definition of the specific existence and articulation of the different levels of the structure of the whole, as they are necessarily implied by the structure of the mode of production considered.

In similar vein, Balibar argues that the problem of relating partial histories, e.g. the history of institutions, sciences, etc. to history in general 'cannot be solved unless history really *constitutes* its object, instead of *receiving* it.'(238)

This last quotation serves as a convenient link with

the work of Barry Hindess and Paul Hirst, who have argued
that the idea of theoretical constitution is incompatible
with history, which 'is condemned by the nature of its
object to empiricism':(239)

> The object of history cannot be conceived as a theoretically constituted object, as an object not limited by what is given. Such a non-given object cannot be part of history; in being constituted theoretically it is constituted independently of the hitherto existing. History must conceive the object of its knowledge as a given object or cease to be historical. But this given real object, far from being real and given prior to investigation, is constituted by definite social and political ideologies.(240)

Rather than conclude that they, like Althusser and Balibar, have expressed the notion of constitution rather too strongly, Hindess and Hirst choose to blame history:(241)

> It is the notion of a Marxist history, of a Marxism confined within the conditions of the historian's practice, which is the contradictory enterprise. Marxism, as a theoretical and a political practice, gains nothing from its association with historical writing and historical research. The study of history is not only scientifically but also politically valueless.

Rather, 'it is the object of Marxist theory to analyse the "current situation"':(242)

> This situation must not be conceived as an object given in the real, social reality at a given moment in time. The analysis of the current situation is not a state description of the social formation. The current situation does not exist independently of the political practice which constitutes it as an object.

The position of these writers, developed further in their more recent works,(243) rests on a radicalisation of Althusser's critique of empiricism to a 'conclusive critique of all epistemology',(244) rejecting any attempt to specify a knowledge-relation between discourse and a realm of independently-existing objects. This is combined with the rejection of an Althusserian 'rationalism' which is accused (rightly) of giving a special place within epistemology to scientific problematics.(245)

This is not the place to examine the Hindess-Hirst account in detail, but the upshot is a radical split between discourse and 'reality':(246)

> if the epistemological notion of 'knowledge' is not a necessary one, then the relation between discourse and its 'objects' need not be represented in terms of both a distinction and a correlation between a realm of discourse and an independently existing realm of

objects. It is then no longer possible (in the absence of the epistemological conception) to refer to objects existing outside of discourse as the measure of the validity of discourse. On the contrary, in the absence of such extra-discursive (and yet specifiable) objects, the entities specified in discourse must be referred to solely in and through the forms of discourse, theoretical, political, etc., in which they are constituted. What is specified in theoretical discourse can only be conceived through that form of discourse (or another, critical or complementary, discourse): it cannot be specified extra-discursively. The question of the 'reality of the external world' is not the issue. It is not a question of whether objects *exist* when we do not speak of them. *Objects* of discourse do not exist. The entities discourse refers to are constituted in it and by it.

This seems a bizarre destination,(247) but it lies in a natural line of development of theories, whether Marxist or not, which misunderstand the scope of the notion of constitution. Althusser's anti-empiricism did not have such dramatic consequences, because it was held in check by his (quite uncritically upheld) distinction between ideology and science, which sustains his further distinction between 'object-of-knowledge' and 'real object'. Without the restraints which a realist theory would provide, there is nothing to prevent the slide into a position which seems pragmatist in both the philosophical and the political sense. The view quoted above is the most powerful demonstration that if one abandons empiricism and takes seriously the idea of constitution, one cannot do without a rationalist or realist theory.(248)

The final version of Marxist theory to be discussed here is that developed in parallel by Jürgen Habermas and Karl-Otto Apel.(249) Habermas agrees with Hegel's critique of Kant to the extent of concluding 'that a radical critique of knowledge is possible only as social theory'.(250) But Hegel and Marx, who attempted this transformation, only succeeded in destroying the theory of knowledge, so that 'since Kant science has no longer been seriously comprehended by philosophy'.(251) Rather than revert to a traditional epistemological problematic, Habermas initiates a process of critical reflection on the natural and human sciences in order to bring out their transcendental grounding in basic 'cognitive interests' of the human species.(252)

It is therefore to be expected that the notion of constitution will play a crucial role in this conception. As Apel admits, the content of the three alleged cognitive interests - technical-instrumental, practical-communicative and emancipatory - is close to the three types of knowledge postulated by Max Scheler: 'Arbeits- or Herrschaftswissen', 'Bildungswissen' and 'Erlösungswissen'. (253) What is new in his and Habermas's account is the recognition of the constitutive role of cognitive interests:(254)

> Habermas' approach to the philosophy of science is characterised above all by the attempt to develop the knowledge-guiding interests of the sciences which are presently possible as transcendental conditions of the possibility of their constitution of objects and to relate these interests to each other.

This constitutive role of the cognitive interests has often been neglected by critics of Habermas. It is no objection to his thesis that for example, much science is not concerned, even remotely, with controlling natural processes, (though it is no doubt required that a fair amount should be, if only potentially, e.g. astrophysics before the Sputnik). Habermas and Apel are claiming, rather, that the object-domain of the 'empirical-analytic sciences' is constituted according to a transcendental interest 'in the possible securing and expansion, through information, of feedback-monitored action [Erfolgskontrolliertes Handeln]. This is the cognitive interest in technical control over objectified processes.'(255)

But if what Habermas and Apel say about the cognitive interest is not easily refutable, it is also not easily confirmed. All they can do is to present an account of the sciences as they are practised (critical reflection) which makes plausible the framework which they propose. This is Habermas's strategy in 'Knowledge and Human Interests', but his modesty in the postscript is not just, I think, a matter of politeness:(256)

> My interpretation of Pierce and Dilthey has I think yielded enough indications for the conjecture that the use of categories like 'bodies in motion' or 'acting and speaking individuals' implies an *a priori* relation to action to the extent that 'observable bodies' are simultaneously 'instrumentally manipulable' whereas 'understandable persons' are simultaneously 'participants in linguistically mediated interaction'.

He makes the same point in his introduction to 'Theory and Practice':(257)

> In the social philosophical essays on Theory and Praxis I have not treated epistemological questions systematically. Nor is that the context within which the history of these problems is treated in my book

Chapter 3

> *Knowledge and Human Interests* or in my inaugural lecture of the same title, if one were to apply rigid standards. Still, I have carried my historical investigations and exploratory considerations sufficiently far, that the program for a theory of science becomes clearly discernible, a theory which is intended to be capable of grasping systematically the constitutive conditions of science and those of its application.

It is these questions of constitution which positivism has 'concealed':(258)

> Once epistemology has been flattened out to methodology, it loses sight of the constitution of objects of possible experience; in the same way, a formal science dissociated from transcendental reflection becomes blind to the genesis of rules for the combination of symbols. In Kantian terms, both ignore the synthetic achievements of the knowing subject.

What then is the status and role of the cognitive interests? First, we must note an important asymmetry between empirical and hermeneutic sciences:

> In the behavioural system of instrumental action, reality is constituted as the totality of what can be experienced from the viewpoint of possible technical control. The reality that is objectified under these transcendental conditions has its counterpart in a specifically restricted mode of experience.(259)

> In the context of communicative action, language and experience are not subject to the transcendental conditions of action itself. Here the role of transcendental framework is taken instead by the grammar of ordinary language....(260)

> the pattern of communicative action does not play a transcendental role for the hermeneutic sciences in the same way that the framework of instrumental action does for the nomological sciences. For the object domain of the cultural sciences is not constituted only under the transcendental conditions of the methodology of inquiry; it is confronted as something already constituted.(261)

In terms of the opposition between 'continuist' and 'separatist' theories of science which was discussed in chapter 2, Habermas is arguing for a greater degree of continuity in the cultural sciences than in empirical science. The hermeneutician(262)

> does not proceed *subject* to transcendental rules, but at the level of *transcendental* structures themselves. He can decipher the experiential content of a historical

text only in relation to the transcendental structure
of the world to which he himself belongs. Here theory
and experience are not divorced, as they are in the
empirical-analytic sciences.
This difference, then, must be added to what has already
been noted about the continuist implications of the 'cognitive interest' concept and Habermas's recent attempts to
restrict these implications.(263) This is not, of course,
just a matter of constitution, but also includes the application of science:(264)

> expressions capable of truth have reference to a reality which is objectified (i.e. simultaneously disclosed
> and constituted) as such in two different contexts of
> action and experience. The underlying 'interest'
> establishes the unity between this constitutive context
> in which knowledge is rooted and the structure of the
> possible application which this knowledge can have.

Indeed, there is a certain ambiguity about whether constitution is a once-and-for-all process with regard to a
given subject matter, or whether it is something which
may change with the development of science. The latter
interpretation seems better able to do justice to the
sorts of shifts of perspective characteristic of science
and, for example, the breakdown of intersubjective understanding in systematically distorted communication (where
the communication partners are forced to 'objectify' each
other).

Finally, we must consider the vexed question of the
general status of the cognitive interests. They are not,
Habermas stresses, a matter for psychology or the sociology of knowledge, since they are invariant; and they are
too abstract to be reducible to biological drives.(265)
At the same time, they are not purely transcendental:

> These systems of reference have a transcendental
> function, but they determine the architectonic of
> processes of inquiry and not that of transcendental
> consciousness as such. Unlike transcendental logic,
> the logic of the natural and cultural sciences deals
> not with the properties of pure theoretical reason
> but with methodological rules for the organisation of
> processes of inquiry. These rules no longer possess
> the status of pure transcendental rules. They have a
> transcendental function but arise from actual structures of human life: from structures of a species that
> reproduces its life both through learning processes of
> socially organised labour and processes of mutual
> understanding in interactions mediated in ordinary
> language.(266)

'Cognitive interest' is therefore a peculiar category, which conforms as little to the distinction between empirical and transcendental or factual and symbolic determinations as to that between motivation and cognition. For knowledge is neither a mere instrument of an organism's adaptation to a changing environment nor the act of a pure rational being removed from the complex of life in contemplation.(267)

Habermas admits: 'The formula quasi-transcendental [268] is a product of an embarrassment which points to more problems than it solves.'(269) He also clarifies somewhat further the status of the two 'lower' interests, the technical and the practical:(270)

As long as these interests of knowledge are identified and analyzed by way of reflection on the logic of inquiry that structures the natural and the humane sciences, they can claim a 'transcendental' status; however, as soon as they are understood in terms of an anthropology of knowledge, as results of natural history, they have an 'empirical' status.

There is some doubt as to whether Habermas still feels committed to the cognitive interest model in any serious way; his most recent work(271) certainly does not deal explicitly with these questions. Moreover, when he does discuss them, it is with the aim of deradicalising their implications by means of the distinctions between action and discourse and between genesis and validity.(272)

In the investigations up to this point I have brought out the interrelation between knowledge and interest, without making clear the critical threshold between communication (which remains embedded within the context of action) and discourses (which transcend the compulsions of action). To be sure, the constitution of scientific object domains can be conceived as a continuation of the objectivations which we undertake in the world of social life prior to all science. But the genuine claim to objectivity which is raised with the instauration of science is based on a virtualization of the pressure of experience and decision, and it is only this which permits a discursive testing of *hypothetical* claims to validity and thus the generation of *rationally grounded* knowledge.

One recent discussion of questions of constitution in terms of the action/discourse distinction can be found in one of Habermas's critiques of Luhmann.(273) Here, Habermas objects to Luhmann's separation of experience (Erleben) and action: 'This traditional opposition cannot stand up to an analysis of the world of experience in terms of constitution.'(274) Such an analysis would show that 'the

114 Chapter 3

construction of a world of objects of possible experience'
is based on 'a systematic interplay of sensual reception,
action and linguistic representation'.(275)
   Here, Habermas retains the idea of a differential constitution of objects of experience, depending on whether
we can or cannot (potentially) communicate with them, but
insists that this is a multiple process and not merely an
epistemological question.(276)
   With regard to the constitution of the world of experience we distinguish between two object-domains (things,
   events; persons, expressions), to which correspond different modes of experience (sensory, communicative),
   two different forms of empirical language (physical and
   intentional language), and two types of action (instrumental, communicative).
In criticisng 'the simple dichotomy of meaningful experience and meaning-guided action',(277) Habermas is implicitly criticising his own earlier formulation of the question of constitution in 'Knowledge and Human Interests'.
Here, cognition was indeed linked to action (Handlungs-
bezug) via the cognitive interests, but the process was
seen too much in transcendental-epistemological terms.
Habermas's reformulation therefore goes some way to meet
the more orthodox Marxist objections of Hans-Jürgen Krahl.
(278)
   Krahl offers an extremely interesting, if ambiguous
and at times rather forced, materialist reformulation of
the concept of constitution.(279) He writes of 'the
practical constitution process, the labour process',(280)
which 'constitutes' objects as useful objects, as objects
of consumption in order to work on them. The epistemological 'problem' of constitution starts from a world of
objects which have already been constituted for practical
purposes.(281) The Marxian problematic of fetishism and
reification(282)
   is in the line of the Kantian critique of reason.
   The latter's emancipatory interest in reason, which
   aims to restore the autonomy of the transcendental
   subject by showing that what it predicates of things
   is its own property, is materialistically translated
   into the critique of production relations which have
   become independent and ossified.
If Krahl's positive account of constitution is not
entirely clear, his objections to Habermas's use of the
term are evident enough. Habermas turns the objective
relationship between humanity and nature into a reified
'transcendental constant'.
   The transcendental subject is not conceived as an
   uncomprehended figure of the social totality of

commodity-producing abstract labour; instead, bourgeois society is obscured in the 'cloudy region' of transcendentality.(283)

Constitution ... is always the constitution of fetishised worlds of experience according to the illusory worlds of jurisprudence. From an ideology-critical point of view, the concept of constitution is penetrated by the categories of fetishisation, reification and alienation. There can therefore be no positive theory of constitution in Marx.(284)

Habermas's revised account of constitution goes some way to meeting these objections, though an orthodox Marxist would no doubt still argue, as did Krahl, that his abstract antithesis between work and interaction fails to do justice to the Marxist concept of labour.(285) The new version, moreover, seems to contain its own difficulties. Habermas's distinction between genesis and validity, like Max Weber's earlier formulation in terms of value-reference and objectivity, does not seem to take seriously enough the consequences of the initial conceptualisation of reality, what Goldmann called the découpage.(286) A more adequate framework seems to me to be provided by Bhaskar's realism and by his distinction between transitive and intransitive objects of knowledge.(287)

...knowledge is a social product, produced by means of antecedent social products; but ... the objects of which, in the social activity of science, knowledge comes to be produced, exist and act quite independently of men. These two aspects of the philosophy of science justify our talking of two dimensions and two kinds of 'object' of knowledge: a transitive dimension, in which the object is the material cause or antecedently established knowledge which is used to generate the new knowledge, and an intransitive dimension, in which the object is the real structure or mechanism that exists and acts quite independently of men and the conditions which allow men access to it.

It is, then, the transitive objects of knowledge which are theoretically constituted, as part of the process by which we attempt to give the best possible description of the intransitive objects of our scientific inquiry and of the empirical phenomena generated by those intransitive objects (structures and mechanisms). The resulting theoretical concepts or transitive objects may initially involve highly speculative departures from perceived reality and our antecedent knowledge of the structures of the world. Where life is particularly hard, as in contemporary microphysics and astrophysics, our concepts may for a time be not just counterintuitive but logically contradictory in the sense that they ascribe incompatible properties to hypothetical entities. In the end, however, the world must be as it is independently of our knowledge of it, and fictionalist and conventionalist philosophies of science are premature expressions of despair.

Bhaskar's distinction was, of course, initially formulated in relation to the natural sciences. How far must it be modified in the name of the social sciences? Bhaskar's answer, which I think is on the right lines, is that social objects may be intransitive in a weaker sense than natural objects; they may be in important respects concept-dependent, in the sense that they 'do not exist independently of the agents' conceptions of what they are doing in their activity'.(288) This does not mean, however, that these conceptions are necessarily veridical. It is, for example, not just inessential for, but incompatible with, the prevalence of 'bourgeois ideology' in a given society that all the members of that society agree that it is prevalent, since they could hardly go on believing ideas which they described in these terms. Social objects also tend to be, in Bhaskar's terms, not just concept-dependent but also activity-dependent, in that they 'do not exist independently of the activities they govern'. Here, in essence, is the truth of conceptions of practical constitution, whether this is conceived in materialist (e.g. Marxist) or idealist (e.g. 'social phenomenological') terms. With these important qualifications, the realist programme is no less applicable to the social than to the natural world.

This naturalist conception of social science may be contrasted with Habermas's insistence, in the 'cognitive interest' model at least, on what he calls the differential constitution of meaning-domains. The situation is complicated here by the fact that Habermas presents empirical science and the 'technical' interest in knowledge - an interest in prediction and control - in classically positivist terms.(289) There thus arises the question of what happens to his argument if one inserts a realist philosophy of science in place of a positivist one.(290)

Habermas clearly has to modify his account of the 'technical' interest in knowledge if realism is accepted, as it surely must be, as at least a credible alternative to positivism, whether or not it is actually superior. (291) There seems to me no reason why Habermas could not refine his account of science in such a way as to do justice to realist or, for that matter, other philosophies of science. Moreover, realism (in the sense of Bhaskar's 'transcendental realism') joins rationalism in taking questions of constitution$_e$ very seriously indeed, so there need be no opposition, prima facie, on that score between Habermas and realism. And third, Habermas's recent stress on questions of validity and truth seems to bring him closer, at least in intention, to satisfying realist desiderata.(292)

On the other hand, there seems to be a fairly serious opposition between realist naturalism, even in the qualified form in which Bhaskar presents it, and critical theory's insistence on the differential constitution of object-domains. If it is the case that in experimental activity '"reality" is disclosed subject to a constitutive human interest in manipulating it',(293) then a concept of constitution which neglects this constraint will no doubt be falsely objectivistic in Habermas's sense. However, as we have seen, Habermas neither has, nor claims to have, produced any conclusive arguments for the existence of a differential constitution$_e$ of meaning-domains. (294) Many of the distinctions he draws in this connection seem forced.(295) Occam's razor suggests that the onus is on the anti-naturalist.

CONCLUSION

I have tried to suggest that the concept of theoretical object-constitution is not incompatible with, indeed is required by, a realist metatheory of science. In the case of the social sciences, realism can and must also incorporate the notion of the practical or, as I previously termed it, ontological constitution of the social - what Touraine has called 'the production of society'. A realist metatheory is compatible with widely differing accounts of this production process: compare Harré's 'Social Being' with Bhaskar's 'Naturalism'. (My own preference, for reasons which I cannot elaborate here, is for the latter's more materialist and structuralist emphasis.)

We must take seriously the idea that sciences constitute their (transitive) object-domain; there are no theory-neutral facts, at least, not once things get interesting.(296) If this is conceded, it becomes vital that we have the 'right' concepts and theories - if we can give any sense to this notion of rightness.(297) The best prospects for handling this situation, without collapsing into relativism, seem to be offered by rationalist and realist epistemologies. Within theory, this notion of constitution is primary; it applies to all sciences,

though it may seem to have a peculiar salience for the social sciences, given their peculiarly low degree of consensus about the range and structure of their object-domain.
But theoretical constitution$_e$ in this sense must somehow be reconciled with the other senses which we have encountered; briefly, the classical Marxist ontological version, which emphasises human practical activity and work: the epistemological extension of this notion, most interestingly canvassed by Habermas, in which theoretical constitution$_e$ is a function of fundamental human interests;(298) and the hermeneutic sense in which social reality is constructed by human agents, both by the imputation of meanings ('making sense together') and by (other forms of) interaction, itself meaningfully structured. These distinctions are, of course, not entirely clear;(299) nor, in a sense, should they be, since these traditions are all trying to grasp a single, if highly complex reality. There are, however, two basic oppositions of which one, I shall argue, is partly spurious.

The first opposition is between 'Marxist' theories emphasising 'real relations' and 'hermeneutic' theories emphasising 'meanings'. Very briefly, I would argue that this opposition has been exaggerated in the past by both 'sides' and by third parties, but that there is nothing to be said for the continuance of apartheid between the two traditions. Social reality is made up both of 'meanings' and of relations such as power and exploitation which are in some sense different from meanings (though they are, of course, symbolically mediated). There will, of course, be arguments about the relative priority of these. In my view, the Marxist tradition is entirely right to stress the priority of material relations. This is, however, a very different matter from excluding all discussion of symbolic relations from Marxism, for fear of falling into idealism. Some Marxists have written as though Marxism never contained a theory of ideology.(300) The relative 'mix' of these 'material' and 'ideal' components in a given situation is in some sense, though not straightforwardly, an empirical matter, and our theories ought to be able to take account of this.(301)

The opposition discussed above is essentially one between two versions of constitution$_o$. The second opposition is between the constitution$_o$ and constitution$_e$ or, as one might put it, between 'practical' and 'theoretical' constitution, where the former covers anything from 'labour' to 'meaning-imputation'. One example of this is Krahl's critique of Habermas. Another is the opposition, neatly presented by Deryck Beyleveld, between a phenomenological and a rationalist sociology of action.(302)

I would express in the following terms my conception of an adequate philosophy of social science: it would be (1) a realist naturalism(303) which recognised (2) the centrality of theoretical constitution, (3) the ontological and heuristic strengths of materialism, and (4) the hermeneutic grounding of social scientific data and the importance of meaningful relations in social life.(304) I have tried to show that (1) and (2) belong together, that the traditional opposition between (3) and (4) is not irreconcilable, and must indeed be reconciled if we are not to remain with 'two sociologies', permanently separate yet locked together, like two negotiating teams which, refusing to recognise each other, insist on sitting in separate rooms.

As for (2) and (3), their prima facie opposition was discussed above in relation to Norman Stockman's work. If theoretical constitution can be shown to involve the differential constitution of meaning-domains, it may seem to follow that naturalism must be abandoned and that the realist project in general must be radically reformulated. On the other hand, the existence of differential interests in description does not necessarily conflict with the realist insistence that there are nevertheless intransitive objects which are independent of alternative descriptions. Second, a realist programme which, like Bhaskar's, is modified in important respects in its application to social reality, seems able without strain to incorporate as much as seems desirable of Habermas's constitution thesis. This seems to me one of the most interesting areas of debate at the present time. (2) and (3) might also be said to be opposed in the sense that (2) implies an independent status for theoretical activity which (3) denies. This is, I think, a mistake. Theoretical knowledge is a part of human practice in general, but it also has its own specificity. For our knowledge of reality, theoretical constitution is prior. In reality itself, our knowledge may in certain circumstances play a part in causally affecting other spheres of reality, but the latter are always prior. How far our cognitive abilities are extended and limited by our practice, and how far our knowledge can feed into our practice and enable us to modify natural and social reality, are empirical questions which can only receive specific answers. At the level of epistemological principles, however, one might expand Martin Hollis's diagnosis to read: 'I take recent philosophy of science to have shown that empirical judgements presuppose theoretical judgements [and an extratheoretical context in which our theorising is embedded] but not to have abolished the need for truth in science'.(305)

4 Max Weber and concept formation in sociology

I have singled out Max Weber for special attention in this book because, as well as producing substantive work of great importance and influence, he devoted a great deal of attention to questions of concept formation and upheld a position diametrically opposed to the one I have been arguing for here. Weber develops his account in explicit opposition to what he sometimes calls an 'antique scholastic epistemology',(1) which claims to capture the most essential features of reality in some more ambitious way than is allowed for by his own notion of ideal-typical concept formation. Weber's attacks on this view bear on its Hegelian version, represented, for example, by the economists Roscher and Knies, but as he implies himself, the same objections apply to realist theories such as Marxism.(2) In other words, Weber's account can be read as a critique of and an alternative to the broadly realist view of concept formation which I am defending here. I shall argue that the antinomies in Weber's account point to the need to adopt something like the view which he attacks.

First, one must reach some judgment on where Weber is to be located in terms of the philosophical disputes of his time and, perhaps more importantly, whether he can be said to have escaped the problematics of traditional philosophy. The view that he did escape has been powerfully argued by Dieter Henrich and John Torrance. According to Henrich,

> Max Weber released the methodology of the sciences from its epistemological context.... For him, the demonstration of scientific objectivity amounts to the proof that it is possible to get to know reality or (in the case of methodology) that it is possible to describe and investigate modes of approach to the reality which is given.(3)

Max Weber is important for philosophy, not because he
advances philosophical theories in his methodology,
but because he does not do this and does not need to
do so.(4)
Torrance takes what seems to me to be a similar line:(5)
Briefly, I would argue that in so far as it [Weber's
methodology] attempts to *prescribe* for social science
it is an academic ideology; that a contradiction therefore
subsists within it between (inherited) ideology
and (emergent) scientific methodology; that Weber had
to clear and defend, by ideological means, a space for
a new social science, sociology, which was conceived
but unborn and whose methods he could only guess at in
advance.
This is, of course, essentially the same problem as can
be raised with reference both to the positivist tradition
and to such thinkers as Marx and Schutz: can the
Gordian knots of traditional epistemology be cut in the
name of 'methodology'?(6) The view taken in this book is
that they cannot, but Weber, like Durkheim, seems to have
felt that they can be cut, or at least avoided.
    Weber did not see himself as a card-carrying philosopher,
but as an empirical scientist who from time to time
had to step into the arena of philosophy (or, as it was
generally known, 'logic') in order to secure his own
methodology.(7) 'Secure' here is intended both in an
intellectual sense and in Torrance's 'ideological' sense.
Weber did not, I think, see philosophies only as ideologies
of science but nor did he take the extreme alternative
view that the special sciences require a complete
philosophical foundation in order to be taken seriously.
What he seems to have in mind, rather, is a notion of
scientific development not dissimilar to Kuhn's, in
which periods of what Kuhn calls 'normal science' are
interrupted by crises of confidence which characteristically
take the form of a critique of prevalent methodological
assumptions and of the concepts currently in use.(8)
    It is significant that Weber does not advance systematic
arguments for the philosophical positions which he
adopts; he tends to present them as generally agreed.
Thus the principle that 'concepts are primarily means of
thought for the intellectual mastery of empirical data and
can only be that' is 'the basic principle of the modern
theory of knowledge which goes back to Kant'; this principle
can be criticised only on the basis of the 'antique-
scholastic epistemology' which sees concepts as aiming at
'the *reproduction* of "objective" reality in the analyst's
imagination'.(9) Such a view, Weber claims in his critiques
of Roscher and Knies, could be consistently sustained

only in Hegelian terms, and would render all knowledge analogous to that of a sequence of mathematical propositions.(10) In this period of his work, Weber argues that the complexity of reality means that it can be known theoretically in only two ways: either via a generalising mode of concept-formation, which concentrates on generic features of empirical phenomena, or by an individualising method which isolates 'individually *meaningful* features' and arranges them in 'universal - but individual - patterns'. What Weber wishes to do is to close off the third alternative, in which one 'accepts the Hegelian theory of concepts and attempts to surmount the *"hiatus irrationalis"* between concept and reality by the rise of "general" concepts - concepts which, as metaphysical realities, comprehend and imply individual things and events as instances of their realisation'.(11)

This view, of Hegelian provenance, is part of a more general orientation which Weber attacks in his essay on Objectivity:(12)

> Nothing, however, is more dangerous than the *confusion* of theory and history stemming from naturalistic prejudices. This confusion expresses itself firstly in the belief that the 'true' content and the essence of historical reality is portrayed in such theoretical constructs or secondly, in the use of these constructs as a procrustean bed into which history is to be forced or thirdly, in the hypostatization of such 'ideas' as real 'forces' and as a 'true' reality which operates behind the passage of events and which works itself out in history.

Weber's central objection, then, to the antique-scholastic epistemology is that it offers an illusory possibility of what Dieter Henrich calls 'Substanzeinsicht', penetrating the complex surface of historical phenomena to a more basic and simpler 'real reality' which underlies them.(13) Henrich is right, I think, to see this as Weber's principal claim. This, taken with his further claim about the complexity of reality, implies the need for selection in science(14) and hence the view that theoretical concepts can only be ideal types.(15) As Weber puts it, with admirable force and clarity, 'Every concept which is not *purely* classificatory diverges from reality.'(16)

I shall return in a moment to the implications of this view for Weber's account of definition and the problems of this account. It is worth noting here, however, that a theme of Roy Bhaskar's 'A Realist Theory of Science' which was briefly noted in chapter 1(17) has considerable relevance to Weber's position. This is Bhaskar's claim that both 'classical empiricism' and 'transcendental idealism' share a commitment to an ontology of 'empirical realism'. (18) For classical empiricism, 'the ultimate objects of knowledge are atomistic events. Such events constitute given facts.'(19) For transcendental idealism, 'the objects of scientific knowledge are models, ideals of natural order etc. Such objects are artificial constructs.' (20) These positions are contrasted with transcendental realism, which 'regards the objects of knowledge as the structures and mechanisms that generate phenomena'.(21) The objection to transcendental idealism is that it cannot sustain the 'intransitive dimension' of knowledge, (22) since on this view,

the objects of which knowledge is obtained do not exist independently of human activity in general. And if there are things which do (things-in-themselves), no scientific knowledge of them can be obtained.(23)

although transcendental idealism rejects the empiricist account of science, it tacitly takes over the empiricist account of being. This ontological legacy is expressed most succinctly in its commitment to empirical realism, and thus to the concept of the 'empirical world'.(24)

Bhaskar's characterisation of transcendental idealism sheds a good deal of light on Weber's philosophy of science. I do not wish to suggest that Weber is wholly committed to transcendental idealism; as I shall argue in a moment, there are also realist elements, especially in his theory of definition. I believe, however, that it forms the dominant element, if anything does, in his philosophical assumptions and tends to drive out the elements which conflict with it.

This is not a particularly radical claim, since the influence on Weber of neo-Kantian philosophy has been well documented.(25) One example is his analysis of causality. Weber's view seems to have been that there are such things as real causal connections, but that there are too many of them for us to handle. We therefore have to select some of them, and selection here involves both the focusing on a particular link or set of links in a causal chain and the simplification of the relations in that chain itself. The establishment of one or more such simplified sequences provides us with approximation to the real causal relations, which are in a strict sense unknowable by virtue of their complexity. As Weber put it, 'In order to gain insight into the real [wirklich] causal connections, we construct unreal ones.' (26)

How does this differ from the realist account cast in terms of causal powers and tendencies? This question brings us back to Weber's initial rejection of Substanzeinsicht, which remains an aspiration, even if one which is never attained, for the realist. Weber repeatedly shies away from the realist implications of, for example, some of his analyses of causality and in particular the distinction between causal and meaningful significance. (27) Generally, these shifts away from realism are legitimated by some reference to the highly problematic notion of Wertbeziehung.

In a passage already cited, Weber spells out his account of ideal-typical concept formation in terms of the concepts of 'church' and 'sect':(28)

[These concepts] ... may be broken down purely in classificatory fashion into complexes of elements [Merkmalscomplexe] whereby not only the distinction between them but also the content of each concept must constantly remain fluid. If, however, I wish to conceptualize 'sect' in a *genetic* fashion, e.g. in reference to certain important cultural significances which the 'sectarian spirit' has had for modern culture, certain characteristics of both become *essential* because they stand in an adequate causal relationship to those effects. However, the concepts thereupon become idealtypical, i.e. in full conceptual purity these phenomena either do not exist at all or only in single instances. Here as elsewhere it is the case that every concept which is not *purely* classificatory diverges from reality.

As we saw earlier,(29) Weber's theory of definition is not at all easy to reconstruct. On the one hand, there is a clear aspiration towards real definition, especially in Weber's earlier work. The starting-point, as Burger shows, is an empirical realist account of real definition, in which general concepts 'are summary representations of common aspects of real phenomena'.(30) This then has to be modified for the cultural sciences, to take account of the fact that putatively definitional properties may be only, in Weber's words, 'more or less present and occasionally absent'.(31) The ideal type is the vehicle of this modification, and fits neatly with Weber's strongly held belief that '*There is no* absolutely "objective" scientific analysis of culture - or ... of "social phenomena" *independent* of special and "one-sided" view-points according to which - expressly or tacitly, consciously or unconsciously - they are selected, analyzed and organized for expository purposes.'(32) Or as Henrich puts it,(33)

There are, then, various attempted real definitions of a particular reality from various points of view. These all describe a real condition [Wirklichkeitsbedingung] of this reality, but they cannot grasp the complex of sufficient conditions [den zureichenden Bedingungszusammenhang]. *Real explications in cultural science are ideal types.* As we noted earlier,(34) it is in keeping with this view that Weber's principal concepts incorporate the results of scientific work and come at the end of the inquiry.(35) On the other hand, this makes it hard to explain Weber's procedure at the beginning of 'Economy and Society', where he presents definitions of his most fundamental concepts as stipulations to be judged on their usefulness. Even here Weber does not seem to be consistent, for he also states, in his prefatory remark to this chapter, that he is attempting 'only to formulate what all empirical sociology really means when it deals with the same problems'.(36) His rejection of holistic concepts, an absolutely central principle of his sociology,(37) seems to lead, as in the case of his reductionist analysis of the concept of the state, to a number of substantive claims about social reality as it is amenable to study by the social sciences. These claims could still be made in a conventionalist form, as they are, for example, in Simmel's 'The Problems of the Philosophy of History',(38) but Weber seems to be committing himself to something more, even if it is hard to see just what this is.(39)

I would suggest that Weber simply is inconsistent in his approach to definition.(40) Somewhat more pretentiously, I think one could say that he starts with a semantic realism derived from Rickert but, again like Rickert and Simmel, rejecting a realist epistemology.(41) As a result, his semantic realism becomes highly qualified, via the ideal type, and once this step is taken it becomes more natural for Weber to introduce his concepts, as he does in 'Economy and Society', by what are, at least in form, nominal definitions.

The important question, however, is what difference all this makes to Weber's sociology. In other words, we must follow up the substantive implications of his definitions. It will be useful to bear in mind three criticisms of Weber's account of concept formation. The first two are essentially positivistic and hermeneutic, respectively; the third is a more general objection to Weber's methodological individualism.

Positivists have tended to assimilate Weber's ideal types to the general class of theoretical concepts.(42) Their value is that they enable us to measure how far phenomena diverge from them.(43) A characteristic form of this operation is the construction of continua between opposed ideal-typical extremes. Science is characterised by a transition from an early classifying stage to a later ordering one, which opens the way to the construction of laws.(44) The 'ideality' of an ideal type means nothing more than, say, the 'purity' of a metal. Weber's prescriptions are not wrong, but they are incomplete in the sense that they govern only the foothills of science.

To this we may counterpose a 'hermeneutic' criticism which stresses the notion of 'adequacy'. Schutz, for example, identifies(45)

> the paradox that dominates Weber's whole philosophy of social science. He postulates as the task of social science the discovery of intended meaning - indeed, the intended meaning of the actor. But this 'intended meaning' turns out to be a meaning which is given to the observer and not to the actor.

In other words, Weber 'naively took for granted the meaningful phenomena of the social world as a matter of *intersubjective agreement* in precisely the same way as we all in daily life assume the existence of a lawful external world conforming to the concepts of our understanding'. (46) Whereas in fact, 'Far from being homogeneous, the social world is given to us in a complex system of perspectives.'(47) Thus although the ideal-typical interpretation of social action is already well under way in the Lebenswelt before the social scientist comes on the scene,(48) the latter's task is nevertheless a more difficult one, and one requiring greater sensitivity, than Weber assumes.

What these two criticisms have in common is the theme that ideal types are in some way too loose and freefloating: the positivist aims to tie them down to precise hypotheses and measuring operations, while the Schutzian is more preoccupied with their descriptive adequacy.(49) The third objection bears on the area where methodology borders on substantive theory and, if the word be allowed, ontology.

The reasons for Weber's methodological individualism are well enough known. Aside from his more general political and 'existential' individualism, and the influence of marginalist economics, there is clearly a very strong internal connection between a verstehende approach and a focus on individual action. As Weber put it, 'The aim of our study - "understanding" - is basically also the reason why verstehende sociology (in our sense) treats the single individual and his or her action as its most basic unit, as its "atom".'(50) If this is accepted, as I think it must be, the problem becomes one of explaining the emergent properties of social structures and the structural determination of action. It is my contention that the union of empiricism and conventionalism in Weber's philosophy of science licenses an evasion of these problems and that this evasion has serious consequences for the foundations(51) of his substantive social theory.

The connection between sociological individualism and what Bhaskar calls empirical realism is clear enough; it can be summed up in the simplifying slogan that 'only people are real': groups, associations, social relations, and social structures in general, are not. Hence statements about all these things are to be taken with a pinch of salt and must be ultimately reducible to statements about individual actions, propensities to act, and so forth. Weber remains loyal to the principle articulated in his early essays that the historian's interest is in the individual aspect of large-scale social phenomena.(52) Although he recognises that sociology is more interested in generalisations,(53) the kernel of the principle is simply transferred to sociology by means of the ideal type and the claim, cited above, that only individuals are 'understandable'.

Reducibility, especially at the level of the more abstract meaning-structures such as 'the protestant economic ethic', must, of course, be understood in a fairly loose sense. Weber's account of the Hindu doctrine of Karma is a good example:(54)

> For the practical effect in which we are interested it is of no importance that the individual pious Hindu did not always have before his eyes, as a total system, the pathetic presuppositions of the Karma doctrine which transformed the world into a strictly rational and ethically determined cosmos. He remained confined to the cage which only made sense through this ideal system and the consequences weighed down upon his action.

The substantive question of methodological individualism will be discussed more fully in the next chapter. I think it is clear, however, that Weber's conventionalism with regard to theoretical concepts means that he treats his reductions in a distinctly casual manner. It also means, as I shall try to show now, that he feels able to base crucial aspects of his sociology on distinctly shaky foundations.

To start right at the beginning, it seems a little odd to begin an exposition of the 'basic concepts of sociology' which is crucially reliant on the notion of the orientation of action, and then to concede that 'in the great

128 Chapter 4

majority of cases actual action goes on in a state of inarticulate half-consciousness or actual unconsciousness of its subjective meaning'.(55) The same approach is used, with more obviously deleterious consequences, in Weber's analysis of domination.

'Naturally', we are told, 'in concrete cases, the orientation of action to an order [Ordnung] involves a wide variety of motives', but 'legitimacy' is sufficiently important to the maintenance of a stable order to furnish a basis of classification.(56) Despite the qualifications with which Weber introduces the notion of legitimacy, it inevitably acquires a privileged status which gives an idealist flavour to the whole analysis.(57) The extent to which a particular regime, or regimes in general, rest on legitimacy rather than, say, the threat of force is a matter of considerable interest which Weber's definitional moves lead him to neglect, at least at the programmatic level with which we are at present concerned.

There is a second, and equally problematic restriction in Weber's account of 'legitimacy' itself; the term is deliberately purged of its original normative connotations just as 'bureaucracy' was purged, in Weber's account, of its pejorative associations. We cannot say that a regime enjoys 'legitimacy' in the eyes of its subjects because it actually is 'legitimate',(58) nor, less crudely, can we distinguish between good or bad grounds of legitimacy. (59) Weber can, of course, reply that he is an empirical scientist who cannot be expected to draw that sort of distinction, but I think it can be shown that this approach gets into serious problems.

First, the analogy with Weber's treatment of bureaucracy does not hold good. 'Bureaucracy' is a term which had acquired generally pejorative connotations at the time Weber was writing.(60) Weber adopts the term but drops the connotations of inefficiency; his 'value-free' ideal type implies, if anything, that bureaucracy in its ideal form tends rather to be efficient, or at least to be 'technically superior' to other modes of administration.(61) Weber's ideal type is undoubtedly something of a mish-mash of conceptual scheme and relatively independent empirical claims, such as the relation between bureaucracy and money economy.(62) This may cause a certain amount of confusion, along with the fact that Weber is not using the word in the familiar sense in which it connoted inefficiency and the further problem that his position on whether the ideal bureaucracy is or is not efficient is not too clear.

But these are surely minor problems, which can be cleared up with a few incisions of conceptual analysis.

The case of 'legitimacy', as John Schaar and Hanna Pitkin have shown, is a good deal more serious.(63) Weber defines legitimacy as 'the prestige of being exemplary or binding':(64) 'Naturally, the legitimacy of a system of domination may be treated sociologically only as the probability that to a relevant degree the appropriate attitudes will exist, and the corresponding practical conduct ensue.'(65) There is little point in objecting to Weber that his slide from 'legitimate' to 'seen as legitimate' (66) means that the social scientist is dropping the evaluative meaning of the term and the potential appeal to reasons involved in it. It is, however, a paradoxical consequence of his redefinition that normative judgments about legitimacy seem even less rational than other value-judgments. If Weber asks a British subject (to use the revealing expression) if the British system of government is legitimate, he can only be asking the respondent either to make an empirical judgment about his or her fellow-citizen's views or, for reasons which must remain obscure, to evince an arbitrary personal opinion. Strictly speaking, indeed, he can only ask the former question, given the way he has defined the term. It is not surprising that Weber is not consistent in this usage.(67) It may also be argued that his way of setting up the problem diverts him from paying serious attention to the origins and locus of 'legitimacy',(68) and to developing an adequate theory of ideology.

I shall go on to show that Weber analyses the concept of rationality in the same way and with similar consequences. This sort of redefinition is, indeed, a characteristic feature of the social sciences in their current state, thanks to the shibboleth of the fact-value distinction.(69) Pitkin suggests three consequences of this process. First, confusion between the ordinary sense of the term and its new 'scientific' sense - a confusion which, as in the case of Weber, affects the social scientists themselves. Second, a suspicion that social scientists 'are somehow destructive or cynical, that they are somehow cowardly or reluctant to make commitments and judgements, that they are somehow intrinsically conservative and supportive of the *status quo*'. (70) Third, the new usages may 'perhaps' infect the political sphere itself.(71) There seems, in fact, little doubt that this process is already well established; we are interested in the 'charisma' and 'credibility' of political leaders, rather than their imagination or sincerity.(72)

After this penetrating diagnosis, Pitkin concludes rather lamely with a plea to combine the insider's perspective with that of the social scientist. I would argue that what is required is a more radical and rigorous attempt to transcend the fact/value distinction in the critique of ideology and to provide a common rational foundation for moral, political and sociological thought. To do this, I think, requires one to reflect further on the nature of some of the concepts which Weber so carefully dismembered and to see that some of them cannot be consistently used in their dismembered form. The best example is Weber's concept of rationality.

Arnold Eisen has recently published a useful short article on The meanings and confusions of Weberian 'rationality'.(74) Eisen argues that Weber's uses of the term are linked by the presence of one or more of six 'component elements': the notions of purpose, calculability, control, 'logical-ness' in the everyday sense, universality and systematic organisation.(75) Having classified some of Weber's characteristic uses of the term in relation to these elements, Eisen concludes, perhaps rather charitably, that 'the meanings of rationality are consistent and conceptually rigorous'.(76) Weber's problems begin where he attempts to 'rationalise' this usage in terms of the distinction between formal and substantive (materiale) rationality, so as to contribute to 'greater consistency in the use of the word "rational" in this field'. Weber introduces this distinction in an economic context, with an explicit reference to contemporary discussions of nationalisation and the contrast between a monetary and a 'natural' economy:(77)

> The term 'formal rationality of economic action' will be used to describe the extent of quantitative calculation or accounting which is technically possible and which is actually applied. The 'substantive rationality', on the other hand, is the degree to which a given group of persons, no matter how it is delimited, is or could be adequately provided with goods by means of an economically oriented course of action ... interpreted in terms of a given set of ultimate values [wertende Postulate].

Here we see Weber once again taking apart a concept which, like 'legitimacy', conventionally has both descriptive and evaluative meaning. 'Legitimacy' was stripped of its evaluative meaning; economic 'rationality' could presumably have been given the same treatment.(78) Each of the two dimensions of Weber's notion reproduced above could be reduced to empirical questions to be answered by measuring the extent of possible and actual calculation in the first place and material satisfaction in the second. Perhaps it was the difficulties of measuring satisfaction without recourse to a normative notion of needs which induced Weber to adopt the alternative strategy of making substantive rationality depend on the observer's evaluative postulates.(79) Whatever his reason for doing so, Weber effectively divides the notion of rationality into one component which is narrowly descriptive and another which is a function of arbitrary values. Thus if asked 'Is capitalism a rational economic system?', Weber must presumably reply that it is formally rational to the extent that calculation can and does take place within it and that whether it is 'substantially rational' or not depends on one's individual values - for example, whether one considers the malnutrition of one third of a population to be a reasonable price to pay for the luxury enjoyed by another third. This account may be contrasted with a Marxist one in which the irrationality of capitalism is located not in technical failures of calculation nor simply in its failure to 'deliver the goods' to the proletariat and other subordinate classes, but in a more fundamental contradiction between social production and private appropriation. The Marxist critique of this contradiction cannot be split up into a technical criticism of capitalist inefficiency and a moral criticism of capitalist injustice; it involves the rejection of this implied antithesis between fact and value.

A more serious criticism of Weber's distinction is most clearly made by Herbert Marcuse, who argues, in essence, that Weber collapses the notion of reason into formal rationality. The latter has substantive implications:(80) it is really 'capitalist rationality'. 'Whatever capitalism may do to man, it must, according to Weber, first and before all evaluation be understood as necessary reason.'(81)

This criticism must not be over-stated; Weber is fully aware of the potential conflict between formal and substantive rationality.(82) Yet the latter concept, in being relativised to arbitrary value-systems, loses any critical purchase on economic reality. All attention is focused on formal rationality (including its substantive conditions).(83) David Beetham is not so far from the mark in saying that formal rationality becomes by default 'the sole consideration in terms of which economic activity is considered in *Economy and Society*'.(84)

Whereas earlier commentators have merely noted the problems of Weber's distinction and its potential as a basis of capitalist apologetics, Eisen relates this irony in the notion of rationality to its original exemplar in the Puritan's irrational commitment to the rationalisation of his Beruf(85) and thus to Weber's overall characterisation of Western capitalism. Whatever Weber's intentions may have been, we can see in his analysis of rationality one of the key places in his work at which his carefully restricted concepts point to a more all-embracing theory of Western civilisation which Weber could not develop explicitly without violating his methodological strictures against speculative philosophies of history and the intrusion of values into scientific analysis. Yet, as Karl Löwith was one of the first to show, Weber's methodological principles were not technical rules of thumb (as they have appeared to be in so many Anglo-Saxon commentaries), but consequences of just such an over-arching theory of the condition of man in Western bourgeois society.(86)

Löwith's seminal article identifies the central theme of the work of both Marx and Weber as the condition of man in bourgeois society. Marx grasps this reality in terms of alienation, Weber in terms of rationalisation. The general argument of Löwith's article is sufficiently well known not to require a full discussion here; I should like, however, to draw attention to Löwith's comments on the intimate connection between Weber's methodology and his overall 'theory' of Western society.

As Löwith points out, Weber believes that science, like the rest of life, has become fragmented, specialised and 'disenchanted' with respect to ultimate values.(87) 'Weber includes his own scientific cognitive orientation in the historical specificity and problematic of the whole of our modern life'.(88)

Löwith illustrates this claim with Weber's attitude to Roscher(89) and Knies; the latter 'is scientifically ambiguous precisely to the extent that his orientation has not yet become fully secular [diesseitig]'.(90) More positively, Weber's entire scientific orientation, and in particular his nominalistic approach to concept formation, is 'the logically consistent expression of a certain specific attitude of man towards reality. The ideal-typical "construction" is based upon a specifically "illusion-free" human being, thrown back on his own resources by a world which has become objectively meaningless and sober and to this extent emphatically "realistic".'(91)

This applies par excellence to concepts like state and nation which are so often, as we would say, 'mystified'. Weber's minimalist concept of the state arises out of his critique of such illusions; it is not merely a matter of methodology but, despite his protestations to the contrary, (92) has a substantial and evaluative significance which is broadly that of Western liberal individualism.(93)

Löwith and others have abundantly demonstrated these

connections between Weber's 'methodology' and his overall theory of Western Society.(94) Yet it is no less clear, I think, that Weber could not himself link the two in a way which would have brought him closer to Marx's more ambitious epistemology. For Marx, human knowledge of reality is partly sustained by that reality itself; he tries to show this with the example of the concept of abstract labour. Connections of this kind sustain a dialectical conception of knowledge involving not just a movement of thought from the whole to the part and back again, but also a practical dimension, which concerns the way in which the advance of knowledge is conditioned by changes in the objects of knowledge.(95) It may be questioned whether Marx can sustain his position as it stands without an unacknowledged reliance on a speculative conception of history which serves as the starting point of this whole process of knowledge.(96) But it is clear that Weber could not possibly even flirt with such an approach. One of the firmest of his methodological principles is that our concepts, like our values, cannot be deduced from some practical, extra-theoretical relation to reality.(97) The kind of potential unity between knowledge and reality postulated by Marx would violate this principle. Thus what I have called Weber's overall theory of Western society has a place, so far as Weber is concerned, only in the pre- and post-scientific stage of his work, as a source of Wertbeziehungen at the beginning and as a set of evaluatively loaded reflections at the end.(98) A more speculative and ambitious social theory can be found in his work, but its formal place, in terms of Weber's methodological prescriptions, is only on the periphery. (99) Criticisms of this aspect of Weber's sociology can be divided into two: those which emphasise the lack of any overall theory of 'Western' capitalism of the kind offered by Marx (hence the arbitrary decisionism of Weber's account of concept formation) and those which argue that he does have some such theory but merely fails, through methodological embarrassment, to make it explicit. On the whole, I think the evidence favours the second view. For present purposes, however, it is enough to note this tension in Weber's work: without some overarching theory of this kind, Weber's account of concept formation is caught between the unattractive alternatives of 'decisionism' (the view that we simply choose our concepts and the causal sequences to be investigated) and empiricism.

To attempt rationally to reconstruct a 'realist' Weber would be a reductio ad absurdum of counterfactual analysis. Two points can, however, be made. First, I have argued that if Weber had seen himself providing real definitions, he would have been more scrupulous in avoiding reductionism and other arbitrary definitional stipulations such as the treatment of legitimacy and rationality which we have examined in this chapter. Second, it may seem that a realist philosophy of science would have ruled out some of his more abstract meaning-structures, such as the protestant economic ethic. This, I think, is not the case. If we assume for the sake of argument that Weber's analysis of the protestant ethic is essentially correct, there seems to be no particular problem in construing it in realist terms as a real tendency within protestant ideology. Its existence is supported by an analysis of relevant writings (again assuming that Weber's reading of Franklin is correct, relevant and generalisable) and more importantly by its ability to explain important aspects of commercial behaviour and of the rise of capitalism (again, pace materialist objections to Weber's thesis). (100)

In sum, then, my criticims of Weber bear on (1) his failure to develop, in a more self-conscious way, his overall background theory of Western capitalism, and especially its connections with his 'methodology'; (2) the related tension between his theory of constitution and his residual empiricism; (3) his evasion of ontological issues such as those raised by his attempted reduction of structure to action.

The third point is one which I attempted to illustrate earlier in relation to Weber's account of domination, in which his stress that authority structures must be reducible to action with a particular orientation seems to give his analysis an unduly idealist emphasis. But even in the analysis of action orientations themselves, Weber's recourse to ideal types, legitimated by his conventionalist philosophy of science, brushes aside the questions which phenomenological sociology makes central to its analysis.(101) There is, of course, a real problem about how seriously we should take Weber's action reductions; if one looks at the upshot of his structural sociology or reads his work in the context of legal theory, one may get a very different picture from that yielded by close attention to his programmatic statements. But such exegetical questions are somewhat beside the point here; what I have tried to show is that Weber's understanding of what he was doing was inadequate and that his difficulties help to illuminate more general dilemmas about concept formation in the social sciences.

5 Concepts of society

In discussing Max Weber's concepts of legitimacy and rationality, I argued that his attempt to purge these terms of their normative force must be judged a failure. It is not as easy as Weber thought to separate formal and substantive rationality. This is a problem of substance, not of language; it is in no way resolved by inventing another term for 'formal rationality' which does not have tiresome overtones of reason and reasonableness. In other words, it is not a matter of deciding to make or not to make value judgments; to get one's concepts totally value-free or to put up with a certain amount of normative contamination; this is a trivialisation of the problem. (1) The real issue is that to think seriously about society as a social scientist involves, as well as some new techniques, the same sort of intellectual operations as have traditionally been performed under the heading of social or political theory and, in particular, a 'reflexive' grasp of the extra-theoretical context in which social theorising is embedded and the associated practical(2) commitments.

This is particularly clear if one examines the concept of 'society' itself. The terms 'social science' and 'sociology' emerged in the wake of the modern concept of society, which can be dated around the late seventeenth and early eighteenth centuries in most European languages. It is, as Bluntschli put it in 1859, a 'concept of the Third Estate',(3) nurtured in the coffee-houses and salons.(4) Paine wrote in 1776 that 'society is produced by our wants, and government by our wickedness'.(5) Government returned the compliment as late as 1908 in politically backward Germany: 'It is, in my opinion, a most perilous error to put "society" in the place of state and church as the decisive [massgebend] organ of human coexistence.'(6) One need only recall the nineteenth century debates over 'the individual and society' to realise that 'society' has always been an intensely political concept. (7)

But if the terms 'social science' and 'sociology' are inextricably linked to 'society', it is no less clear that many social scientists and sociologists have been embarrassed by this reference, feeling that the concept of society either is too vague, like the concept of 'life' in biology or, on the contrary, has unequivocal holistic or anti-individualist associations of an undesirable kind. Alternative terms such as 'social relations', 'social facts', 'social structure(s)', or 'social action/interaction' may function as euphemistic escape-routes from the intrinsic vagueness or the undesirable commitments understood to be associated with the concept of society.

There is scope, no doubt, for a full historical examination of sociology's love-hate relationship with the concept of society along the lines of Alan Dawe's penetrating discussion of theories of social action.(8) In this chapter I shall draw some distinctions between alternative conceptions of society in terms of the categories introduced by Roy Bhaskar in 'A Realist Theory of Science'. I shall isolate three concepts of society: a negative concept, underpinned by empiricism, which rejects 'society' as a pre-scientific category which is not open to the necessary operationalisation; an empirical realist concept which reifies society as a substantive entity with its own laws of motion; and a 'transcendental idealist' concept which is partially exemplified by Simmel and Max Adler. To these three concepts I shall oppose a fourth, predicated on transcendental realism, which attempts to incorporate the moment of truth in the first three.(9)

In line with the argument developed earlier in this thesis, I shall try to show that the choice of a frame of reference, an ontology of the social, should not be seen as a mere 'definitional question', with little if any importance for the analyses which follow it. As Dawe has shown, for example, the choice of an 'action' framework has very often led, in a curious dialectical way, to 'the concept of a dominating and constraining social system'. (10) Other consequences are more direct and account for the remarkable passion, as well as the confusion, of discussions of 'methodological individualism'.

The empirical realist rejection of 'society' is implicit throughout the empirical research tradition. If it is rarely made explicit, it is because it goes without saying, challenged only by mavericks such as the researchers of the Institut für Sozialforschung.(11) Lachenmeyer's classically positivistic programme includes the rationale

of most empirical research practice. Drawing on Quine's notion of referential opacity, he roundly asserts that 'there is no such entity as a "role"'. Parsons, he goes on, should have called his book 'The "Social System"':
This term cannot be used as if it were a primitive term standing in one-to-one correspondence with empirical events. If it is to be analyzed as a thing, it must be analyzed as a term, not an empirical event, and therefore must be in quotation marks.(12)

Individual actors and their actions are observable, empirical events. When these actors and their actions are summated and then described in terms that purport to refer to more than the summation, one is dealing with inferred entities, labels, abstractions, etc. that are derived from these empirical events but are not observable empirical events in and of themselves.(13)

Lachenmeyer therefore objects to the term 'social structure' because
it conveys the impression that sociologists are dealing with phenomena that have the stability of the phenomena of the physical sciences. The word 'structure' implies the existence of perceptual wholes like buildings or cars or chairs when in actuality the parameters of social phenomena are not as easily extrapolated from the empirics of human behaviour.(14)

In short, the term 'social structure' should be abandoned in favour of the compound predicate 'the patterned relations between men' which is often used to define it.(15)

What Lachenmeyer seems to be arguing for is a sociology which focuses on the details of 'patterned relations between' individuals at the expense of any idea that these relations are themselves determined or 'patterned' by more general social processes - the latter, one suspects, would be ruled out of order as unobservable.(16) The nature of 'individual actors and their actions', by contrast, does not seem to be problematic for Lachenmeyer.

David Papineau has recently provided a more sophisticated expression of this position. Papineau argues for an ontological reduction of social facts: 'The individualist does not want to deny that there are norms, institutions, economic structures, etc. All he wants to insist is that they do not exist external to individual reality, but only as complex (and perhaps therefore not that easily detectable) aspects of it.'(17) As Papineau points out, this is a different position from an explanatory reductionism which holds that social facts, if they exist, are only fully explained when they are broken down analytically:(18)

there seem to be some perfectly good senses in which
one might be an individualist on the 'what' question,
as I am, and yet a holist on the 'why' question. I
even suggested that it could make sense to be a holist
(Durkheimian) on the 'what' question and a kind of
individualist on the 'why'.

Papineau rejects 'the claim that in explaining a social
fact it is essential to give an explanation of all the
individual facts that make it up'.(19) But 'while we can
get by without individual reductions, they do have a number of attractions'.(20)

In so far as social facts are in the end constituted
by aggregates of individual facts and nothing more, it
should always be possible, in long-term principle at
least, if not in foreseeable practice, to uncover the
underlying connections between the individual components comprising those social facts which would enable
us, if we so wished, to give typical or actual individual reductions.(21)

It is ... undeniable that we in some sense will have
a deeper understanding of what is going on when we can
explain our macro-generalisations: we will see how
they are expectable consequences of individual truths
which are applicable in a wider range of contexts than
the specific kind of social circumstance under examination.(22)

Explanations in terms of social facts, then, are an intermediate stage, 'as long as we remain short of a detailed
social psychological underpinning for our macro-theories.'
(23) Social facts are not analogous to unobservable
entities which, on a realist view of science, produce
observable phenomena.(24)

Any difficulties about defining social facts in individual terms are of less ontological significance.
It is not so much a matter of their existing on a
separate level from individual reality as of our not
yet having decided, so to speak, exactly which bits
of individual reality they are to be reduced to.

Here we have a set of arguments to the effect that only
individual terms have a real reference; this empiricism,
it should be noted, is compatible with both a positivistic conception of social science and a more interactionist or 'phenomenological' approach. In either form, I
think it is clear that these positions rest precisely on
what Bhaskar calls the epistemic fallacy, the conflation
of the real and the empirical.(25) But there is another
form of empirical realism which sees no problems in
ascribing a sui generis reality to macro-social phenomena,

Chapter 5

including 'society' itself. In Comte's classic phrase, 'A *society* ... can no more be decomposed into *individuals* than a geometric surface can be resolved into lines, or a line into points.'(26)

A very important way in which sui generis views of society have been mediated is by the use of organic or 'organismic' analogies. Although such analogies go back at least as far as Plato, their systematic application to social phenomena, and the clear distinction between organism and mechanism, is a feature of nineteenth-century thought.(27) Mannheim distinguishes clearly between the German romantic use of such analogies and their later use in the work of Spencer and others. Schelling, for example, called the state 'einen objektiven Organismus der Freiheit', but 'he never thinks of it as a biological or social organism but as a mental and spiritual one.'(28)

The use of organic analogies became more extravagant in the later decades of the nineteenth century. Herbert Spencer is often cited as an extreme exponent of this way of thinking, and it is easy to find in his work, besides the bald assertion that 'A society is an organism',(29) notorious analogies such as that between nerve fibres and telegraph wires.(30) But Spencer turns aside the more obvious lines of criticism in the following disclaimer: (31)

> Here let it once more be distinctly asserted that there exist no analogies between the body politic and a living body, save those necessitated by the mutual dependence of parts which they display in common. Though, in foregoing chapters, sundry comparisons of social structures and functions in the human body have been made, they have been made only because structures and functions in the human body furnish familiar illustrations of structures and functions in general. The social organism, discrete instead of concrete, asymmetrical instead of symmetrical, sensitive in all its units instead of having a single sensitive centre, is not comparable to any particular type of individual organism, animal or vegetal.

Other writers, especially in the German-speaking world, were less cautious in pursuing Spencer's analogies, and thus fuelled the hostility to reified conceptions of society which one finds in Simmel, Max Weber and others. (32) What counts, however, is not so much the use of organic analogies as the more general aspiration to a 'system' analysis, which may also use models of mechanical equilibrium or of information transfer.(33)

Paradoxically, Spencer was also a political and economic individualist, and, moreover, his explanations are in part cast in an individualist form: 'Given the structures and instincts of the individuals as we find them, and the community they form will inevitably present certain traits.'(34) It was this individualism which Durkheim objected to in Spencer:(35)

> He admits, it is true that once it is formed society reacts on individuals. But it does not follow that society itself has the power of directly engendering the smallest social fact; from this point of view it exerts an effect only by the intermediation of the changes it effects in the individual. It is, then, always in human nature, whether original or acquired, that everything is based....
> if such a method is applied to social phenomena, it changes fundamentally their nature.

Durkheim's own position, to which I now turn, is not made entirely clear in the above passage,(36) nor, perhaps, in the 'Rules' as a whole.(37) However, I think it is clear, despite what is implied by the quotation above and by some of the rhetoric in the 'Rules' and elsewhere, that Durkheim did not really believe that society exists independently of the individuals who compose it. 'Society', he wrote in 'The Elementary Forms of the Religious Life', 'exists and lives only in and through individuals.'(38)

In general, Durkheim gives more attention to the explanatory role of social facts than to their ontological status. He is more committed, in other words, to holistic patterns of explanation than to a holistic ontology of the social. Occasionally he flirts with the latter, but mostly because he believes (mistakenly) that this is required to establish the case for the possibility of explaining social facts by other social facts.(39) At the same time, however, he is intoxicated by 'society' in the most general sense of the term, in which it does not so much denote any particular social structure as gesture towards the social totality and the phenomenon of socialisation or societation (Vergesellschaftung). For Durkheim, however, this reference involves much more than it does for, say, Simmel or Max Weber. Most importantly, perhaps, it is partially concretised in Durkheim's concept of the social species, 'l'espèce sociale'.(40)

Durkheim introduces this concept as a middle path between histoire événementielle and the sort of reification of 'humanity' associated with Comte.(41)

> This concept of the social species has the very great advantage of furnishing us a middle ground between ... the nominalism of historians, and the extreme realism of philosophers. For the historian, societies represent just so many heterogeneous individualities, not

comparable among themselves. Each people has its own physiognomy, its special constitution, its law, its morality, its economic organisation, appropriate only to itself; and all generalisations are well-nigh impossible. For the philosopher, on the contrary, all these individual groupings, called tribes, city-states and nations, are only contingent and provisional aggregations with no exclusive and separate reality. Only humanity is real, and it is from the general attributes of human nature that all social evolution flows....
One escapes from this alternative once one has recognised that, between the confused multitude of historic societies and the single, but ideal, concept of humanity, there are intermediaries, namely, social species.(42)

The concept of social species, however, is explicitly introduced in terms of the need to distinguish the normal and the abnormal;(43) and its use leads Durkheim on to extremely shaky ground.(44) I have suggested that neither Spencer nor Durkheim can be identified with a view which, in Alpert's words 'implies that society is an ontological reality, a substantial entity having corporate existence apart from, or ... over and above, the individuals who comprise it'.(45) At the same time, however, neither of them can be understood if one does not take into account their leanings in this direction.

Rather than engage in the antiquarian pleasures of disinterring what Stark has called 'extreme forms' of organicism in such writers as Bluntschli, Schäffle, von Lilienfeld and others,(46) I shall now turn to more recent general versions of social system theory. Walter Buckley is a useful guide to this terrain. Buckley argues that the excessively crude models, whether mechanical or organic in form, which have been used in most sociological systems theory, 'are quite inappropriate in dealing with the type of system represented by the sociocultural realm'. (47) Rather than this sort of misplaced concreteness, one needs to construct (or borrow from cybernetics) models of organisation sufficiently general and complex, though built from simple units, to embrace behaviour systems of any type - physical, biological, psychological, or sociocultural'.(48)

Buckley endorses the familiar criticism of the functionalist tendency to 'overemphasise the more stable, overdetermined, and supported normative aspects of the social system at the expense of other, equally important aspects without which dynamic analysis is impossible.'(49) He therefore looks with approval at what he calls the 'process model' of the social system exemplified by the

Chicago School under the influence of Simmel and von Wiese;
this 'is most congenial to, if not a forerunner of, the
modern systems view we are exploring'.(50) This is particularly true of the conventionalist gloss which is
given to the concept of structure:(51)

> In essence, the process model typically views society
> as a complex, multifaceted, fluid interplay of widely
> varying degrees and intensities of association and dis-
> sociation. The 'structure' is an abstract construct,
> not something distinct from the ongoing interactive
> process but rather a temporary, accommodative repre-
> sentation of it at any one time.

Despite the apparently diverse formulations, I think this
is essentially the sense of 'social structure' which was
cited above from Lévi-Strauss: one which 'has nothing to
do with empirical reality but with models which are built
up after it'.(52) More generally, I think one could
demonstrate a shift within social systems theories from
the reification of social systems and the uncritical use
of organic and other analogies to a more conventionalist
style of theorising which seems characteristic of Buckley's book. In the latter mode, the emphasis seems to be
on the heuristic usefulness of models, rather than the
possibility of giving them a realistic interpretation in
the particular system under discussion. As Buckley, puts
it,(53)

> modern systems theory ... can be seen as a culmination
> of a broad shift in scientific perspective striving
> for dominance over the last few centuries. This sci-
> entific world-view, product of a constant dialectic
> between conceptions of physical and those of biologi-
> cal science, have [sic] led away from concern for
> inherent substance, qualities, and properties to a
> central focus on the principles of *organisation per se*,
> regardless of what it is that is organised.

It seems then, that sociological system theories
which are so often accused of the reification of social
reality, have an opposite (but perhaps complementary)
tendency towards a nominalist and conventionalist interpretation of their theories. It will be recalled that
Parsons attacked as positivistic empiricism 'the *identification* of the meanings of the concrete specific propositions of a given science, theoretical or empirical, with
the scientifically knowable totality of the external
reality to which they refer'.(54) Parsons declares himself opposed to 'fictionalism' and in favour of 'analytical realism', in which(55)

> it is maintained that at least some of the general
> concepts of science are not fictional but adequately

'grasp' aspects of the objective external world. This is true of the concepts here called analytical elements .... These concepts correspond, not to concrete phenomena, but to elements in them which are analytically separable from other elements. But despite this apparent commitment to a non-empirical realism, Parsons's development of action analysis seems rapidly to move in a direction in which his concepts are either given a conventionalist interpretation or, in so far as they make up the action frame of reference, are part of 'the indispensable logical framework in which we describe and think about the phenomena of action'.(56) As for structural-functionalism itself, it is characterised in 'The Social System' as a provisional and 'second-best' approximation to the laws expressing the real interrelations between roles, values and needs.(57)

The above suggestions about the Parsonian system are presented only very tentatively. In general, however, there does seem to be evidence of a dialectic - the other side of the coin which Dawe has described - in which theories which stress system determination, the more elaborate they become, shift towards a conventionalist metatheory. In so doing, they approach the conception of society which, following Bhaskar, I call transcendental idealism.

Transcendental idealist theories of society arise in response to the perceived excesses of those which either treat society as a supra-individual entity or uphold a naively individualistic position. The central figure here is, I think, Simmel; I shall also discuss Max Adler, whose position on this issue has an apparent affinity with Simmel's, and Max Weber, whose emphasis is very different.

We have already noted in chapter 3 some of the ambiguities of Simmel's concept of society as it appears in How is Society Possible?.(58) Chapter 3 was organised around the antithesis between constitution$_e$, the theoretical constitution of, for example, 'society' as an object in the mind of the sociologist, and the practical constitution$_o$ of 'society' in human praxis, interaction, etc. It is, however, easy to see a priori two possible mediations of these two concepts of constitution. In the first, the cognitive process is guided by the exigencies of practical intervention in the world; in a stronger version, the world may be said, à la Vico, to be knowable to the extent that it is man-made. (This idea seems to be clearly present in Marx and parts of the Marxist tradition, especially in Alfred Schmidt's works.) In the second version, the constitution$_o$ of reality in general or social reality in particular is to some degree a product of cognitive acts of constitution$_e$ - interpretations, definitions of the situation etc.

As we saw in chapter 3, Simmel seems to equivocate between two questions:
(1) How is society possible as an object of knowledge (for social theorists and other members of society)?
(2) How is society possible as a practical accomplishment of its members?
If Simmel's answer to question (2) is taken to be 'By acts of knowledge',(59) the two questions collapse into one, yielding an idealist conception of the empirical genesis and foundation of society.(60) Alternatively, one can take Simmel (and a fortiori Max Adler) to be really asking 'How is sociology possible?'; then, however, 'sociology' must surely be understood in a more general sense than usual - as something like 'intellectual representations of social relations'. This would mesh in neatly with Simmel's insistence that the social a prioris are to be understood as constitutive 'categories of reality' and not merely tools in the hand of the social theorist.(61)

In talking of a transcendental idealist conception of society, I do not, however, wish to confine this category to peripheral aspects, contentiously interpreted, of the thought of Simmel and Adler. What I have in mind is a more diffuse conception which eschews the concept of society, preferring that of 'sociation' and related categories of 'process'. And there is no doubt that this is a central theme of Simmel's work:(62)

> one should properly speak, not of society, but of sociation. Society merely is the name for a number of individuals, connected by interaction ... society certainly is not a 'substance', nothing concrete, but an event: it is the function of receiving and affecting the fact and development of one individual by another.

Earlier, in 'Über soziale Differenzierung',(63) Simmel had argued more aggressively that 'society' is no more the object of sociology than 'the cosmos' is the object of astronomy; the latter actually studies, for example, the movements of individual stars. Again in The Field of Sociology,(64) Simmel emphasises that 'Sociology ... is founded upon an abstraction from concrete reality, performed under the guidance of the concept of society'. (65)

Schrader-Klebert, as we saw, argues that Simmel's concept of society should be seen as a regulative idea in Kant's sense - 'the hypothetical concept of the subject-matter (Sache) which is to arise successively in scientific cognition'. This interpretation is certainly supported by the quotation above and by the following more inductivist formulation from a lecture given by Simmel in 1899: 'We cannot start from a concept of society, for society is the sum of the ways in which human beings act with or against one another. Only when we know all these ways will we have the concept of society. Definitions are valueless and empty.'(66) 'Society', Simmel seems to believe, cannot be analysed in a wholly positive manner as a substantive reality. Nor, however, can it be simply dissolved into individual scraps of social knowledge, since it is the abstract principle of society or social determination which constitutes these findings as social knowledge. The concept of society is not really transcendentally given, despite Simmel's references to Kant, but one which can be, in Schrader-Klebert's phrase, 'reflexively recovered'.(67) It is, however, legitimated not only by our cognitive interests but also by the nature of reality:(68)

Abstractions alone produce science out of the complexity or the unity of reality. Yet however urgently such abstractions may be demanded by the needs of cognition itself, they also require some sort of justification of their relation to the structure of the objective world. For only some functional relation to actuality can save one from sterile inquiries or from the haphazard formulation of scientific concepts.

Max Weber, as we saw in chapter 3, does not attempt to give his sociology any transcendental foundation. His (negative) concept of society, however, has a considerable affinity with Simmel's. We have already noted(69) the consistently hostile attitude to the abuse of holistic concepts which Weber displayed in his letter to Liefmann:(70)

If I have become a sociologist (according to my letter of accreditation), it is mainly in order to exorcise the spectre of collective conceptions which still lingers among us. In other words, sociology itself can only proceed from the actions of one or more separate individuals and must therefore adopt strictly individualistic methods.

As Emerich Francis has shown, Weber scarcely ever uses the word 'society' (except, of course, in the title of his principal work); it seems clear that he associated the term with spuriously scientific sociologies which treat society as a substantial entity.(71) 'Gemeinschaft' appears rather more frequently, and does not seem to raise the same anxieties in Weber. In the case of both terms, however, he generally uses the processual forms Vergemeinschaftung and Vergesellschaftung; this is, of course, in keeping with Tönnies's own ideal-typical formulation of the antithesis: 'I do not know of any condition of culture and society in which elements of Gemeinschaft and elements of Gesellschaft are not simultaneously present, that is, mixed.'(72)

If one takes into account Weber's more general strategy of reducing social structural phenomena to complexes of action,(73) I think one can begin to see that a common feature in much turn-of-the-century sociology, at least in Germany,(74) was a relatively abstract and 'negative' concept of society. This was, no doubt, a corollary of the contemporary attraction to the concept of action, at least for Weber. With Simmel, the influences seem to be of a more general philosophical kind, while Tönnies was strongly influenced by Schopenhauer's concept of the will. (75)

Transcendental idealist concepts of society were carried further in interactionist and 'phenomenological' sociology.(76) Blumer, for example, put it in these terms: 'The human being is not swept along as a neutral and indifferent unit by the operation of a system ... cultural norms, status positions and role relationships are only frameworks inside of which [the] process of formative transaction goes on.'(77) Schutz cites with approval Simmel's 'underlying idea ... that all concrete social phenomena should be traced back to the modes of individual behaviour'.(78) The same idea is developed further in Berger and Luckmann's highly ambiguous book:

In contrast to some of the dominant fashions of theorising in contemporary sociology, the ideas we have tried to develop posit *neither* an ahistorical 'social system' *nor* an ahistorical 'human nature'. ... We cannot agree that sociology has as its object the alleged 'dynamics' of social and psychological 'systems', placed *post hoc* into a dubious relationship.(79)

The central question for sociological theory can ... be put as follows: How is it possible that subjective meanings *become* objective facticities.... In other words, an adequate understanding of the 'reality *sui generis*' of society requires an inquiry into the manner in which this reality is constructed. (80)

The theme of 'reality construction' has of course been pushed to an extreme in recent sociology.(81) A speculative explanation of the appeal of this approach might involve a sense of alienation from institutions seen as reified, pretentious and in need of 'deflating'. This was, of course, a crucial theme of the protest movements of the 1960s, expressed in the academic context in the slogan that a professor is merely a person with a different opinion. More generally, Anton Zijderveld claims that 'modern society has become abstract in the experience and consciousness of man'. The abstract character of modern society is primarily the result of 'segmentation of its institutional structure.... As a result of this pluralism society has lost ... much of its existential concreteness.' (82) This is expressed not only in impersonal role relationships but also in abstract art-forms. Alain Touraine, who, unlike Zijderveld, is not in any sense a Schutzian, makes a similar case in 'La Société Invisible': 'Society has disappeared.... On the one hand, one sees nothing more than the economy in a state of growth or crisis and international strategies: on the other hand, we react only to personal lived experience, to the invention of a culture.'(83)

There is, however, perhaps another current, linked to the names of Max Adler and Adorno, in which a transcendental idealist concept of society shifts towards what I would call a transcendental realist conception. The two salient features of this process are first, a stronger emphasis on social determination and second, an awareness of the extra-theoretical origins and political significance of the concept of society.

Max Adler, as we have seen, closely followed Simmel in demanding an epistemological foundation for sociology. However, the works in which he developed this theme should be seen in the context of his keen awareness of the historical development of the concept of society. Adler notes that Marx, in 'The Holy Family', recognises the illusory nature of the image of society as made up of isolated individuals. Like Hegel, Marx(84)

> takes as the starting-point of [his] sociological treatment of the problem of society the conception of bourgeois society as a mere appearance of the atomistic independence of its elements.... In Marx, this appearance is shown to be the necessary product of a particular historical form of human sociation, namely the form in which all acts of sociation must merely be performed by isolated individuals who are not conscious of their sociation, a form which is overcome by the removal of this social order.

This sense of the problematic nature of sociation in bourgeois society is developed further by Adorno.(85) The sense in which Adorno uses the term 'society' is not the sense in which we speak of hunting and gathering

societies or individualistic societies, where the term
refers to a mode of production or reproduction. Adorno's
'emphatic' concept of society denotes 'the moment of
sociation ... i.e. that there exists between human beings
a functional connection ... which takes on a certain
kind of independence in relation to them'.(86)
   Adorno's concept of society is in some respects very
close to Simmel's. Both see sociation as a functional
relation.(87) The affirmation of society does not mean a
depreciation of the individual, though it does involve an
emphasis that individuals are constituted by society and,
like all other social phenomena, can only be understood
in relation to the social totality. Hence Adorno's hostility to those, whether empirical researchers or theorists, who dispense with the concept of society:(88)
   It is on account of this functional structure that the
   notion of society cannot be grasped in any immediate
   fashion, nor is it susceptible of drastic verification,
   as are laws of the natural sciences. Positivistic
   currents in sociology tend therefore to dismiss it as
   a mere philosophical survival. Yet such realism is
   itself unrealistic. For while the notion of society
   may not be deduced from any individual facts, nor on
   the other hand be apprehended as an individual fact
   itself, there is nonetheless no social fact which is
   not determined by society as a whole. Society appears
   as a whole behind each concrete social situation.
In a characteristically Marxian turn, Adorno argues that
the abstraction implicit in the concept of society is not
a matter of the sociological theorist's banal reflection
that 'everything is connected with everything else';(89)
rather it is the essence of the exchange process which is
fundamental to society in the modern sense.(90) More
ambitiously still, he argues that there is a conceptuality
(Begrifflichkeit) in social relations themselves, most
notably in the exchange relation:(91)
   It is futile to ask whether ... [such] ... essential
   connections are 'real', or merely conceptual structures.
   The person who attributes the conceptual to social
   reality need not fear the accusation of being idealistic. What is implied here is not merely the constitutive conceptuality of the knowing subject but also a
   conceptuality which holds sway in reality [Sache]
   itself.
      Exchange value, merely a mental configuration when
   compared with use value, dominates human needs and
   replaces them; illusion dominates reality. To this
   extent, society is myth and its elucidation is still
   as necessary as ever. At the same time, however, this

illusion is what is most real, it is the formula used
to bewitch the world.
This theme of the interpenetration of thought and reality
is central to Adorno's concept of society (as it is to his
thought in general). What he does, in essence, is to
restore the polemical edge which the concept had in the
bourgeois revolutions of the eighteenth and nineteenth
centuries and in the liberal problematic of 'the individual' versus 'society' or 'the state'. Adorno has a post-
Marxian concept of the individual, but he restores the
pathos of the original discussion, believing that reification and social control are now immeasurably stronger:(92)
'The more the subjects are grasped by society, and ... the
more completely they are determined by the system, the
more the system maintains itself not simply by the use of
force against the subjects, but also through the subjects
themselves.'(93) This theme is brought out in more concrete terms in Adorno's discussion of the relationship
between sociology and psychology.(94) The susceptibility
of 'the masses' to irrational appeals, in particular those
of fascism, requires psychological analysis as well as a
sociological investigation of mass movements: 'For the
masses would hardly succumb to the brazen wink of untrue
propaganda if something within them did not respond to
the rhetoric of sacrifice and the dangerous life.'(95)
Thus the relationship between sociology and psychology
has been fundamentally misconceived where it is seen only
in terms of the classification of the sciences or their
pluridisciplinary integration:

> Where any thought at all has been devoted to the rela-
> tion between social theory and psychology, it has not
> gone beyond merely assigning the two disciplines their
> place within the total scheme of the sciences: the
> difficulties their relation involves have been treated
> as a matter of employing the right conceptual model.
> Whether social phenomena are to be derived from
> objective conditions or from the psyche of socialised
> individuals, or from both: whether the two types of
> explanation complete or exclude one another, or
> whether their relationship itself requires further
> theoretical consideration - all this is reduced to
> mere methodology.(96)

The way social and individual, objective and psychic,
moments relate to one another is supposedly dependent
on the mere conceptual schematisation imposed on them
in the busy academic process; plus the usual reserva-
tion that a synthesis would at this stage be premature,
that more facts have to be gathered and concepts more
sharply defined.(97)

Thus although 'all varieties of psychologism that simply take the individual as their point of departure are ideological',(98)

> a psychology that turns its back on society and idiosyncratically concentrates on the individual and his archaic heritage says more about the hapless state of society than one which seeks by its 'wholistic approach' or an inclusion of social 'factors' to join the ranks of a no longer existent *universitas literarum*.(99)

> the difference between individual and society is not merely quantitative, and it is seen this way only from the blinkered perspective of a social process that from the outset moulds the individual into a mere agent of his function in the total process. No future synthesis of the social sciences can unite what is inherently at odds with itself.(100)

Adorno develops a similar argument in relation to the theories of Weber and Durkheim. Weber's stress on the 'understanding' of social phenomena and Durkheim's insistence that they should be treated as things are equally one-sided and partial.(101) Each must be understood both in respect of its partial justification and as an expression of a 'false' state of society. An atomistic, individualising sociology reflects an atomised and administered society;(102) Durkheim's opposite stress on social constraint expresses, but does not analyse, the reification to which such a society is also prone.(103) Taken together, they demonstrate in a quite unmysterious and unpretentious manner the need for a dialectical theory of society which does justice to both of these contradictory moments.(104)

What would such a theory look like in practice? Adorno is notoriously long on critique and short on positive statements; indeed one of his central claims is that the latter must be treated with suspicion as sources of reification. For all this, however, a clear and powerful account can be found in his writings. His concept of society is intimately linked to his account of the relation between theory and data. As we have seen, 'society' is a theoretical concept par excellence: 'Because society can neither be defined as a concept in the current logical sense, nor empirically demonstrated, while in the meantime social phenomena continue to call out for some kind of conceptualisation, the proper organ of the latter is speculative theory.'(105) Such theorising is not to be seen as an alternative to empirical research, but as complementary, though relatively autonomous. The important distinction is not between theory and research, but between research which is conducted with an eye to the social totality and that which deliberately brackets out any such 'speculative' reference. The former was essentially the approach of the Institute for Social Research. Adorno argued, for example, that the analysis of class conflicts must seek them out in areas remote from the visible conflict between capital and labour in, for example, interpersonal relationships and in the psychological domain.(106) One of the main themes of his work in the sociology of music was to elucidate the effects in this domain of the exchange relation, reification and fetishism.(107) The principle is the same throughout; however specific the theme of a particular investigation, sociology should be concerned with 'the essential laws of society, (which) are not what the richest possible empirical findings have in common'.(108) As Adorno put it in an autobiographical essay:(109)

> Whether one proceeds from a theory of society and interprets the allegedly reliably observed data as mere epiphenomena upon the theory, or, alternatively, regards the data as the essence of science and the theory of society as a mere abstraction derived from the ordering of the data - these alternatives have far-reaching substantial consequences for the conception of society. More than any specific bias or 'value judgement', the choice of one or the other of these frames of reference determines whether one regards the abstraction 'society' as the most fundamental reality, controlling all particulars, or on account of its abstractness considers it, in the tradition of nominalism, as a mere *flatus vocis*. These alternatives extend into all social judgements, including the political.

I have suggested that what one finds in Adorno is a transcendental idealist concept of society, similar to Simmel's, but one which is fundamentally transformed in a realist direction by being located in a materialist theory - a theory which is more reflexive than, or reflexive in a different way from, that of Simmel.

I shall now go on to examine Bhaskar's sketch of a realist theory of society(110) and compare it with other recent works dealing with the relation between action and structure. First, it is helpful to ask just what conception of society a realist theory is committed to. I suggest that the essential principle of such a theory is the reality of structures(111) and of the relations within and between structures (in particular, causal relations). In other words, it is required of whatever social structures and mechanisms are postulated that they be in some sense real, rather than heuristic devices, and that they explain satisfactorily (without being reducible to) the observable phenomena of social life.

This is, I think, enough to distinguish a realist conception of society or social structure from empirical realist ones, such as Radcliffe-Brown's or Nadel's, or transcendental idealist ones such as those of Lévi-Strauss(112) and Leach. What constraints does it set, though, on candidates for social structural mechanisms? In principle, none. The realist distinction between the real and the empirical is precisely designed to legitimate the postulation of entities which are observable only via their effects, for which they provide the best available explanation in terms of current theory.(113) The realist does not, therefore, need to rule out entities such as the conscience collective or the Protestant ethic - indeed they must be given a realist interpretation as causally efficacious structures if they are to be allowed an explanatory role.(114)

There is widespread agreement among contemporary sociologists that the concept of conscience collective was not well suited to the explanatory work which Durkheim wanted it to perform, and he himself virtually abandoned it.(115) Similarly, one may want to limit the explanatory role of systems of ideas such as the Protestant economic ethic; (116) certainly a historical materialist version of realism will insist on systems of ideas being subject to further causal explanation.(117) But these issues are separate from the question of constraints on a realist ontology of the social.

It is, nevertheless, the case that realist theories as different as those of Harré(118) and Bhaskar uphold a relational ontology of the social. Bhaskar adopts the strategy of a 'pincer movement'.(119) Society is not reducible to people and their actions, since it is a condition of those actions. At the same time, society does not exist independently of individuals and their actions. (120) We are therefore back with Berger and Luckmann's question: 'How is it possible that human activity [Handeln] should produce a world of things [choses]?'(121) But this question is badly posed; what is at issue is not the Robinsonian creation of social structures which then reform the individuals who created them. To put the matter in this way 'encourages, on the one hand, a voluntaristic idealism with respect to our understanding of social structure and, on the other, a mechanistic determinism with respect to our understanding of people'.(122) People do not create society, but reproduce or transform it.(123)

That this is not merely a verbal difference is shown, I think, by the incoherence of the concept of reification associated with Berger's formulation.(124) A non-reified society, on this analysis, is a classically existentialist one, of a kind inconceivable outside the head of Jean-Paul Sartre. In Bhaskar's 'transformational model', by contrast,(125)
> a non-alienating society ... can no longer be conceived as the immaculate product of unconditioned ('responsible') human decisions, free from the constraints (but presumably not the opportunities) inherited from its past and imposed by its environment. Rather it must be conceived as one in which people self-consciously transform the social conditions of existence (the social structure) so as to maximise the possibilities for the development and spontaneous exercise of their natural (species) powers.

For Bhaskar, 'Society is both the ever-present *condition* (material cause) and the continually reproduced *outcome* of human agency.'(126) 'Society stands to individuals, then, as something that they never make, but that exists only in virtue of their activity.'(127) I have already cited Bhaskar's theses of the activity - and concept - dependence of social structures and alluded to the epistemological implications of these claims.(128) At an ontological level, they strengthen the case for a relational conception of the social which was made negatively by way of a critique of attempts to ground the social in individuals, groups (with society being seen as a sort of super-group), masses or whatever.(129) The connections between action and structure are made, in large part, through 'positions' and 'practices' which are specified relationally.(130) A further advantage of the relational conception is that(131)
> It allows one to focus on a range of questions, having to do with the *distribution* of the structural conditions of action, and in particular with differential allocations of: (i) productive resources (of all kinds, including for example cognitive resources) to persons (and groups) and (ii) persons (and groups) to functions and roles (for example in the division of labour).

Here again there is a close parallel with Giddens's discussion of the problems raised by Steven Lukes's oversharp dualism of power and structure.(132) There is thus an interesting and encouraging convergence between Bhaskar's 'philosophical critique of the contemporary human sciences'(133) and some of the most interesting contemporary sociological writing on the relations of action and structure, and related issues of ideology and critique. (134) How far such work retains the concept of society in a prominent position is a matter of secondary importance, so long as sociologists continue to do justice to the themes with which it has always been inextricably associated.

CONCLUDING REMARKS

I hope that the above discussion of the concept of society has helped to clarify and specify the general argument of this book, as outlined in the Introduction. What I have been arguing for is a realist philosophy of science and a realist ontology of the social as discussed in chapter 1. This ontology views society as both a condition and a continuously reproduced outcome of action. What is provided here is a real definition of society, i.e. a definition which makes truth-functional claims about reality (along the lines discussed in chapter 2, section b). Such a definition is therefore distinct from ordinary usage, in the sense that it may involve abstract theoretical concepts, and yet is likely at the same time to be linked in complex ways to our contemporary and historical experience of sociality (2c).

Society has to be constituted$_e$ as an object of inquiry, just as it is continuously reproduced (constituted$_o$) by human action (chapter 3). Durkheim's reification of society and Weber's reduction of society to sociation each underplay one term of the complex relation between 'action' and 'structure'. Chapter 5 is thus intended as an illustration of my overall argument and as a kind of microcosm of the book as a whole.

Finally, I should mention three objections which might be raised against the argument of this book. The first concerns the interpretation of social theorists (or for that matter natural scientists) in categories derived from the philosophy of science. This is, of course, a highly imprecise and uncertain activity(135) and some sociologists have concluded that this sort of labelling is best left to the Kremlin. It will be clear that I do not share this view. However one characterises the relationship between philosophy and the social sciences, it seems undeniable that philosophical uncertainties are in large measure responsible for the endemic conceptual disarray of social theory. It is simply naive to believe that a 'sociological epistemology' which brushes aside the traditional problems of philosophy will be able to evade these difficulties.

Chapter 5

A more serious objection concerns the status of the realist programme. I think it must be conceded that the viability of this programme needs to be demonstrated in more detail on the terrain of philosophy. In this book I have concentrated on furnishing subsidiary arguments in favour of the realist programme, rather than raising and attempting to meet the objections which may be raised from other philosophical traditions. This very necessary dialogue will no doubt be pursued elsewhere; at present it has scarcely begun.

The third objection was mentioned in the Introduction. It is that abstract discussion of problems of concept formation is sterile; what social theorists should be doing is constructing substantive theories whose conceptual merits will come out in the wash of intertheoretical discussion. For the reasons stated above, I feel that this view, however tempting it may seem in the present state of sociological theorising, rests on a misunderstanding of the conceptual problems of the social sciences. Chapter 5 is a gestural response to this third objection, in that it attempts to point out the substantive promise of a more adequate concept of society.

What is clear, I think, is that positivism has influenced the direction of social theory in ways which are now felt to be unsatisfactory. This influence has been direct, in licensing empiricist research programmes, and indirect, in constraining conceptions of hermeneutic alternatives. An alternative alliance, made up of a realist philosophy of science and new forms of naturalistic social theory, offers interesting possibilities for future research in the social sciences.

Notes

INTRODUCTION

1 Emerich Francis, Kultur und Gesellschaft in der Soziologie Max Webers, in 'Max Weber. Gedächtnisschrift der Ludwig-Maximilians-Universität München', Berlin, Duncker & Humblot, 1966.
2 A.R. Radcliffe-Brown, 'A Natural Science of Society' 2nd edn, Chicago, Free Press, 1957, p.55.
3 Claude Lévi-Strauss, 'Structural Anthropology', London, Allen Lane, 1968, ch.15, Social Structure, p.279. Cf. Edmund Leach's claim that social structure in 'practical situations' 'consists of a set of ideas about the distribution of power between persons and groups of persons', 'Political Systems of Highland Burma', London, Bell 1954, p.4.
4 Emile Durkheim, 'The Rules of Sociological Method', Chicago, Free Press, 1964, p.141.
5 See chapter 2 below.
6 P. Lazarsfeld and R. Boudon, Les Fonctions de la Formalisation en Sociologie, 'Archives Européennes de Sociologie', vol.4, 1963, reprinted in R. Boudon, 'La Crise de la Sociologie', Geneva, Droz, 1971. Karl Popper has consistently upheld a similar view, expressed in his famous table which contrasts 'statements or propositions or theories and their truth' (which are important) with 'words or concepts and their meanings' (which are not). K. Popper, 'Objective Knowledge', Oxford University Press, 1972, pp.309f. Cf. ibid., pp.123f. and Popper, 'Conjectures and Refutations', 3rd edn, London, Routledge & Kegan Paul, 1969, pp.18ff.
7 See the argument by Michael Scriven quoted on page below.
8 This rapprochement is clearly brought out in Karl-

Otto Apel, 'Analytic Philosophy of Language and the Geisteswissenschaften', Dordrecht, Reidel, 1967, and in G.H. von Wright, 'Explanation and Understanding', London, Routledge & Kegan Paul, 1971.
9 'Understanding Social Life. The Method Called Verstehen', London, Allen & Unwin, 1975.
10 Roy Bhaskar, 'A Realist Theory of Science', 2nd edn, Brighton, Harvester Press, 1978.
11 Roy Bhaskar, 'The Possibility of Naturalism', Brighton, Harvester Press, 1979.
12 I have attempted to develop some of these implications in my contribution to Gareth Morgan (ed.), 'Beyond Method: A Study of Organisational Research Strategies' (forthcoming). The bibliography of this article contains references to some of the work which has already been done in a number of sciences, notably psychology and linguistics, in terms of a realist framework.

CHAPTER 1   CONCEPTS OF SCIENCE

1 For a careful attempt to disentangle some of these views, see Peter Halfpenny, 'Explanations in Sociology: Positivist and Interpretivist Models', PhD thesis, Essex, 1976; Manchester University Press, forthcoming. Note that, for Halfpenny, realism is a variant of positivism; cf. below, pp.14f.
2 At least one which does not rely on some sort of covering law theory. Cf. G.H. von Wright, op.cit., ch.1.
3 These two terms, of which the first stems from Locke, are introduced by Peter Winch in 'The Idea of a Social Science', London, Routledge & Kegan Paul, 1958, pp.3-10. Winch himself, of course, offers a further possibility: that of the virtual identity of philosophy and social science.
4 Cf. Roy Bhaskar, 'The Possibility of Naturalism', pp.5-11.
5 For an excellent overview, see Anthony Giddens, Positivism and its Critics, in Tom Bottomore and Robert Nisbet (eds), 'A History of Sociological Analysis', London, Heinemann, 1978 and in Giddens, 'Studies in Social and Political Theory', London, Hutchinson, 1977. See also Norman Stockman, Positivism and Antipositivism, in Sociological Metatheory, PhD thesis, Aberdeen, 1979.
6 Mainly in the United States. It had barely penetrated the United Kingdom, despite A.J. Ayer's pioneering 'Language, Truth and Logic', London, Gollancz,

158 Notes

1936, when it was overtaken by what is sometimes called the 'second phase' of analytic philosophy, which drew on Wittgenstein's later work and on that of J.L. Austin.

7   For a more general account, see in particular Peter Achinstein and Stephen Barker (eds), 'The Legacy of Logical Positivism', Baltimore, Johns Hopkins Press, 1969.
8   Central to this view was a crude theory of meaning and reference. Language is merely the medium through which empirical statements pick out features of the world. But the medium is not always sufficiently pure, and it may lead us astray. In particular, we may be led to use language in a 'metaphysical' way which does not refer at all. The characteristic source of such confusions is the conflation of empirical science and philosophy; the latter, being an a priori science, cannot make justifiable substantive claims about reality.
9   See, for example, Rudolf Carnap, 'The Logical Syntax of Language', London, Kegan Paul Trench, Trubner, 1937, part V, and Carnap, Logical Foundations of the Unity of Science, in 'International Encyclopedia of Unified Science', vol.1, no.1, University of Chicago Press, 1938.
10 This was the title of a series of articles: Richard Rorty (ed.), 'The Linguistic Turn', University of Chicago Press, 1967.
11 'The Logical Structure of the World', London, Routledge & Kegan Paul, 1967. First published in 1928.
12 Intellectual Autobiography, in P.A. Schilpp (ed.), 'The Philosophy of Rudolf Carnap', The Library of Living Philosophers, vol.XI, La Salle, Illinois, Open Court, 1963, p.18. Carnap later (in the 1930s) came to join Otto Neurath in his support of a 'physicalistic' language basis.
13 See, for example, Moritz Schlick, 'Allgemeine Erkenntnislehre', 2nd edn, Berlin, Springer, 1925, p.18; C.G. Hempel, Fundamentals of Concept Formation in Empirical Science, 'International Encyclopedia', vol.II, no.7, 1952, p.1.
14 Ibid., pp.18ff.
15 The Scientific Conception of the World: The Vienna Circle, in Otto Neurath, 'Empiricism and Sociology', ed. Marie Neurath and Robert S. Cohen, Dordrecht and Boston, Reidel, 1973, p.306. This collective manifesto was written by Neurath - see p.318, n.2. It is hardly accidental that both Neurath and Carnap were interested in artificial languages - Neurath in his diagrammatic language, ISOTYPE, and Carnap in Esperanto.

Notes

16 Ibid., p.315.
17 Carnap, Logical Foundations, p.52. See also p.61, where Carnap stresses that this reduction of scientific languages is a first step towards the ultimate ideal of the unity of scientific laws. Cf. P. Oppenheim and H. Putnam, Unity of Science as a Working Hypothesis, in H. Feigl, M. Scriven and G. Maxwell (eds), 'Concepts, Theories and the Mind-Body Problem', Minnesota Studies in the Philosophy of Science, vol.II, University of Minnesota Press, 1958.
18 Hence the term 'logical empiricism'. In Toulmin's sharp formulation, 'the hybrid system of logical positivism ... professed to put an end to all metaphysics but succeeded, rather, in rewriting the metaphysics of Hume & Mach in the symbolism of Russell & Whitehead' (Stephen Toulmin, From Logical Analysis to Conceptual History, in Achinstein and Barker, op. cit., p.40).
19 Cf. Dudley Shapere, Toward a Post-Positivistic Interpretation of Science, in Achinstein and Barker, op.cit., p.128.
20 Cf. Giddens, Positivism, in Bottomore and Nisbet, op.cit., p.252: 'The original view of most of the Vienna Circle was that scientific knowledge rests upon a bedrock of indubitable fact, expressed in the immediacy of sensations as specified by Mach.' Neurath, as Giddens notes, was an exception to this consensus.
21 Gerard Radnitzsky, 'Contemporary Schools of Metascience', vol.1, Akademiförlaget Göteborg, 1968, p.64.
22 Cf. Herbert Feigl, The Origin and Spirit of Logical Positivism, in Achinstein and Barker, op.cit., p.17: 'In picturesque language it is the "upward seepage of empirical juice" which provides a meaning for the otherwise altogether unvisualisable (non-intuitive) concepts.'
23 Cf. David Kaplan, Significance and Analyticity, in Jaako Hintikka (ed.), 'Rudolf Carnap, Logical Empiricist', Synthese Library, vol.73, Dordrecht and Boston, Reidel, 1975.
24 Herbert Feigl, The 'Orthodox' View of Theories, in M. Rudner and S. Winokur (eds), 'Analyses of Theories and Methods of Physics and Psychology', Minnesota Studies in the Philosophy of Science, vol.4, University of Minnesota Press, 1970.
25 See, in particular, Peter Achinstein, 'Concepts of Science', Baltimore, Johns Hopkins Press, 1968. Such arguments, of course, apply a fortiori to the cruder

160 Notes

version of positivism which simply reduced theoretical to observational terms.
26 See, for example, Mary Hesse, 'The Structure of Scientific Inference', London, Macmillan, 1974, p.292. Popper's insensitivity to the problem of meaning-change between different theories, and to questions of language in general (cf. 'Objective Knowledge', pp.123f.) makes it legitimate, despite his objections, to put him, for present purposes, in the positivist camp.
27 See, for example, 'Objective Knowledge', pp.71f, 258f., 342-7.
28 Cf. Martin Hollis and Edward Nell, 'Rational Economic Man. A Philosophical Critique of Neo-Classical Economics', Cambridge University Press, 1975, pp.104-10.
29 Stephen Toulmin, 'Human Understanding', part I, Oxford, Clarendon Press, 1972, p.127.
30 Cf. Hollis and Nell, op.cit., ch.4; Bhaskar, op.cit., esp. p.168.
31 This feature of moral discourse is brought out well in J.M. Brennan, 'The Open-Texture of Moral Concepts', London, Macmillan, 1977.
32 At the same time, of course, positivism reduces explanation to description in the sense that it assimilates theoretical concepts to empirical facts and laws to their instances. Explanation is nothing more than the description of constant conjunctions.
33 While empiricism does not entail physicalistic reductionism, it is not difficult to see why it appealed to the logical empiricists. On some problems of the reductionist thesis in general, see C.G. Hempel, Reduction: Ontological and Linguistic Facets, in S. Morgenbesser, P. Suppes and M. White (eds), 'Philosophy, Science and Method. Essays in Honor of Ernest Nagel', New York, St Martin's Press, 1969.
34 Reprinted in O. Neurath, 'Empiricism and Sociology', ed. Marie Neurath and R.S. Cohen, Dordrecht and Boston, Reidel, 1973.
35 'Empiricism and Sociology', p.361. Cf. p.357: 'He who keeps free from metaphysics, understanding [Verstehen] and similar strivings, can, as a sociologist, use only behaviouristic phrases, as are proper to a discipline with a materialist foundation.'
36 Ibid., p.363.
37 Ibid.
38 Ibid., p.360.
39 Ibid., p.361.

40 One of the few exponents of a radically positivist sociology was George Lundberg, in his 'Sociology', 4th edn, New York, Harper & Row, 1968.
41 As Giddens notes, in Bottomore and Nisbet, op.cit., p.255, the replacement of 'method' by 'methodology' - the latter term distinguished from earlier conceptions of philosophy - is symptomatic of this influence. Cf. Jürgen Habermas, 'Knowledge and Human Interests', London, Heinemann, 1972, esp. pp.80f. Also Albrecht Wellmer, 'Methodologie als Erkenntnistheorie', Frankfurt, Suhrkamp, 1967.
42 See, for example, Hans Zetterberg, 'On Theory and Verification in Sociology', 3rd edn, New Jersey, Bedminster Press, 1965, ch.1, Sociology as a Humanistic Discipline. This chapter was added to the third edition of the book.
43 Ibid., ch.4. I shall try to suggest in the course of this book that one can separate this legitimate naturalist aspiration from the exaggerated and misconceived form which it took in positivism.
44 I tried to bring out these connections in 'Understanding Social Life. The Method Called Verstehen'.
45 On the links between this tradition and continental hermeneutics, see Karl-Otto Apel, op.cit.; also von Wright, op.cit.
46 Cf. Bhaskar, op.cit.
47 Cf. the discussion in chapter 2.
48 This constitutes an essential difference from natural science, even if one accepts a 'protophysics' made up of pre-understandings of natural phenomena. Cf. Anthony Giddens, 'New Rules of Sociological Method', London, Hutchinson, 1976, pp.146-54.
49 Max Weber, 'Economy and Society', vol.1, pp.7f. Quoted here in the translation by E. Matthews in W.G. Runciman (ed.), 'Max Weber, Selections in Translation', Cambridge University Press, 1978, p.11.
50 Cf. the notion of 'thick description', developed by Gilbert Ryle and taken up by the anthropologist Clifford Geertz, in 'The Interpretation of Cultures', London, Hutchinson, 1975.
51 T. Abel, The Operation Called <u>Verstehen</u>, 'American Journal of Sociology', vol.54, 1948. Cf. W. Outhwaite, op.cit., pp.47ff, 84ff. There is also the particular problem for positivists that motives and their analogues seem not to be logically independent of the actions of which they are alleged to be the motives, and therefore cannot, according to the party line, be analysed in terms of causal relations with them.

52 Chapter 2(c).
53 Hans-Georg Gadamer, 'Truth and Method', London, Sheed & Ward, 1975, pp.269ff.
54 Ibid., esp. pp.xiii, 446f. Paul Ricoeur, Herméneutique et Critique des Idéologies, translation in Paul Ricoeur, 'Essays on Hermeneutics', ed. John Thompson, Cambridge University Press, 1980.
55 Cf. Outhwaite, op.cit., pp.80f.
56 See, for example, J. Habermas, Zu Gadamers 'Wahrheit und Methode', in K.-O. Apel et al., 'Hermeneutik und Ideologiekritik: Theorie-Diskussion', Frankfurt, Suhrkamp, 1971, esp. pp.52ff. Gadamer's reply in the same book is reprinted in English in a shorter version in H.-G. Gadamer, 'Philosophical Hermeneutics', University of California Press, 1976. See also Habermas's earlier discussion of Gadamer in his 'Zur Logik der Sozialwissenschaften', 2nd edn, Frankfurt, Suhrkamp, 1971, pp.251-90; available in English in Fred Dallmayr and Thomas McCarthy (eds), 'Understanding and Social Inquiry', Notre Dame University Press, 1977, pp.335-63. For two further views, see Claus von Bormann, Die Zweideutigkeit der hermeneutischen Erfahrung, in Apel, et al., op.cit., and Rüdiger Bubner, 'Dialektik und Wissenschaft', Frankfurt, Suhrkamp, 1973, 2nd edn, 1974, pp.89-111.
57 Martin Hollis, 'Models of Man', Cambridge University Press, 1977; Deryck Beyleveld, Epistemological Foundations of Sociological Theory. An Examination of Recent Critiques of 'Positivism', PhD thesis, University of East Anglia, 1975.
58 Roy Bhaskar, 'A Realist Theory of Science'. Idem, 'Naturalism'. Cf. Russell Keat and John Urry, 'Social Theory as Science', London, Routledge & Kegan Paul, 1975; Ted Benton, 'The Philosophical Foundations of the Three Sociologies', London, Routledge & Kegan Paul, 1977.
59 The scope of a priori theory is, however, much broader for rationalism than for realism. Cf. Beyleveld, op.cit., chapter 6, esp. pp.424f., 431-4; Bhaskar, 'A Realist Theory of Science', esp. postscript to the 2nd edn, pp.258ff.; and Bhaskar, 'Naturalism', p.64 and n.65.
60 Hollis, op.cit., pp.178f.; Bhaskar, 'Naturalism', p.63.
61 Hollis, op.cit., p.20. The special thesis can survive without the general one (ibid., p.186) but the two tend to support each other.
62 Ibid., p.179. Cf. Beyleveld's claim, developed throughout his thesis and especially in ch.6: 'In

163 Notes

this chapter I have argued for a Rationalist epistemology as constituting the only way to combine the hard-headed attitude which logical positivism exhibits towards facts with the insight that knowledge is an activity governed by paradigmatic assumptions.'
63 Ibid., p.171.
64 Lukes calls these rational 1 and rational 2 criteria respectively, Some Problems About Rationality, section III, 'Archives Européennes de Sociologie VIII',2, 1967, reprinted in Bryan Wilson (ed.), 'Rationality', Oxford, Blackwell, 1974.
65 'The Limits of Irrationality', 'Archives Europeennes de Sociologie VIII', 2, 1967; reprinted in Wilson, op. cit.
66 Hollis, op.cit., pp.171ff. Beyleveld takes the strong line that all law-like generalisations, if true, are true a priori. (See esp. pp.425f.)
67 Cf. Hollis, op.cit., pp.165ff.
68 Hollis admits this in the final pages of his book, pp.186-90. Beyleveld explicitly argues for actionalism against structuralism, but seems to have an impoverished conception of the latter (e.g. p.20).
69 Another strong version of realism is upheld by Rom Harré. See, in particular, 'The Principles of Scientific Thinking, London, Macmillan, 1970; 'The Philosophies of Science', Oxford University Press, 1972, and R. Harré and E.H. Madden, 'Causal Powers', Oxford, Blackwell, 1975. Mary Hesse has upheld a more muted realism in 'The Structure of Scientific Inference', esp. ch.12, and in other works. (This chapter contains (pp.287ff.) a useful critique of E. Nagel's contention ('The Structure of Science', London, Routledge & Kegan Paul, 1961, ch.6, p.152) that the opposition between realism and instrumentalism is merely 'a conflict over preferred modes of speech'.
70 'A Realist Theory of Science', p.241.
71 Ibid., p.56f. This ontological distinction between domains of reality should not be confused with the positivist's epistemological distinction between observation and theory. The positivist remains bound to an empiricist ontology based on experience and expressed, as Bhaskar notes, in the incoherent concept of the 'empirical world'.
72 Ibid., p.9. Cf. p.12: 'It is a condition of the intelligibility of experimental activity that in an experiment the experimenter is a causal agent of a sequence of events but not of the causal law which the sequence of events enables him to identify.'

73 'A Realist Theory of Science', p.250. This, for Bhaskar, implies the impossibility of a correspondence theory of truth (p.249). Hesse, by contrast, retains a modified correspondence theory.
74 Ibid., p.249.
75 Hollis, op.cit., p.190.
76 This does not, of course, rule out in principle the idea of collective actions, structures of action, and so forth. But rationalists have so far seemed disinclined to embrace these concepts and seem less well placed to handle them than, for example, realists. More generally, rationalist philosophies of science do not deal adequately with the empirical moment in science (especially experimentation) and with contingency in the world. Cf. Beyleveld, op.cit., pp.430f.
77 Ibid., p.21.
78 Alan Ryan, Deductive Explanation in the Social Sciences, part II, 'Proceedings of the Aristotelian Society', supplementary volume XLVII, 1973, p.179. Hollis quotes this against himself (op.cit., p.98f.) but says in reply that the proposition must be restricted to autonomous actions. This begs the question, in so far as people are not autonomous and rational, as we must a priori assume them to be.
79 Ibid., pp.123-41.
80 Bhaskar, 'Naturalism', p.139. This is not, I think, to rule out the heuristic role of deductive 'theories' such as game theory, decision theory and perhaps neo-classical micro-economic theory.
81 Ibid., p.44.
82 Ibid., pp.48f. Cf. Ted Benton's criticisms of this position in Realism and Social Science, 'Radical Philosophy', no.27, 1981.
83 Ibid., pp.57ff.; Nb. n.53, p.59.
84 Ibid., p.59.
85 Ibid., p.59.
86 Ibid., p.63.
87 Ibid., p.65.
88 Ibid., p.64 and n.65.
89 Cf. Hollis and Nell, op.cit.
90 There is scope here for a systematic investigation of rhetorical procedure in the social sciences, along the lines perhaps of Gernot Böhme's interesting work on natural science. Cf. G. Böhme, The Social Function of Cognitive Structures: A Concept of the Scientific Community Within a Theory of Action, in K. Knorr, H. Strasser and H.G. Zilian (eds), 'Determinants and Controls of Scientific Development', Dordrecht and Boston, Reidel, 1975. Also G. Böhme,

Notes

Die Ausdifferenzierung wissenschaftlicher Diskurse, in N. Stehr and R. König (eds), 'Wissenschaftssoziologie', Sonderheft 18, 'Kölner Zeitschrift für Soziologie und Sozialpsychologie', Opladen, Westdeutscher Verlag, 1975.
91 'A Realist Theory of Science', p.248. Cf. p.258 for Bhaskar's criticisms of a stronger formulation of incommensurability.
92 Steven Lukes, 'Power. A Radical View', London, Macmillan, 1974, p.27.
93 Hollis, op.cit., p.178 and pp.174-80 passim.
94 Lukes, 'Power', p.26. Cf. W.B. Gallie, Essentially Contested Concepts, 'Proceedings of the Aristotelian Society', New Series, LVI, 1955-6; also William E. Connolly, 'The Terms of Political Discourse', Lexington, Mass., D.C. Heath, 1974.
95 Cf. Steven Lukes, Relativism, Cognitive and Moral, 'Proceedings of the Aristotelian Society', Supplementary Volume, 1974.
96 Steven Lukes, On the Relativity of Power, in S.C. Brown (ed.), 'Philosophical Disputes in the Social Sciences', Brighton, Harvester Press, 1979, p.270. Lukes writes (pp.272f.) that he has 'as a matter of fact, been pleasantly surprised at the extent to which it is possible to appeal to the proponents of contending views in this area by calling their background assumptions into question in this way'.
97 Ibid., p.271. Cf. Steven Lukes, Power and Authority, in Bottomore and Nisbet, op.cit., esp. p.669, para.2.
98 Op.cit., p.179.
99 The terms structure and mechanism may, of course, be used to mean anything from patterns of action to large-scale collective phenomena. Rom Harré, who takes a strongly realist position in the philosophy of science, also favours broadly interactionist varieties of social theory. See R. Harré and P.F. Secord, 'The Explanation of Social Behaviour', Oxford, Blackwell, 1972. In a more recent book, 'Social Being', Oxford, Blackwell, 1979, Harré gives a stronger realist gloss to his social psychology, and is sceptical of the claims of macrosociology. See, for example, his discussion of social change, esp. pp.347ff.
100 Cf. note 97 above.
101 'Naturalism', ch.3.
102 Op.cit., p.143.
103 Harré and Secord, op.cit., p.125. Cf. p.161.
104 In that, for example, it resuscitates the possibility of naturalism, which positivism may be said to have

166 Notes

killed with kindness, and allows a far greater role to empirical discovery. (For a rationalist view of the latter, see Beyleveld, op.cit., pp.430f.)
105 Penguin translation, 1973, p.106.
106 Ibid., p.331.
107 My translation. Cf. 'Capital', vol.I, Harmondsworth, Penguin, 1976, p.174.
108 The most impressive recent work to make this case is Derek Sayer's book, 'Marx's Method. Ideology, Science and Critique in "Capital"', Brighton, Harvester Press, 1979. See also John Mepham and D.-H. Ruben (eds), 'Issues in Marxist Philosophy', 3 vols, Brighton, Harvester Press, 1979.
109 'Capital', vol.III, Harmondsworth, Penguin, 1981, p.956.
110 L. Kolakowski, 'Marxism and Beyond', London, Paladin, 1971, pp.59-87.
111 Cf. p.15 above and the fuller description in chapter 3, below.
112 Anthony Cutler, Barry Hindess, Paul Hirst and Athar Hussain, 'Marx's Capital and Capitalism Today', 2 vols, London, Routledge & Kegan Paul, 1977 and 1978. Roy Edgley has developed a more orthodox account based on the idea that a theory can have a critical relation to its object. This account he sees as incompatible with realism or, as he calls it, 'epistemological materialism'. See his articles in: 'Radical Philosophy' nos. 15 and 21; Mepham and Ruben, op.cit., vol.3. However, this notion of critique seems impossible to sustain except on realist premises, once Edgley has rejected transcendental idealism.
113 On this 'immanent method', see Gillian Rose, 'The Melancholy Science', London, Macmillan, 1978.
114 Theodor Adorno, 'Negative Dialectics', New York, Seabury Press, 1973, p.53. Cf. Adorno, 'Vorlesung zur Einleitung in die Soziologie', Frankfurt, Junius-Drucke, 1973, pp.27, 30-6, 88f., 126-30. See also Susan Buck-Morss, 'The Origin of Negative Dialectics' Brighton, Harvester Press, 1977, and Rose, op.cit., p.61.
115 Cf. Paul Hirst, 'Durkheim, Bernard and Epistemology', London, Routledge & Kegan Paul, 1975; Keat and Urry, op.cit., ch.4; Benton, op.cit.
116 Bhaskar, 'A Realist Theory of Science', pp.24ff. Cf. chapter 4, below.

CHAPTER 2 CONCEPTS IN SCIENCE

1 Even the more mathematised natural sciences are discussed by scientists in 'everyday' terms. Cf. Michael Mulkay, 'Science and the Sociology of Knowledge', London, Allen & Unwin, 1979, esp. ch.3. See also Gernot Böhme, The Social Function of Cognitive Structures, and Die Ausdifferenzierung Wissenschaftlicher Diskurse.
2 'The Mind and Society', London, Cape, 1935, vol.I, para.119.
3 It is an index of the strength of this view that the word 'semantic' has acquired a distinctly pejorative aura.
4 Op.cit., p.42. Cf. Lewis Carroll, 'Alice', Oxford University Press, 1971.
5 Lazarsfeld and Boudon, op.cit. and P. Lazarsfeld and M. Rosenberg (eds) 'The Language of Social Research', Chicago, Free Press, 1955. Cf. Charles Lachenmeyer, 'The Language of Sociology', Columbia University Press, 1971.
6 'Truth and Method', p.412.
7 'A System of Logic', London, Longmans, 1868, vol.I, book I, ch.III, para.1.
8 F.A. Trendelenburg, 'Geschichte der Kategorienlehre', Berlin, 1846.
9 'Journal of Philosophy', vol.39, 1942, p.312. On Cassirer's own programme, see 'The Philosophy of Symbolic Forms', Yale University Press, 1957, vol. III and Zur Theorie des Begriffs, 'Kantstudien', vol.33, 1928, p.135: 'The theory of logical-scientific concept formation must be preceded by a theory of linguistic concept formation.'
10 Maurice O. Crosland, 'Historical Studies in the Language of Chemistry', London, Heinemann, 1962, p.xiv.
11 Quoted by Crosland, ibid., pp.170f.
12 Quoted in Stephen Toulmin and June Goodfield, 'The Architecture of Matter', London, Hutchinson, 1962, p.218.
13 G. Baldamus, 'The Structure of Sociological Inference', London, Martin Robertson, 1976, p.37. Cf. Maurice Natanson, 'Philosophy of the Social Sciences' New York, Random House, 1963, p.14: 'The reason that the vocabularies of social scientists cannot be cleared up in some concerted operation and rendered uniform is that terminology is most often the reflection of an implicit Weltanschauung. Furthermore, the reluctance of many theoreticians and methodologists

with regard to adopting a kind of theoretical Esperanto is rooted in the fact that among them there are serious philosophical differences. Language can reflect underlying consensus; it cannot create it.'
14 London, Routledge & Kegan Paul, 1963.
15 Ibid., p.160.
16 Ibid., pp.162f. Ossowski gives us an example of the way in which the extension of the Durkheimian concept of religion differs from that of more conventional accounts.
17 New York, Atherton Press, 1967, p.17. See also 'The Terms of Political Discourse'.
18 Ibid., p.18.
19 Ibid., p.108.
20 Ibid., p.104.
21 London, New Left Books, 1975, pp.224f.
22 A recent book which takes seriously the analogies between sociological paradigms and literary genres is Richard Brown, 'A Poetic for Sociology', Cambridge University Press, 1977. See also Joseph Gusfield, 'Community. A Critical Response', Oxford, Blackwell, 1975. A central question here is, of course, the role of metaphor in the social sciences. See David Perman's comments on Brown in The Artful Face of Sociology, 'Sociology', vol.12, no.3, 1978 and Perman's earlier paper: Metaphor, Cliche and Sociological Theory. For a very different, solidly structuralist, approach see Claudine Normand, 'Metaphore et Concept', Brussels, Edition Complexe, 1976.
23 'Truth and Method', esp. pp.364f., 375f., 407, 411f. and 'Philosophical Hermeneutics', p.86.
24 Cf. ch.1, n.113, p.21 above.
25 'Capital', vol.I (Penguin edition), p.677.
26 'Capital', vol.III (Penguin edition), p.957.
27 Ibid., p.953. Cf. Norman Geras, Marx and the Critique of Classical Political Economy, in Robin Blackburn (ed.), 'Ideology in Social Science', London, Fontana, 1972, pp.284-305.
28 Weber, 'Economy and Society', vol.I, p.14. Cf. his letter to Robert Liefmann, cited in Wolfgang Mommsen, 'The Age of Bureaucracy', Oxford, Blackwell, 1974, p.110, and Mommsen, Max Weber's Political Sociology and his Philosophy of World History, 'International Social Science Journal', vol.17, 1965, p.40n. See also Reinhard Bendix, Two Sociological Traditions, in Reinhard Bendix and Guenther Roth, 'Scholarship and Partisanship: Essays on Max Weber', University of California Press, 1971, ch.15, pp.282-98.

29 'Rules', p.104.
30 Cf. n.17, p.7, above.
31 Not, of course, for its own sake, but for the sake of greater precision. For positivists, such innovations were not of substantial importance, since on this view science consists only of empirical statements and logical operations.
32 Cf. p.7 , above.
33 Bridgman's operationalism represents another possible strategy. (P.W. Bridgman, 'The Logic of Modern Physics', New York, Macmillan, 1954.)
34 Cf. Achinstein, 'Concepts of Science'.
35 J.L. Austin, 'Philosophical Papers', 2nd edn, Oxford, Clarendon Press, 1970, p.182.
36 Ibid., p.185. Cf. Hanna Pitkin, 'Wittgenstein and Justice', University of California Press, 1972, pp.313f.
37 See, for example, Anthony Kenny, 'Action, Emotion and Will', London, Routledge & Kegan Paul, 1963; A.I. Melden, 'Free Action', London, Routledge & Kegan Paul, 1961.
38 Op.cit.
39 Ibid., pp.9f. Cf. pp.251f.
40 David Walsh, Science, Sociology and Everyday Life, in Chris Jenks (ed.), 'Rationality, Education and the Social Organisation of Knowledge', London, Routledge & Kegan Paul, 1977, p.49. Cf. David Walsh, Sociology and the Social World, in Paul Filmer, Michael Phillipson, David Silverman and David Walsh, 'New Directions in Sociological Theory', New York, Collier-Macmillan, 1972. See also the seminal work by the originator of ethnomethodology, Harold Garfinkel, 'Studies in Ethnomethodology', Englewood Cliffs, New Jersey, Prentice-Hall, 1967.
41 Loc.cit.
42 Ibid., p.51.
43 'Truth and Method', pp.364f.
44 'Philosophical Hermeneutics', p.26.
45 Ibid., p.19.
46 'Truth and Method', p.394.
47 Ibid., pp.411f.
48 Ibid., p.376.
49 Ibid., p.375. Cf. also Semantics and Hermeneutics (1972), reprinted in 'Philosophical Hermeneutics', esp. p.86: 'Precisely defined, unambiguous terms live and communicate only in so far as they are embedded in the life of the language, and hence it is obviously essential that they enrich their power of making things clear - a power previously limited

by their univocality - with the communicative power of multivocal, vague ways of speaking. To be sure, science can ward off such muddying of its concepts, but methodological "purity" is always attainable only in particular areas - the context of world-orientation resting upon our linguistic relationship to the world precedes it. For an example, one need only think of the concept of "force" in physics and the connotations that are heard along with "force" and that make the insights of science meaningful to the layman.'

50 Pp.101f.
51 R. König (ed.), 'Handbuch der empirischen Sozialforschung', 2nd edn, Stuttgart, Enke, 1967, p.4.
52 Grundlagenprobleme der soziologischen Forschungsmethoden (Modelle, Theorien, Kategorien), in F. Karrenberg und H. Albert (eds), 'Sozialwissenschaft und Gesellschaftsgestaltung. Festschrift für G. Weisser', Berlin, Duncker & Humblot, 1963.
53 Ibid., p.35.
54 Ibid., p.36.
55 'Gesammelte Aufsätze zur Wissenschaftslehre' (GAW hereafter), 3rd edn, Tübingen, Mohr, 1963, p.190; translated as 'The Methodology of the Social Sciences', E. Shils and H. Finch (eds), Chicago, Free Press, 1949, p.90. But cf. Weber's significantly different formulation in 'Roscher and Knies', New York, Free Press, 1975, pp.175f. (GAW, p.131); cf. Burger, op.cit., p.204, n.31.
56 He gives the example of E. Faris's review, 'American Sociological Review', vol.18, 1953.
57 Ibid., p.40.
58 Hollis, 'Models of Man', p.99.
59 'A Realist Theory of Science', p.259; 'Naturalism', pp.64f. and n.65. See chapter 5 below.
60 T. Carver (ed.), 'Karl Marx. Texts on Method', Oxford, Blackwell, 1975, p.198.
61 Sayer, op.cit., pp.8f.
62 Ibid., p.9.
63 Louis Althusser and Etienne Balibar, 'Reading Capital', London, New Left Books, 1970.
64 Cf. R. Aron, 'D'une sainte famille à l'autre', Paris, Gallimard, 1969, p.73.
65 'The sighting is thus no longer the act of an individual subject, endowed with the faculty of "vision" which he exercises either attentively or distractedly; the sighting is the act of its structural conditions, it is the relation of imminent reflection between the field of the problematic and _its_ objects and its problems.'

66 Althusser and Balibar, op.cit., p.226.
67 Cf. the final sentence of his essay, where he seems to equate theoretical practice with the production of the concepts which enable one to solve theoretical problems: 'In the problems of theoretical practice, all that is ever at issue, beneath their peculiar form as theoretical problems, i.e. beneath the form of the production of concepts which can give their knowledge are the tasks and problems of other practices,' (ibid., p.308). See also Althusser, The Object of Capital, sec.6, Althusser and Balibar, op. cit., pp.154-7), and the Three Generalities model in 'For Marx', London, Allen Lane, 1969, pp.182-93, in which primacy is assigned to generalities II or theoretical concepts. Cf. in Althusserian vein, Eric Esaer, Les principaux concepts pour une science sociale, 'Revue de l'Institut de Sociologie', vol.49, no.4, 1976, and, of course, the work of Nicos Poulantzas.
68 Weber explicitly attacks the idea 'that the goal of the cultural sciences ... is to construct a closed system of concepts, in which reality is synthesised in some sort of *permanently* and *universally* valid classification and from which it can again be deduced' (GAW, p.184; translation, p.84). Cf. GAW, pp.208f.; translation, p.106.
69 For a late statement of Weber's views, see 'Economy and Society', vol.I, ch.1, part 1, section 11, pp.19f. The fullest discussion of ideal types is in Weber's essay on 'Objectivity', but he recognised that even this was 'sketchy' and therefore might lead to misunderstanding (in a footnote to his essay on Knies, GAW, p.131, n.1; 'Roscher and Knies', p.277, n.95). Cf. Burger, op.cit., pp.115-40.
70 'Rules', p.37.
71 This example and the discussion as a whole is largely based on Richard Robinson, 'Definition', Oxford University Press, 1954, reprinted 1962. I have also referred to an article by Kasimierz Ajdukiewicz, Three Concepts of Definition, in T.M. Olshewsky (ed.), 'Problems in the Philosophy of Language', New York, Holt, Reinhart & Winston, 1969. Ajdukiewicz distinguishes 'nominal' (i.e. lexical), 'real' and 'arbitrary' (positive) definitions.
72 I say 'characteristically' because some statements, such as 'God is love', might be taken to express a real definition, without having a readily assignable truth-value, while the reference to 'nature' might seem inappropriate in some circumstances, e.g.

'Warsaw is the present capital of Poland.' (Ajdukiewicz gives this as an example of a real definition, though Robinson (op.cit., p.24) disallows real definitions of particulars.)
73 Robinson, op.cit., pp.29f.
74 Ibid., p.153.
75 Ibid., p.189.
76 He suggests that Marx's definition of value in terms of labour 'is not really an attempt to describe the facts at all but the expression of a moral ideal ... that the products of labour should all go to the labourers', p.167.
77 Ibid., pp.24f.
78 'Principia Mathematica', Cambridge University Press, 1910, vol.I, pp.11f.
79 Morris Weitz, Analysis and the Unity of Russell's Philosophy, in P.A. Schilpp (ed.), 'The Philosophy of Bertrand Russell', Library of Living Philosophers, New York, Tudor Press, 1944, 1951, p.111. Cf. Arthur Pap, 'Semantics and Necessary Truth', Yale University Press, 1958, pp.270f.
80 R. Bierstedt, Logic, Language and Sociology, PhD thesis, Columbia, 1950, p.102. This is perhaps to put it too strongly, if Bierstedt's intention is to rule out a priori theory altogether. But this may not be intended, since this passage arises out of a criticism of 'committees on definitions' (see below). Bierstedt, like Robinson, accepts that there is no clear distinction between real and nominal definitions, but he goes on to argue that 'only in the case of newly-introduced term can the definition be purely nominal' (p.90). See also R. Bierstedt, Nominal and Real Definitions in Sociological Theory, in his 'Power and Progress. Essays on Sociological Theory', New York, McGraw-Hill, 1974.
81 Robinson, op.cit., p.40.
82 Baldamus, op.cit., p.146 and note, p.172.
83 'Die Wissenformen und die Gesellschaft', 'Werke', 2nd edn, Bern, Francke Verlag, 1960, vol.8, pp.99ff. My translation. For an English translation, see Max Scheler, 'Problems of the Sociology of Knowledge', ed. Kenneth Stikkers, London, Routledge & Kegan Paul, 1980, p.107. Cf. also Gottfried Salomon, 'Historischer Materialismus und Ideologienlehre', vol.I, 'Jahrbuch für Soziologie II', Karlsruhe, 1926, esp. p.393: Skeptizismus, Nominalismus, Sensualismus, Empirismus, wirken revolutionär, indem sie die geltenden Nomen und Formen in ihrer Autorität und Apriorität bestreiten.'

173 Notes

84 'Wissensformen', pp.430-8, Max Webers Ausschaltung der Philosophie.
85 Leszek Kolakowski, 'Positivist Philosophy. From Hume to the Vienna Circle', Harmondsworth, Penguin, 1972, pp.13-16.
86 For example Herbert Blumer, whose debate with Lundberg about clear concepts defined ab initio is reported by Bierstedt in Ll. Gross (ed.) 'Symposium on Sociological Theory', Evanston, Illinois, Row, Paterson, 1959. Cf. also Blumer's article The Problem of the Concept in Social Psychology, 'American Journal of Sociology', vol.44, 1940. Another candidate would be Eubank's Conceptual Approach - see his contribution to H.E. Barnes and H. Becker (eds), 'Contemporary Social Theory', New York, Appleton Century, 1940.
87 Stephen Toulmin and Michael Scriven were prominent in developing these ideas in the philosophy of science.
88 As early as 1950, Bierstedt's thesis aimed to transport to sociology 'some of the premises of a realistic philosophy of science'. (Preface)
89 See ch.2, n.4, above.
90 Cf. Boudon and Lazarsfeld, op.cit.
91 'The Foundations of Economics', London, W. Hodge, 1950, p.51. Cf. Karl Menger: 'Definitions are dogmas; only the conclusions drawn from them can afford us any new insight' (quoted approvingly by Karl Popper, 'The Logic of Scientific Discovery', London, Hutchinson, 6th impression, 1972, p.55).
92 'An Autobiographical Study', 2nd edn, London, Hogarth, 1946, pp.106f. Cf. Claudine Normand, op. cit., pp.46ff, 124f.
93 Though he characterises them rather unusually, restricting the term 'nominal definition' to the introduction of a new term with a stipulated meaning ('Fundamentals of Concept Formation in Empirical Science', p.9) 'real definitions' therefore include descriptive specifications of meaning (pp.9ff.).
94 Ibid., p.11.
95 'Expression' here refers to an extensionalist conception of meaning. Cf. p.48: 'If ... (a) term has so far been used solely in prescientific discourse, then the only way of ascertaining whether a proposed set of precise criteria affords a "valid" gauge of the characteristic in question is to determine to what extent the objects satisfying the criteria coincide with those to whom the characteristic in question would be assigned in prescientific usage.'
96 See above, pp.7f.

97 Lundberg, 'Sociology', esp. p.42 (favourable citation of Humpty Dumpty), p.58 (support of operationalism). See also his article on Operational Definitions in the Social Sciences, 'American Journal of Sociology', vol.47, no.5, 1942. Cf. H.P. Fairchild's preface in his 'Dictionary of Sociology', New York, Philosophical Library, 1944.

98 In particular, the creation in the USA in 1937 of a 'Committee on Conceptual Integration' to try to reach agreed definitions of sociological terms. See Hornell Hart's Abridged Report of the Sub-Committee on Definition of Definition, 'American Sociological Review', vol.8, 1943, pp.333-42. Bulletin 64 (1954) of the American SSRC reports on a similar enterprise with regard to historical terms, organised by Charles Beard and Sidney Hook. See also the more sophisticated and less prescriptive efforts of the Committee on Conceptual and Terminological Analysis (COCTA). The best source for the latter is Giovanni Sartori, Fred W. Riggs and Henry Teune, 'Tower of Babel. On the Definition and Analysis of Concepts in the Social Sciences', International Studies Association, Occasional Paper no.6, University of Pittsburgh, 1975.

99 P.W. Bridgman, op.cit.; C.K. Ogden and I.A. Richards, 'The Meaning of Meaning', London, Kegan Paul, 1923; Alfred Korzybski, 'Science and Sanity', 4th edn, Lakeville, Conn., International Non-Aristotelian Publishing Co., 1958; Stuart Chase, 'The Tyranny of Words', London, Methuen, 1938.

100 Above, ch.2, n.86.

101 As does the opposition to them: in Joachim Rohlfes's hostile characterisation, for historicism 'a highly developed and precise system of concepts (Begrifflichkeit) was suspect in that it conflicted with the [historicist] idea of the *individuum ineffabile*' (Beobachtungen zur Begriffsbildung in den Geschichtswissenschaften, in E. Jäckel and E. Weymar (eds), 'Die Funktion der Geschichte in Unserer Zeit', Stuttgart, Klett, 1975, p.20).

102 Natanson, op.cit., p.14.

103 See L. von Wiese and H.E. Becker, 'Systematic Sociology', London, Chapman & Hall, 1932, pp.128ff.; and E.E. Eubank, The Conceptual Approach to Sociology, in Barnes and Becker, op.cit. See also the lists of concepts compiled for several years at the Maison des Sciences de l'Homme, Paris, and published in 'Social Science Information', 1967-75.

104 M. Scriven, Definitions, Explanations and Theories, in H. Fiegl, M. Scriven and G. Maxwell (eds),

175 Notes

'Concepts, Theories and the Mind-Body Problem', Minnesota Studies in the Philosophy of Science, vol. 2, University of Minneapolis Press, 1958, p.100.
105 Ibid., p.166.
106 Scriven, loc.cit.
107 In Minnesota Studies in the Philosophy of Science, vol.1, 1956, p.48.
108 Cf. Pitkin, op.cit., pp.313f.
109 'Philosophical Hermeneutics', p.127.
110 Cf. Gillian Rose, op.cit., p.61.
111 T.W. Adorno, 'Negative Dialectics', p.5.
112 Ibid., p.52.
113 Ibid., p.43.
114 Ibid., p.151.
115 'Vorlesung zur Einleitung in die Soziologie', p.88.
116 Ibid., p.27. Cf. Adorno's treatment of the concept of society, which I shall discuss in chapter 5. Elsewhere, Adorno cites approvingly Nietzsche's assertion in 'The Genealogy of Morals', New York, Doubleday, 1966, Second Essay, Section XIII: 'All those concepts in which a total process is comprehended semiotically, resist definition; only that is definable which has no history' (quoted in the Frankfurt Institute for Social Research, 'Aspects of Sociology', London, Heinemann, 1973, p.16).
117 'Models of Man', pp.178f. Some implications of this position are discussed above, pp.12-20.
118 'A Realist Theory of Science', p.211.
119 Ibid., p.174.
120 Ibid., p.173.
121 'Naturalism', p.63. Cf. p.17 above.
122 Althusser and Balibar, op.cit., p.146.
123 B. Ollman, 'Alienation', Cambridge University Press, 1971, p.35.
124 Ibid., p.69.
125 Ibid., p.172.
126 Cf. Hegel's critique of definition in the 'Science of Logic', London, Allen & Unwin, 1929, vol.II, section 3, ch.IIA(b)1. Ollman's interpretation nevertheless seems highly speculative. For a brief attempt to sort out the tangled discussion of internal relations, see Bhaskar, 'Naturalism', pp.53ff.
127 Notes on Wagner in Terrell Carver, op.cit., quoted above, p.34. See Carver's introduction.
128 Quoted by Rancière, 'Lire le Capital', vol.III, Paris, Maspéro, 1973, p.62.
129 'Capital', vol.I (Penguin edn), pp.185f.
130 Cf. Sayer, op.cit., p.174, n.10.

131 F. Tönnies, 'Philosophische Terminologie in Psychologisch-soziologischer Absicht', Leipzig, Thomas, 1906. This was written for the Welby Prize and the English translation was published in 'Mind', vols. VIII and IX.
132 Ibid., p.34 (section 55).
133 Ibid., p.90.
134 'Rules', pp.34f. (Inserts from the French original are taken from 'Les Regles de la Méthode Sociologique', Paris, Presses Universitaires de France, 1973, p.34.)
135 Ibid., p.42.
136 Ibid., pp.42f.
137 Ibid., p.43. Cf. p.57 of the 'Rules' on the definition of the 'normal' and the 'pathological'.
138 Paul Hirst, op.cit., p.179.
139 Cf. Steven Lukes, 'Emile Durkheim', London, Allen Lane, 1973, pp.31ff.
140 Hirst, op.cit., p.97.
141 GAW, pp.208f.; translation p.94.
142 Ibid., p.195 (emphasis added). Cf. his characterisation of his own definitions at the beginning of 'Economy and Society' as 'inevitably abstract and remote from reality'.
143 'Economy and Society', vol.I, p.20.
144 Ibid., vol.II, p.399.
145 Cf. Karl Bosl, Der 'Soziologische Aspekt' in der Geschichte, 'Historische Zeitschrift', 20, 1965, esp. pp.625f.
146 Thomas Burger, op.cit., p.29. According to Burger, Weber adopts the notion of the ideal type to avoid two embarrassing implications of this position:
   1 In the case of concepts, 'definitional properties' may only, as Weber put it, be 'more or less present and occasionally absent'.
   2 In the case of laws, those of economics, sociology, etc., do not hold universally.
147 Cf. Burger, op.cit., pp.68f.
148 E. Meyerson, 'La Déduction relativiste', Paris, Payot, 1925.
149 G. Bachelard, 'Le Nouvel Esprit scientifique', Paris, Presses Universitaires de France, 1934; 'La Philosophie du non', Paris, Presses Universitaires de France, 1966.
150 Cf. Paul Forman, Weimar Culture, Causality and Quantum Theory, 'Historical Studies in the Physical Sciences', vol.3, 1971. Something which Forman confines to a footnote but which is highly relevant to my argument here is the whole discussion about

Notes

abstraction vs 'Anschaulichkeit' in scientific theorising. Cf. C.F. von Weizsäcker, 'The World View of Physics', London, Routledge & Kegan Paul, 1952. Also relevant here is the work of the 'Erlangen School' of 'protophysics'. (On the latter, see Gernot Böhme (ed.), 'Protophysik', Frankfurt, Suhrkamp, 1976. See also G. Böhme and M.V. Engelhardt (eds), 'Entfremdete Wissenschaft', Frankfurt, Suhrkamp, 1979.
151 'Rules', p.44.
152 L'état actuel des études sociologiques en France, 'La Riforma sociale', 1895, reprinted in E. Durkheim, 'Textes 1, Eléments d'une Théorie Sociale', (ed. V. Karady, Paris, Editions de Minuit, 1976, p.95.
153 'Rules', p.18.
154 Ibid., p.37.
155 Loc.cit.
156 London, Cape, 1973, p.58.
157 Marxism, psycho-analysis and geology.
158 'Structural Anthropology', p.279.
159 'Sociologie de l'action', Paris, Seuil, 1965, p.52.
160 Ibid., p.471.
161 Pierre Bourdieu et al., 'Le Métier de sociologue', 3rd edn, Paris and The Hague, Mouton, 1980, p.27.
162 Ibid., p.56.
163 'Social Research', vol.35, 1968, p.69.
164 Ibid., p.705. Bourdieu here goes beyond a simple 'separatism' to suggest, in a way that recalls Marx, the unification by theory of the appearances of immediate reality and the relations underlying these appearances.
165 This is fairly clear in the case of Bourdieu; cf. 'Métier', parts 2 and 3, esp. pp.35, 51ff., 90 and 218. Keat and Urry also point out realist elements in Lévi-Strauss's work - as does Godelier ('Perspectives in Marxist Anthropology', Cambridge University Press, 1977, pp.44ff.). Touraine's philosophical commitments are rather less clear.
166 Isaiah Berlin, A Note on Vico's Concept of Knowledge, in G. Tagliacozzo and H. White (eds), 'Giambattista Vico. An International Symposium', Baltimore, Johns Hopkins Press, 1969, p.371.
167 Ibid., p.372.
168 Ibid., p.375. Cf. also I. Berlin, 'Vico and Herder', London, Hogarth, 1976, and Leon Pompa, 'Vico', Cambridge University Press, 1975.
169 One of the vehicles of this continuity was, for example, Dilthey's concept of 'Erlebnis'.
170 Above, ch.2, n.155.

171 L'état actuel des études sociologiques en France', pp.94f.
172 'Capital', vol.III, ch.48, section III. Cf. the reference to astronomy in vol.I, ch.12 (Penguin edition, p.433): 'a scientific analysis of competition is possible only if we can grasp the inner nature of capital, just as the apparent motions of the heavenly bodies are intelligible only to someone who is acquainted with their real motions, which are not perceptible to the senses.' See also Paul Thomas, 'Marx and Science', 'Political Studies', vol.24, no.1, 1976.
173 'Capital', vol.I, preface to the first edition, Harmondsworth, Penguin, 1976, p.90.
174 'Economic and Philosophical Manuscripts', in 'Karl Marx. Early Writings', Harmondsworth, Penguin, 1975, p.355.
175 'Capital', vol.I, p.174.
176 C. Menger, 'Untersuchungen über die Methode der Sozialwissenschaften und der Politischen Ökonomie insbesondere', Leipzig, 1883, translated as 'Problems of Economics and Sociology', University of Illinois Press, 1963.
177 Ibid., pp.40f., translation, pp.60f. Cf. J.R. Hicks and W. Weber, 'Carl Menger and the Austrian School of Economics', Oxford, Clarendon Press, 1973. See also Burger, op.cit., pp.140-53. For a more recent version of Menger's distinction, see Edgar Salin, 'Politische Ökonomie', Tübingen, Mohr, 1967, p.180; Hans Neisser, Der Gegensatz von 'anschaulich' und 'rational' in der Geschichte der Volkswirtschaftslehre, 'Archiv für Soziologie und Sozialpolitik', vol.65, no.2, 1931.
178 Menger, 'Untersuchungen', p.79; 'Problems', p.88.
179 Alfred Schutz, Choice and the Social Sciences, in L. Embree (ed.), 'Life World and Consciousness. Essays in memory of Aron Gurvitsch', Northwestern University Press, 1972, p.573.
180 Göran Therborn, 'Science, Class and Society', London, New Left Books, 1976, pp.109f.
181 The marginal utility principle 'bases economic thought on the broad experiences of daily life and the psychology of choice between alternatives' (ibid.). Cf. Felix Kaufmann's interesting attempt to link the contrast between objective and subjective theories of value to that between 'explanation' and 'understanding' respectively. Logik und Wirtschaftswissenschaft, 'Archiv für Sozialwissenschaft und Sozialpolitik', vol.54, no.3, 1925.

Notes

182 Therborn, op.cit., p.11. Cf. Hilferding's critique of Böhm-Bawerk, of which a part is translated in Tom Bottomore and Patrick Goode, (eds), 'Austro-Marxism', Oxford, Clarendon Press, 1978.
183 Schutz's notion of 'relevance' seems to me to function in this way. It is possible that 'meaningful adequacy' was merely part of the public face of economic theory and of no great interest within the discipline. In sociology, it was seen as a 'relevant' problem by the sociological community itself, or at least by a substantial part of it.
184 GAW, p.161f.; translation p.64f. Some indication of Weber's view of the relationship between sociology and history is provided in 'Economy and Society', ch. 1, pt 1, section 11, and the first paragraph of ch.1, pt 4 (Bedminster Press edn, pp.19 and 29).
185 GAW, p.188; translation, p.88.
186 Ibid., p.131; 'Roscher and Knies', p.175.
187 GAW, 3rd edn, p.393, 1st edn, p.369. This is Weber's essay on marginal utility theory.
188 'The Crisis of European Sciences and Transcendental Phenomenology', Northwestern University Press, 1970.
189 In his earlier 'Vienna Lecture', printed as an appendix to the English translation of the 'Crisis', he also discusses Greek thought.
190 'Crisis', pp.48f.
191 Ibid., pp.296f.
192 Ibid., p.59.
193 Ibid., pp.31f.
194 Ibid., pp.283ff.
195 'Ideen zu einer reinen Phänomenologie und phänomenologischen Philosophie', vol.III, 'Husserliana', vol.V, The Hague, Nijhoff, 1952, p.160. Cf. ibid., p.151.
196 Husserl himself, of course, was much more interested in psychology - at a pinch, perhaps social psychology - than sociology. His unpublished manuscripts, however, do contain references to a programme for sociology. Cf. R. Toulemont, 'L'Essence de la société selon Husserl', Paris, Presses Universitaires de France, 1962; and Stephen Strasser, Grundgedanken der Sozialontologie E. Husserls, 'Zeitschrift für philosophische Forschung', vol.29, no.1, 1975.
197 Some writers, such as Robert Gorman ('The Dual Vision. Alfred Schutz and the Myth of a Phenomenological Social Science, London, Routledge & Kegan Paul, 1977, esp. ch.5), have canvassed the possibility of more radically phenomenological sociologies, in Gorman's

case existentialist, but so far not very plausibly. Cf. also Fritz Sander, Der Gegenstand der reinen Gesellschaftslehre, 'Archiv für Sozialwissenschaft und Sozialpolitik', vol.54, no.2, 1925.
198 London, Heinemann, 1972: first published as 'Der sinnhafte Aufbau der sozialen Welt', Vienna, Springer-Verlag, 1932.
199 'The Phenomenology' is all written from within the standpoint of the 'natural attitude' with the exception of chapter 2. In the Husserl colloquium at Royaumont in 1957, Schutz explicitly rejected Husserl's account of intersubjectivity: 'we must conclude that Husserl's attempt to account for the constitution of transcendental intersubjectivity in terms of operations of the consciousness of the transcendental ego has not succeeded. It is to be surmised that intersubjectivity is not a problem of constitution which can be solved within the transcendental sphere, but is rather a datum [Gegebenheit] of the life-world. It is the fundamental category of human existence in the world and therefore of all philosophical anthropology' (Alfred Schutz, 'Collected Papers', vol.II, 'Studies in Social Theory', ed. Arvid Brodersen, The Hague, Nijhoff, 1964, p.82). Cf. Robert Gorman, op.cit., esp. pp.31ff, 106f.
200 Ibid., p.138.
201 'Collected Papers', vol.II, pp.16f. Cf. Richard Grathoff, Ansätze zu einer Theorie sozialen Handelns bei Alfred Schutz, in R. Bubner, K. Kramer, R. Wiehl (eds), 'Neue Hefte für Philosophie', vol.9, 1976, p.124: 'Life and thought are after all two different things, and science remains a concern of thought even when it deals with life - for example life in the social world.' See also Richard Grathoff (ed.), 'The Theory of Social Action', Indiana University Press, 1978, esp. Grathoff's introduction, p.xxii; Parsons, pp.76 and 123.
202 'The Phenomenology', p.221.
203 Ibid., p.10.
204 Ibid., p.241.
205 Ibid., p.10.
206 'Collected Papers', vol.I, 'The Problem of Social Reality', ed. Maurice Natanson, The Hague, Nijhoff, 1962, p.131. Note the Husserlian framework in which Schutz's dualism is expressed; the whole paragraph (from which this quotation is extracted) shows this even more clearly.
207 Subjective Action and Objective Interpretation, 'The Annals of Phenomenological Sociology', vol.I, 1976,

p.251. These postulates set the context for the more familiar social scientific postulates of 'logical consistency', 'subjective interpretation' and 'adequacy' which appear, in different forms, in 'Collected Papers' (CP), vol.I, pp.34f. and elsewhere.
208 Ibid., pp.35f. (This is an excerpt from Schutz's critique of Parsons, part of which was published as The Social World and the Theory of Social Action in CP, vol.II.) Note the 'realist' language in which Schutz discusses science here.
209 'The Phenomenology', p.9.
210 CP, vol.I, pp.34f. The only use of the term that I am aware of in 'The Phenomenology of the Social World' is a very different one: Schutz attempts to reduce Weber's 'causal adequacy' to 'meaningful adequacy' by reconceptualising the former as 'agreement with past experience' (pp.233f.).
211 A. Zijderveld, The Problem of Adequacy, 'Archives Européennes de Sociologie', vol.13, no.1, 1972, p.185.
212 As Hanna Pitkin puts it: 'The argument that really, strictly speaking, only the individual actor knows what he is doing is so patently false that only someone in the grip of conceptual puzzlement might persuade himself of its truth' (op.cit., p.254). See also chapter 11, pp.241-63, passim.
213 Grathoff, 'The Theory of Social Action'.
214 Choice and the Social Sciences, in L. Embree (ed.), 'Life World and Consciousness. Essays in Memory of Alan Gurvitsch', Evanston, Northwestern University Press, 1972, p.583.
215 Ibid., p.573.
216 Ibid., p.582. For a similar analysis see Arthur Spiethoff, Anschauliche und reine Volkswirtschaftstheorie, in E. Salin (ed.), 'Synopsis. Festgabe für Alfred Weber', Heidelberg, L. Schneider, 1948, pp.569-664.
217 Parsons, Retrospect, in Grathoff, 'The Theory of Social Action', p.123.
218 Zum Rationalismusstreit in der gegenwärtigen Philosophie, 'Kritische Theorie', I, Frankfurt, Fischer, 1968, p.146.
219 Adorno, 'Vorlesung zur Einleitung in die Soziologie', p.132. See also Adorno's contributions to Adorno, et al., 'The Positivist Dispute in German Sociology', London, Heinemann, 1976.
220 'Theory and Practice', London, Heinemann, 1974, p.265.
221 See, in particular, his inaugural lecture at Frankfurt, reprinted as an appendix to 'Knowledge and

Human Interests'. Cf. the similar judgment made from a very different background by G.-G. Granger, 'Pensée formelle et sciences de l'homme', Paris, Aubier-Montagne, 1968, pp.217f.
222 Preface to 2nd edition of 'Theory and Practice', pp. 7ff., 14ff. On the term 'quasi-transcendental', see below, chapter 3, pp.112f.
223 'Knowledge and Human Interests', passim.
224 Cf. J. Habermas, Der Universalitätsanspruch der Hermeneutik, in Apel, et al., 'Hermeneutik und Ideologiekritik'. Cf. A. Wellmer, 'Critical Theory of Society', New York, Herder & Herder, 1971, pp.42-51.
225 Which he discusses very fully in 'Zur Logik der Sozialwissenschaften'.
226 A Postscript to 'Knowledge and Human Interest', 'Philosophy of the Social Sciences', vol.3, no.2, 1973, p.172.
227 See Apel's article, Szientistik, Hermeneutik, Ideologiekritik, reprinted in 'Hermeneutik und Ideologiekritik'; The Apriori of Communication, 'Acta Sociologica', vol.13, no.1, 1972; and Types of Social Science in the Light of Human Cognitive Interests, in S.C. Brown (ed.), 'Philosophical Disputes in the Social Sciences', Brighton, Harvester Press, 1979, pp.1-50.
228 A Postscript to 'Knowledge and Human Interests', pp.174f. Cf. ibid., pp.168ff.
229 R. Döbert, J. Habermas and C. Nunner-Winkler (eds), 'Die Entwicklung des Ichs', Cologne, Hain/KNO, 1977, p.27. Quoted and translated by Thomas McCarthy, 'The Critical Theory of Jürgen Habermas', London, Hutchinson, 1978, p.335.
230 Chapter 3 is an attempt in this direction.
231 Cf. A. Giddens, 'Central Problems in Social Theory', London, Macmillan, 1979, pp.245ff.
232 Ibid., pp.250ff.
233 Ibid., p.248.
234 This is not to deny that what are here presented as quantitative differences may be based on a qualitative one. Bhaskar argues, for example, that social scientific theory is necessarily incomplete ('Naturalism', pp.61f.).

CHAPTER 3 CONSTITUTION

1 There is no entry in the 'Encyclopedia of Philosophy', New York, Macmillan and the Free Press, 1967. There is, however, a useful article by W. Hogrebe in

'Historisches Wörterbuch der Philosophie', Darmstadt, Wissenschaftliche Buchgesellschaft, 1976, part III, section 4, pp.999-1002. For the history of the term, see Hogrebe's article and also Robert Sokolowski, 'The Formation of Husserl's Concept of Constitution', The Hague, Nijhoff, 1964, pp.214ff.

2 Knowledge as Interpretation: An Historical Survey, 'Philosophy and Phenomenological Research', vols. 10 and 11, 1950.

3 My translation. Cf. Marx, 'Early Writings'.

4 Marx, The 18th Brumaire of Louis Bonaparte, in K. Marx and F. Engels, 'Selected Works', London, Lawrence & Wishart, 1969, p.97.

5 Henceforth referred to as 'constitution$_e$' and 'constitution$_o$'. Compare Bhaskar's distinction between the transitive and intransitive dimensions ('A Realist Theory of Science', p.17 and passim). I take constitution$_o$ to involve more than the banal claim that society is constituted by, in the sense of made up of, human activities. What I have in mind is the more activist idea of the production of society or, better, its reproduction.

6 In Kurt Wolff (ed.), 'Georg Simmel', Columbus, Ohio State University Press, 1959.

7 W.I. and D.S. Thomas, 'The Child in America', New York, Knopf, 1928, p.572.

8 Marx, 2nd and 8th 'Theses on Feuerbach' in 'Early Writings', pp.422f. Cf. this passage from the 1844 manuscripts ('Early Writings', p.354) 'subjectivism and objectivism, spiritualism and materialism, activity and passivity (Leiden), lose their antithetical character, and hence their existence as such antitheses, only in the social condition; it can be seen how the resolution of the <u>theoretical</u> antitheses themselves is possible <u>only</u> in a practical way'.

9 At this point, the concept of constitution may be thought to collapse into empiricism and thus abolish itself. A la limite this is true, but this does not mean that to allow any interaction with the objects known is to break out of the 'constitution' framework. Realists can assert the constitutive role of human subjects in formulating descriptions of things <u>and</u> that it is meaningful to ask how far our descriptions capture the real structures and processes at work in reality. Experimentation, in particular, may cause us to 'bump up against' reality and modify our conceptions accordingly. (Cf. Bhaskar, 'A Realist Theory of Science', p.250 and passim.)

10 Besides the standard commentaries, see Habermas, 'Knowledge and Human Interests', section 12, and Habermas's introduction to F. Nietzsche, 'Erkenntnistheoretische Schriften', Frankfurt, Suhrkamp, 1968.
11 'The Gay Science', New York, Random House, 1974, Bk III, section 121.
12 'The Will to Power', ed. O. Levy, Edinburgh and London, Foulis, 1910, vol.II, Bk III, section 481.
13 Ibid., section 552 (pp.60f.).
14 A Comparison of Decisions Made on Four 'Pre-Theoretical' Problems by Talcott Parsons and Alfred Schutz - unpublished seminar paper c.1960.
15 It is clear, I hope, from the context that Garfinkel's last phrase is not to be taken as an expression of empiricism.
16 Varieties of Positivism, in Paul Filmer et al., 'New Directions in Sociological Theory', London, Collier-Macmillan, 1972, p.49.
17 Ibid., p.54. Here Walsh comes close to the well-known formulation of Peter Winch: 'Reality is not what gives language sense. What is real and what is unreal shows itself in the sense that language has.' Understanding a Primitive Society, 'American Philosophical Quarterly', 1964; reprinted in Winch, 'Ethics and Action', London, Routledge & Kegan Paul, 1972, p.12. Cf. 'The Idea of a Social Science', p.23: 'social relations are expressions of ideas about reality', and ch.5, passim.
18 Ibid., p.6. Note the form of argument characteristic of this tradition, in which cognitive ('interpretative') processes have an ontological upshot in producing '"real" things'.
19 See D.-H. Ruben, 'Marxism and Materialism', Brighton, Harvester Press, 1979, and Beyleveld's unpublished critique of Ruben and Bhaskar, Transcendentalism and Realism.
20 Paul Natorp, Kant und die Marburger Schule, 'Kant-Studien', vol.17, 1912. Cf. W.H. Werkmeister, Cassirer's Advance Beyond Neo-Kantianism, and Fritz Kaufmann, Cassirer, Neo-Kantianism, and Phenomenology, both in P.A. Schilpp (ed.), 'The Philosophy of Ernst Cassirer', The Library of Living Philosophers, vol.VI, Evanston, Illinois, 1949. See also Andrew Arato, The Neo-Idealist Defense of Subjectivity, 'Telos', no.21, 1974, and Gillian Rose, 'Hegel Contra Sociology', London, Athlone Press, 1981.
21 On Husserl's relationship to Kant, see in particular Iso Kern, 'Husserl und Kant. Eine Untersuchung über Husserls Verhaltnis zu Kant und zum Neukantianismus', The Hague, Nijhoff, 1964.

22 Cf. Fritz Kaufmann, op.cit.
23 Some of Adler's work is available in English in Tom Bottomore and Patrick Goode (eds), 'Austro-Marxism'. See also Alfred Schmidt, 'The Concept of Nature in Marx', London, New Left Books, 1971.
24 See, for example, an interesting unpublished paper by David Rasmussen, delivered in Sheffield in 1978: Towards a Theory of Social Constitution.
25 'Critique of Pure Reason', Preface to 2nd edn, B xvi; Kemp Smith translation, London, Macmillan, 1964, p.22.
26 This is, of course, part of his redefinition of the term 'transcendental' to denote all cognition 'which is occupied not so much with objects as with the mode of our knowledge of objects in so far as this mode of knowledge is to be possible *a priori* (ibid., Introduction, B 25; translation, p.59). Cf. Ernst Cassirer, Transcendentalism, 'Encyclopedia Brittannica', 14th edn, 1928.
27 The Kemp Smith translation gives 'subjective constitution' for 'subjektive Beschaffenheit' (e.g. pp.82, 84), but this again seems to have the sense of 'make-up'.
28 B 221; translation, p.210.
29 B 222f.; translation, p.211.
30 Cf. Hogrebe, Konstitution.
31 'Ideen zu einer reinen Phänomenologie und Phänomenologischen Philosophie', III, p.128.
32 Cf. Sokolowski, op.cit., p.184; Gadamer, 'Truth and Method', pp.204-14; Kern, op.cit., p.84.
33 I. Kant, 'Critique of Judgement', trans. J.C. Meredith, Oxford University Press, 1952, p.4.
34 Ibid., p.14.
35 H.W. Cassirer, 'A Commentary on Kant's "Critique of Judgement"', London, Methuen, 1938, p.114.
36 Ibid., p.117. Cassirer emphasises, however, that, at the same time, 'Kant adheres strictly to his distinction between the constitutive principles of the understanding (the principle of mechanical causation in particular) and the regulative principle of causal reflection' (p.346).
37 Ibid., p.11. Aesthetic judgments, moreover, are ones 'whose determining ground cannot be *other than subjective*'. 'Critique of Judgement', quoted by Cassirer, op.cit., p.179.
38 Ibid., p.117.
39 Cf. W.H. Werkmeister, op.cit., esp. p.761. This is, of course, precisely the shift which Habermas documents in a more general context in 'Knowledge and Human Interests'.

40 Paul Natorp, 'Allgemeine Psychologie', Tübingen, Mohr, Bk I, p.2, my translation.
41 New Haven, Yale University Press, 1953. Cf. S.M. Itzkoff, 'Ernst Cassirer: Scientific Knowledge and the Concept of Man', University of Notre Dame Press, 1971.
42 In Schilpp, 'The Philosophy of Ernst Cassirer'.
43 P. Natorp, 'Platons Ideenlehre', 2nd edn, Leipzig, F. Meiner, 1921, p.1 - quoted by Fritz Kaufmann, op. cit., p.818. Cf. Werkmeister, op.cit., p.765.
44 Fritz Kaufmann, op.cit., p.804.
45 H. Vaihinger's 'The Philosophy of "As If"' was published in 1911 (English version, translated by C.K. Ogden, London, Kegan Paul, 1925) but was 'substantially completed by 1877' (John Passmore, 'A Hundred Years of Philosophy', Harmondsworth, Penguin, 1968, p.544, n.6). See also n.5 on Cohen and Lange.
46 Ibid., pp.320f. On a further set of connections - between positivism and phenomenology - see H. Lübbe, Positivism and Phenomenology, in Thomas Luckmann (ed.), 'Phenomenology and Sociology', Harmondsworth, Penguin, 1978.
47 The exception, of course, is Cassirer, who differed from 'orthodox' Marburg neo-Kantianism in accepting the specificity of realms of thought other than natural science: language, myth, the Geisteswissenschaften, etc. (Cf. Schilpp, 'The Philosophy of Ernst Cassirer'.)
48 For what is, in my view, a misinterpretation of Weber in this sense, see David Goddard, Max Weber and the Objectivity of Social Science, 'History and Theory', vol.12, 1973.
49 'Die Grenzen der Naturwissenschaftlichen Begriffsbildung', Tübingen, Mohr, 1902. References here are to the 3rd and 4th edition, 1921. Also 'Kulturwissenschaft und Naturwissenschaft', Tübingen, Mohr, 1899, 6th and 7th edn, 1926, translated as 'Science and History', New York, Van Nostrand, 1962. The latter work, Rickert insists, is not a substitute for the detailed arguments of the former. ('Science and History', p.xi - preface to the 6th and 7th German edition.)
50 See his earlier book, 'Der Gegenstand der Erkenntnis', Tübingen, Mohr, 1892. He intends, however, that the 'logical theory' advanced in 'Grenzen' should 'serve to combat naturalism and to establish an idealist philosophy oriented to history'. ('Grenzen', Vorwort p.V.)
51 Cf. Kern, op.cit., pp.395f. and section 37, passim.

Notes

52 'Kulturwissenschaft und Naturwissenschaft', pp.30f., my translation. 'Science and History', pp.32f. Cf. 'Grenzen', pp.24ff., and, in relation to history, p.220: 'Even when history knows too little about its objects, it also knows too much about them. It can therefore never limit itself to narrating what actually happened or to an idiographic procedure; it must everywhere separate the essential from the inessential' (my translation).
53 Cf. 'Grenzen', p.220: 'what is an exception for natural science constitutes [bildet] the rule for history'.
54 'Kulturwissenschaft und Naturwissenschaft' (K&N), p.81. 'Science and History' (S&H), pp.83f. Translation slightly modified. Cf. K&N, pp.87f., S&H, p.90: 'historical individualities ... are constituted [entstehen] on the basis of a theoretical relation of things [Gegenstände] to values.'
55 'Grenzen', p.251.
56 Ibid., p.214.
57 Ibid., p.390.
58 Ibid., 1st edn, p.390. Quoted by Thomas Burger, op. cit., p.42.
59 'Grenzen', p.494. The earlier part of this quotation is discussed with disapproval by Lukács in 'History and Class Consciousness', London, Merlin, 1971, pp.150ff.
60 'Historical centres' is Rickert's term for the 'spiritual' beings with which history is concerned.
61 For criticisms, see Raymond Aron, 'La Philosophie Critique de l'histoire'; Habermas, 'Knowledge and Human Interests', p.340; Outhwaite, op.cit., pp.42f.; Burger, op.cit., p.55. See also W.G. Runciman, 'A Critique of Max Weber's Philosophy of Social Science', Cambridge University Press, 1972, pp.92f.
62 Arato, op.cit., pp.108-61.
63 Ibid., p.125.
64 Ibid., p.128. Cf. Habermas, loc.cit.
65 Arato, op.cit., p.133.
66 The Free Press, New York, 1977. This is a translation of the 2nd German edn, 1905, with notes added from the 3rd edn.
67 Ibid., p.VII, preface to the 2nd German edn. Simmel stresses that 'In the first edition of the book, this basic problem was not yet sufficiently clear to me .... In consequence, the present text must be regarded as a completely new book' (ibid., p.IX). Cf. the introduction by Guy Oakes, p.31.
68 Ibid., p.VII. Simmel's argument seems to be that the

illusion of immediate knowledge is stronger in the case of history. Cf. his essay on the constitutive concepts of history, in 'Fragmente und Aufsätze', Hildesheim, G. Olms, 1967. Translated in Guy Oakes (ed.), 'George Simmel. Essays on Interpretation in Social Science', Manchester University Press, 1980.
69 'Problems', p.IX, Simmel tries to establish a rather problematic connection between historical realism and historical determinism. 'It is necessary to emancipate the self from historicism in the same way that Kant freed it from naturalism' (ibid., pp.VIIIf.).
70 Ibid., p.82.
71 Ibid., p.87. Cf. the autobiographical fragment, reprinted as Anfang einer unvollendeten Selbstdarstellung, in Kurt Gassen and Michael Landmann (eds), 'Buch des Dankes an Georg Simmel', Berlin, Duncker & Humblot, 1958.
72 Ibid., p.200.
73 Pp.62f. Cf. p.98 and section 9, pp.77-87, passim.
74 P.201. Cf. Alfred Schutz, 'The Phenomenology of The Social World', p.10 and CP I, pp.5f.
75 'Uber sociale Differenzierung', Leipzig, Duncker & Humblot, 1890. Introduction, Zur Erkenntnistheorie der Sozialwissenschaft, p.2. Cf. Wolff, 'The Sociology of Georg Simmel', p.14.
76 Ibid., p.10.
77 'The Sociology of Georg Simmel', p.22.
78 In Wolff, 'Georg Simmel', pp.337-56.
79 Ibid., p.338. Cf. ibid., pp.340f.
80 Ibid., p.341.
81 E.g. p.335: 'We do not ask merely: How is it possible that there are the empirically developing, particular formations which are brought together under the general concept of "society"? We ask beyond this: How is society as such possible, as an objective form of subjective minds?'
82 Max Adler, for example, complains that Simmel, having raised the epistemological question (which Adler himself takes entirely seriously), does no more than reveal the '*psychological* preconditions of social interaction'. 'Das Rätsel der Gesellschaft. Zur Erkenntniskritischen Grundlegung der Sozialwissenschaft', Vienna, Saturn-Verlag, 1936, p.205. Cf. more recently Hans-Joachim Lieber and Peter Furth, Zur Dialektik der Simmelschen Konzeption einer Formalen Soziologie, in Gassen and Landmann, op.cit., pp.39-59.
83 See also, for example, his account, even in the excursus, of the 'three social a prioris', which are

presented as 'categories of reality' which are not merely tools in the hand of the social theorist but constitutive of social interaction itself. Cf. Uta Gerhardt, 'Rollenanalyse als kritische Soziologie', Neuwied and Berlin, Luchterhand, 1971, p.39.
84 Der Begriff der Gesellschaft als Regulative Idee. Zur Transzendentalen Begründung der Soziologie bei Georg Simmel, 'Soziale Welt', 19, 2, 1968, pp.97-118.
85 'Critique of Pure Reason', B 675. Schrader-Klebert, op.cit., p.104.
86 Wolff, 'The Sociology of Georg Simmel', esp. pp.13ff.
87 Arato, op.cit., p.157. Arato notes, however, that Simmel 'partially retained the viewpoint of transcendental constitution' (p.142).
88 This is Arato's view, ibid., p.161.
89 The degree of continuity between Rickert and Weber is a matter of considerable dispute. Burger stresses Rickert's influence and barely mentions that of Simmel. For a review of the debate, see John Torrance, Max Weber: Methods and the Man, 'Archives Européennes de Sociologie', vol.IX, 1974, pp.127-65, esp. pp.128ff.
90 At least in his early methodological essays. The term appears only once in 'Economy and Society', in a very weak sense (I, 1,1, I, 9; translation p.18). A good deal of the original notion remains, however, in Weber's various assertions about what verstehende sociology is interested in. (Ibid., sections 4, 7, 8, 9, 11.) For Weber's earlier use of the term, see esp. GAW, pp.170-8, 182ff.; translation, pp.72-9, 82ff., 110ff.
91 GAW, passim; esp. pp.193, 200f., 206f., 290.
92 GAW, p.184; translation, p.84.
93 Ibid., p.175; translation, p.76.
94 Ibid., p.161; translation, p.64.
95 Beyleveld, op.cit., pp.182f. Cf. Dieter Henrich, 'Die Einheit der Wissenschaftslehre Max Webers', Tübingen, Mohr, 1952. There remains the problem of specifying the range of the two sorts of categories, but to see it in these terms is at least half the battle, given the large number of exaggeratedly 'Kantianized' accounts of Weber's position in the literature. (See, for example, Goddard, op.cit.)
96 GAW, 183f.; translation, 83f. Cf. Thomas Burger, op.cit., pp.87-93, whose translation of this passage (p.89) I have used (and slightly augmented). As Burger points out, 'What Weber claims here is the objectivity of those historical accounts which are written with the help of "subjective" ... value-viewpoints.'

97 GAW, p.213; translation, p.111.
98 One can of course substitute 'theoretical presuppositions' for values as Runciman thinks Weber should have done ('Critique', ch.4), without essentially changing the terms of the problem. The result, however, might be different, given that there is a stronger case against cognitive than against moral relativism. (Cf. Steven Lukes, Relativism, Cognitive and Moral.)
99 Cf. Lucien Goldmann, 'Marxisme et sciences humaines', Paris, Gallimard, 1970, p.251: 'The fundamental methodological problem of any human science - above all if one places oneself in a structuralist and historical perspective - lies in the découpage of the object of study.... Once this découpage has been made and accepted, the results of the research will be practically predictable.'
100 GAW, p.170; translation, p.72. I have again cited Burger's translation (op.cit., p.88). This may sound like a 'perspectival' or 'paradigmatic' holism which denies the meaning-invariance of propositions across paradigms. Such a reading would, I think, be a mistake for two reasons. First, Weber retains a concept of propositional truth. Second, as I have suggested, he presupposes that the 'one-sided' viewpoints can be compared with reality.
101 GAW, pp.212f.; translation, p.110.
102 'Economy and Society', I, p.13.
103 Paul Lazarsfeld, Historical Notes on the Empirical Study of Action, 'American Sociological Review', 1965; published in a fuller version in Lazarsfeld's 'Qualitative Analysis', Boston, Alleyn & Bacon, 1972. Lazarsfeld cites the opinion of Paul Kecskemeti that '*Handlung* stands in the centre of Weber's methodological writings, only tangential to his thinking, and played no role at all in his substantive work.' Lazarsfeld, however, characteristically, has a much too narrow conception of what a sociological account of action would involve: namely, the sort of empirical attitude studies which he conducted himself.
104 Cf. Schutz's 'The Phenomenology of the Social World', ch.1.
105 This contrast must of course be qualified. In the famous introduction to his sociology of religion Weber invokes a classically Rickertian concept of Wertbeziehung: 'Any product of modern European civilisation, studying any problem of universal history, is bound to ask himself to what combination of circum-

Notes

stances the fact should be attributed that in Western civilisation, and in Western civilisation only, cultural phenomena have appeared which (as we like to think) lie in a line of development having *universal significance and value*' (quoted from 'The Protestant Ethic and the Spirit of Capitalism, p.13).
106 Cf. Johannes Weiss, 'Max Webers Grundlegung der Soziologie', Munich, UTB Verlag Dokumentation, 1975, pp.33f.
107 Arato makes this point, perhaps rather too sharply: 'Rickert's difficulties in distinguishing between the constitutive activity of the historian and the creative activity of the historical actor are thus brought to an ultimate climax by Weber, because he seems to insist with far greater vehemence than Rickert that (1) values (among them the value of scientific truth) emerge only in the form of historical value-realisations (in conflict with one another), as historical "goods" created by historical actors and that (2) cultural meaning can constitute only the basis of the most arbitrary ("ideal-typical") constructive activity of historians' (op.cit., p.133).
108 Runciman, op.cit., ch.4.
109 This last point is the important insight conveyed by Troeltsch's joking reference to Weber's 'wissenschaftsfreie Wertposition'.
110 Cf. ch.3, note 101, above (GAW, p.212f).
111 Herbert Spiegelberg, 'The Phenomenological Movement', 2 vols, The Hague, Nijhoff, 1960, vol.I, p.110. Sokolowski, op.cit., p.214.
112 Leszek Kolakowski, 'Husserl and the Search for Certitude', New Haven and London, Yale University Press, 1975, esp. p.67.
113 'Ideen', p.129. Cf. Schutz's distinction between two kinds of social theory, 'The Phenomenology', p.248.
114 Husserl makes a play here on two words, 'Einheit' and 'Fluss'.
115 Fritz Kaufmann, op.cit., p.810. See also Iso Kern, op.cit.
116 'zwischen Sinnbildung und Creation' (quoted by Sokolowski, p.197).
117 Clarification of an Error of Principle (quoted by Sokolowski, p.135). I have slightly modified his translation. Cf. Kolakowski, 'Husserl and the Search for Certitude', p.71.
118 Sokolowski, op.cit., p.134. Note the crucial ambiguity here in the identification of 'perception' and 'constitution'.

119 Quoted in ibid., p.135. Translation again slightly modified.
120 Ibid. Cf. note 2, where he quotes Husserl's reference to 'die Rätsel, die Mysterien, die Probleme um den letzten Sinn der Gegenständlichkeit der Erkenntnis'
121 Ibid., pp.138, 196.
122 Ibid., p.198. Cf. pp.138f., 158f.
123 Ibid., pp.137f.
124 Phenomenology, 'Encyclopedia Britannica', 14th edn, 1946. This may have been written by Heidegger and published under Husserl's name, but the idea seems canonical. Alfred Schutz uses almost the same words in presenting Some Leading Concepts of Phenomenology: 'The phenomenologist, we may say, does not have to do with the objects themselves; he is interested in their *meaning*, as it is constituted by the activities of our mind' (vol.I, p.115).
125 Kolakowski, 'Husserl and the Search for Certitude', p.65.
126 Above, chapter 2, section b. Exceptions are a few references to constitution in everyday life and in the positive sciences ('Cartesian Meditations', The Hague, Nijhoff, 1960, pp.25, 52n., quoted by Barry Hindess, 'Philosophy and Methodology in the Social Sciences', Brighton, Harvester Press, 1977, p.60). In the earlier part of his work, before he came under Frege's influence (and before he used the term 'constitution'), he had relied on an empirical rather than a transcendental ego, but he abandoned this position because of its relativistic implications (Beyleveld, op.cit., pp.107f.). Note that this explanation does not apply to Schutz, who effectively abandons the transcendental framework. Cf. Gorman, op.cit., esp. p.138.
127 Op.cit., p.112.
128 Beyleveld attempts to retain the concept for his 'rationalist actionism'. Habermas and Apel retain a transcendental framework to some extent, but the 'transcendental' subject becomes the human species (Habermas) or is replaced by the pragmatic presuppositions of language (Apel).
129 'Husserl and the Search for Certitude', p.57.
130 Some Leading Concepts of Phenomenology, p.115.
131 Ibid., p.111. This is, of course, an exposition of phenomenology in general, but Schutz stresses his 'conviction ... that future studies of the methods of the social sciences and their fundamental notions will of necessity lead to issues belonging to the domain of phenomenological research' (p.116). Cf.

Notes

      in the same volume Phenomenology and the Social Sciences.
132 CP, vol.I, p.5.
133 Ibid., p.6. Cf. 'The Phenomenology', p.10.
134 (Rather than transcendental.)
135 The first of these is a commonplace of Schutz-interpretation; see, for example, Gorman, op.cit.; Hindess, op.cit., pp.49-77, esp. 59-61; Beyleveld, op.cit.; for the second and third, I have relied heavily on Burke Thomason's 'The Social Reality of Reification', PhD thesis, University of Sussex, 1978; 'Making Sense of Reification', London, Macmillan, 1982. References here are to the thesis.
136 Gorman, op.cit., p.137.
137 'The Phenomenology', p.44. Cf. Husserl's Importance for the Social Sciences, CP, vol.I, p.145.
138 Ibid., p.17. Cf. Thomas Luckmann on what Schutz calls 'regional typologies': 'the regional typology of a historical life-world is acquired by the *worldly* ego in the process of socialisation. It determines its habitual perceptions of what is social and what is not' (On the Boundaries of the Social World, in Natanson, op.cit., p.81).
139 Cf. Gorman, op.cit., p.144.
140 Beyleveld, op.cit., p.135. Cf. ch.2, passim. Beyleveld has brought out these implications most clearly, but they are also recognised by other critics.
141 Ibid., p.136. This latter consequence seems to be embraced by Garfinkel when he writes that for a 'congruence' as opposed to a correspondence theory of truth 'the way in which something is of interest to a witness is all the way in which that thing is real' (A Comparison).
142 Cf. Thomason, op.cit., pp.60f. He rejected, however (as I noted above, p.46n), what he saw as the 'radicalisation' of the concept from 'explication' to 'creation'. See section 3 below, pp.
143 'The Phenomenology', p.41.
144 Ibid., p.42. Cf. a passage from On Multiple Realities, CP, vol.I, p.210.
145 Ibid., p.41.
146 GAW, pp.12n; 'Roscher and Knies', p.217f.
147 'The Phenomenology', p.52.
148 Cf. above, pp.50ff. There are various versions of these postulates - see Thomason, op.cit., pp.74f.
149 Ibid., pp.82f.
150 Ibid., p.178.
151 Ibid., pp.228f.

152 Beyleveld, op.cit., p.128. It does not suspend the empirical ego, he continues, but only its products.
153 On Multiple Realities, CP, vol.I, p.229.
154 I.e. presumably less solid than it appears to be.
155 'The Phenomenology', p.248. Cf. Z. Bauman, 'Hermeneutics and Social Science', London, Hutchinson, 1978, ch.8, where Bauman gives Schutz a radically Kantian gloss.
156 Cf. Richard Grathoff (ed.), 'The Theory of Social Action', 1978. The fact that Schutz envisaged this sort of separate development as early as 1932 shows that his characterisation of the relationship between his work and Parsons's was not just an ad hoc solution prompted by deference.
157 Some Leading Concepts of Phenomenology, CP, vol.I, p.115. N.b. also the notion of sciences as finite provinces of meaning (e.g. Symbol, Reality and Society, CP, vol.I, p.346) and the sophisticated conventionalism of Felix Kaufmann's 'Methodenlehre der Sozialwissenschaften', Vienna, Springer, 1936; abridged as 'Methodology of the Social Sciences', New York, The Humanities Press, 1958.
158 Cf. Anton C. Zijderveld, The Problem of Adequacy, pp.18ff.; Gorman, op.cit., p.131.
159 Positivism, neo-Kantianism and phenomenology unite in arguing, in their different ways, that this is not an appropriate subject of rational discussion, so it is hardly surprising that Schutz agreed. An alternative, explicitly relativistic position would hold that it is sheer hubris to think that one can make any categorical statement about social reality. It should be clear that Schutz does not take this view. On ontological commitments, see W.V.O. Quine's 'Ontological Relativity and Other Essays', New York and London, Columbia University Press, 1969. Also John Wisdom, Scientific Theory; Empirical Content, Embedded Ontology, and Weltanschauung, 'Philosophy and Phenomenological Research', vol.33, 1972.
160 Anthony Giddens, in 'New Rules of Sociological Method', summarised in 'rule' D2, p.162, seems to imply (despite his disclaimer on p.20) a more unified conception of sociology. The division is nowhere so clearly exemplified as in the differences between Harré's 'Social Being' and Bhaskar's 'Naturalism'.
161 In particular, the deeply ambiguous book by Peter Berger and Thomas Luckmann, 'The Social Construction of Reality', Harmondsworth, Penguin, 1967. The authors seem to go beyond Schutz in the ontological claims they make about the way 'knowledge' enters

Notes

162 into the construction of social life itself.
See, for example, Gorman's claim that 'Existential phenomenology avoids [Husserl's] dilemma by adjuring (sic) all claims to scientific objectivity, while, at the same time, carefully building its argument with non-solipsistic knowledge' (p.144).
163 See the quotations from Garfinkel and Walsh, above, pp.5f. The same tendency can be found in the 'Heideggerian' wing of ethnomethodology - Blum, McHugh, et al.
164 Garfinkel has undoubtedly taken the lead in this rejection.
165 London, Kegan Paul, 1895, vol.III, p.426.
166 Ibid., pp.467f. Cf. Habermas, 'Theory and Practice', p.152: 'Hegel does not link the constitution of the "I" to the reflection of the solitary "I" on itself, but instead understands it in terms of formative processes.'
167 As far as the term goes, he seems to use it in the same sense as Kant (though, of course, to make very different claims). Cf. the Preface to the 2nd edition of the 'Logic': 'The objective concept of things constitutes their own reality.'
168 Cf. the passage from the 'Philosophy of Religion' quoted by Lukacs in 'History and Class Consciousness', p.218 n.20: 'There is no immediate knowledge. Immediate knowledge is where we have no consciousness of mediation; but it is mediated for all that.' Cf. also J.B.S. Haldane's preface to the Johnstone and Struthers translation of the 'Science of Logic', London, Allen & Unwin, 1929, p.10: 'Into every form of experience reflection thus enters, not as constituting it *ab extra*, but inherent in its very nature.' Cf. Furio Cerrutti, Hegel, Lukacs, Korsch, in O. Negt (ed.), 'Aktualität und Folgen der Philosophie Hegels', Frankfurt, Suhrkamp, 1970, pp.199-214, esp. pp.202f.
169 Hegel, 'Science of Logic', Introduction, p.54. Cf. the introduction to the 'shorter logic'.
170 'Phänomenologie des Geistes', Hamburg, Meiner, 1952, pp.63-6. 'The Phenomenology of Spirit', trans. A. Miller, Oxford, Clarendon Press, 1977, pp.46-9. I say partially independent, because this critique seems to presuppose the notion of 'absolute knowledge' and therefore refers one back to Hegel's positive claims.
171 Ibid., p.66; translation, p.49.
172 Cf. 'Philosophy of History', trans., J. Sibree, London, Constable, 1956, p.11.

196 Notes

173 Cf. p.21 , above.
174 For discussions of this theme, see Martin Jay, 'The Dialectical Imagination', London, Heinemann, 1973, ch.2.
175 Above, p.70.
176 Cf. Jindrich Želeny, 'The Logic of Marx', Oxford, Blackwell, 1980, p.31: 'To the individual-empiricist, contemplative interpretation of experience Marx counterposes the historical-collectivist, practical conception.'
177 This has been frequently argued in the literature. Perhaps the best recent work is Derek Sayer, op.cit.
178 Cf. Hegel, 'Method is the consciousness of the form of the inner self-movement of its content', 'Logik', Jubiläumsausgabe, 1958, vol.I, p.51; and 'Encyclopedia', para.139: 'What is inside, is also present outside, and vice versa. The appearance shows nothing which is not in the essence, and in the essence there is nothing which is not manifest.' The latter statement is, of course, more complicated than it appears. Cf. Herbert Marcuse, 'Reason and Revolution', 2nd edn, London, Routledge & Kegan Paul, 1955, pp.142ff. and George Lukács, 'The Ontology of Social Being. Hegel's False and His Genuine Ontology', London, Merlin, 1978, p.82, and (on the relation between method and content) the second volume, 'Marx's Basic Ontological Principles', p.49.
179 In Bhaskar's terms, we construct transitive objects which may, with luck, correspond to intransitive ones. Lukács argues that the same positing process is true of work in general: 'Zur Ontologie des Gesellschaftlichen Seins. Die Arbeit', Neuwied & Darmstadt, Luchterhand, 1973, ch.1, esp. pp.14f, 24.
180 Marx clearly does not believe that these relations can be immediately known: there is, of course, the difference that Marx seems to envisage a closer fit between knowledge and reality than Kant's separation of phenomena and noumena would allow.
181 'The German Ideology', Part I, ed. Chris Arthur, London, Lawrence & Wishart, 1974, p.42.
182 'The German Ideology', London, Lawrence & Wishart, 1965, p.491. Translation modified.
183 Cf. p.34 , above.
184 Sayer, op.cit., pp.8f.
185 Cf. chapter 1, pp.20f. above; also Leszek Kolakowski, Karl Marx and the Classical Definition of Truth, in his 'Marxism and Beyond'.
186 See, for example, the use made of the concept of 'synthesis' by Max Adler; Alfred Sohn-Rethel,

'Intellectual and Manual Labour', London, Macmillan, 1978, esp. pp.4, 35ff.; and Habermas, 'Knowledge and Human Interests', esp. pp.31ff. It would be extremely useful to have a study which traced the links between neo-Kantianism and Marxism, in the way in which those between neo-Kantianism and phenomenology have been traced. Cf. G. Rose, 'Hegel Contra Sociology'
187 He claims that Kant's critical philosophy was virtually unknown among Marx's contemporaries. Max Adler, 'Kausalität und Teleologie im Streite um die Wissenschaft', in 'Marx-Studien', vol.I, eds. M.A. and R. Hilferding, Vienna, Ignaz Brand, 1904, pp.312ff.
188 E.g. Karl Vorländer, 'Kant und der Sozialismus', Berlin, Reuter & Reichard, 1900.
189 Max Adler, 'Kant und der Marxismus', Berlin, E. Laub, 1925, translated in Bottomore and Goode, op.cit., p.63. Cf. their Introduction, pp.15ff.
190 'Kausalität und Teleologie', p.291. Cf. p.430: Marx 'treibt aus dem seine ganze Fruchtbarkeit erst erschliessenden Wunderboden Kantschen Denkens neue, bedeutungsvolle Bildungen hervor'.
191 I.e. Kant's 'Bewusstsein überhaupt', Fichte's 'absolute ego' and Hegel's 'objective mind' ('Kant und der Marxismus', p.162; cf. p.172). The essay from which these passages come is partly reprinted in Bottomore and Goode, op.cit., pp.62-8. This is, of course, the claim, which one finds very often in the Marxist tradition, that all epistemology or all philosophy is really something other than what it appears to be. (Cf. Krahl, below.)
192 'Kausalität und Teleologie', p.426. Adler is discussing the view of Windelband and Rickert that the distinction between the natural and the human sciences lies essentially ('epistemologically') in their different relation to the subject (p.425). This, he says, is not enough, since a subjective attitude is not part of science. Cf. Adler's late work, 'Das Rätsel der Gesellschaft. Zur Erkenntniskritischen Grundlegung der Sozialwissenschaft', Vienna, Saturn-Verlag, 1936, esp. the Introduction: Worum die Soziologie mit Erkenntnistheorie anfangen muss. There is also a brief statement of this view in 'Die Staatsauffassung des Marxismus', 'Marx-Studien', vol.IV, Vienna, 1922, esp. p.30.
193 Cf. 'Kausalität und Teleologie', pp.285ff., 291, 398ff., 426.
194 'Das Rätsel der Gesellschaft', p.19.
195 Ibid., pp.87ff. Cf. p.143: 'We know that, everywhere we are confronted by an objective state of affairs,

198 Notes

      this is only another expression for the transcendental-social function of consciousness.'
196 'Kant und der Marxismus', p.153: 'The individual consciousness is <u>a priori socialised</u>' ('Das Rätsel der Gesellschaft', p.178). Cf. Wittgenstein's arguments against the possibility of a private language.
197 'Kausalität und Teleologie', p.382.
198 Ibid., p.383. Cf. 'Das Rätsel der Gesellschaft', pp.178f.: 'The essential thing is that the social should be recognised as an element of the logical process of thought itself. It is therefore one of the conditions of all experience. The social is therefore not a product of human coexistence, of the intellectual activity [Denkverkehr] of the individuals or of their co-operative and mutually antagonistic interaction. Rather, the social is a form of consciousness which first makes possible all historical coexistence and all social development. This form of consciousness is however a form of <u>existence</u>. And so the social does not exist first, say, in a normative form, whether as an inner moral imperative or as external regulation. It exists, rather, as something natural, as a form of being. Only this being, however, is social being; this natural phenomenon is social nature.' It is in this sense that Adler's concept of <u>Verstehen</u> is 'transcendental, i.e. constitutive of social experience' ('Das Rätsel', p.147). I think this is more than the fairly uncontroversial claim that human knowledge is only possible on the basis of sociality: Adler seems to believe that the basis of sociality is itself grounded in a cognitive relation.
199 Pp.86f. above.
200 'Das Rätsel', p.205. This question is discussed in chapter 5, below.
201 This is gradually being published in West Germany by Luchterhand and in Britain by the Merlin Press.
202 'The Ontology of Social Being', vol.2, 'Marx's Basic Ontological Principles', pp.14f.
203 'Marx', p.49. Cf. p.103 and vol.1, 'Hegel', p.78. Lukács notes (ibid., p.82) that the same is true of Hegel.
204 'Marx', p.99.
205 'Arbeit', p.65.
206 Penguin edn, pp.90ff.
207 'Marx', p.62.
208 'Hegel', p.71
209 Lukács explains the importance of work for sociality by saying that it forms the bridge between pre-social

(organic) and social being. 'All other categories of this form of being are essentially already of a social character. Their properties and their modes of effectivity develop only where social being is already constituted.... Only work has ... an expressly transitional character' ('Arbeit', p.8). 'In work, all the determinations which make up the essence of what is new in social being are already contained in nuce' (p.9).
210 Ibid., p.70.
211 Pp.14f.
212 P.24.
213 'Die Arbeit besteht aus teleologischen Setzungen, die jeweils Kausalreihen in Gang setzen. Diese schlicht-konstatierende Feststellung eliminiert jahrtausendalte ontologische Vorurteile' (Georg Lukács, Die Ontologischen Grundlagen des Menschlichen Denkens und Handelns, in 'Autorität - Organisation - Revolution', The Hague, von Eversdijck, 1972, p.142).
214 Above, p.196-7, n.186.
215 Op.cit., p.4. He goes on: 'It is around this notion that the major arguments of this book will revolve.' Cf. pp.35ff.
216 Ibid., p.75. Among the most basic of these abstract concepts are those of absolute space and time and Galileo's concept of inertial motion.
217 Ibid., pp.98f.
218 P.179.
219 P.180.
220 Herbert Marcuse, 'One Dimensional Man', London, Routledge & Kegan Paul, 1964. Cf. Jürgen Habermas, Technology and Science as Ideology, in 'Toward a Rational Society', London, Heinemann, 1971. See also Brian Easlea, 'Liberation and the Aims of Science: An Essay on Obstacles to the Making of a Beautiful World', London, Chatto & Windus for Sussex University Press, 1973.
221 Alfred Schmidt, 'The Concept of Nature in Marx', p.108.
222 Cf. pp.108f.: 'the very criticist question of the conditions of possible knowledge is "abstract" in the Hegelian sense and lost any object for Marx through Hegel's critique of Kant. The highest form of epistemology, for Marx as for Hegel, is the philosophy of world history. The process of cognition should not be described as a relation of Subject and Object which can be fixed for all time.' Also p.121: 'Marx both retained Kant's thesis of the non-identity of

Subject and Object and adopted the post-Kantian view, no longer exclusive of history, that Subject and Object entered into changing configurations'.
223 P.12. Cf. p.26: 'Marx went beyond Feuerbach in bringing not only sensuous intuition but also the whole of human practice into the process of knowledge as a constitutive moment.'
224 Schmidt, op.cit., pp.121f. The textual evidence that Marx, and not just Horkheimer, held these interesting views is less than overwhelming; Schmidt has been accused with some justification of over-interpreting some of Marx's utterances in an epistemological sense. (See G.A. Cohen's review in 'Radical Philosophy', 2, 1972.) Schmidt's claim that Marx identifies a special kind of constitutive practice, different from ordinary 'technological' practice and from the 'transforming practice' of the 'Theses on Feuerbach' (Preface, p.12) seems similarly under-supported.
225 Schmidt, op.cit., p.33; 'The German Ideology' (1965 edn), p.59.
226 Schmidt, op.cit., p.114.
227 Ibid., p.119.
228 P.120. The quotation is from 'Capital', vol.I, Harmondsworth, Penguin, 1976, p.133.
229 Schmidt criticises Jean-Yves Calvez ('La Pensée de Karl Marx', Seuil, Paris, 1956) for presenting 'Marxist materialism as a theory of the constitution of reality, which leans so far towards Kant that the elaborated material of nature is deprived of any inherent structure of its own' (Schmidt, op.cit., p.226, n.127). Cf. Calvez, op.cit., pp.140, 347, 378f.
230 Cf. n.174, p.196, above, on 'Identitätsphilosophie'; Schmidt, op.cit., p.121; also Dieter Henrich, Karl Marx als Schüler Hegels, in Henrich, 'Hegel im Kontext', pp.187-207, esp. pp.193f., 205. 'Identitätsphilosophie' is only one of the issues at stake here; there is also, lurking in the background, the opposition between 'voluntaristic' and 'deterministic' tendencies within historical materialism.
231 The scare quotes denote recognition of the substantial differences within this tradition, both between the original authors of 'Lire le Capital' and the early and later Althusser (see Althusser's 'Essays in Self-Criticism', London, New Left Books, 1976 and Rancière's essays in 'Radical Philosophy', 1974,) and with, for example, Barry Hindess and Paul Hirst, whose thought developed within this tradition.
232 This seems true even of Hindess and Hirst, who claim

Notes

to eschew epistemologies. (On this claim, see esp. the introduction to Hindess, 'Philosophy and Methodology in the Social Sciences', pp.1-22.

233 Raymond Aron, 'D'une sainte famille à une autre', p.73. Aron waspishly calls this 'une interrogation que le normalien appellera kantienne et qu'Engels aurait appellée petite-bourgeoise'. Etienne Balibar admits as much in this revealing specification of 'the general problem underlying Althusser's enterprise': 'What type of philosophy of sciences is capable of discussing, recognising and proving the scientific character of historical materialism [Marxism],' (and, he adds for good measure, psychoanalysis) (From Bachelard to Althusser: The Concept of 'Epistemological Break', 'Economy and Society', vol.7, no.3, 1978).

234 Part II of the English edition of 'Reading Capital'. See especially chs 6 and 8.
235 Above, p.35.
236 'Reading Capital', p.146.
237 Ibid., p.178.
238 Ibid., p.249. 'Constitutes' it, in other words, in theoretical terms: 'Marx's analysis constitutes his object (the "productive forces") by constructing the history of its successive forms, i.e. forms which have a determinate place in the structure of the mode of production.

'In his determination of the object of a component theory, Marx's method thus completely *abolishes* the problem of "reference" of the empirical designation of the object of a theoretical knowledge, or of the ideological designation of the object of a scientific knowledge. In fact, this determination now depends entirely on the theoretical concepts which make it possible to analyse in a differential way the successive forms of a connexion, and the structure of the mode of production to which this connexion belongs.' Cf. Balibar's criticism of Granger for misunderstanding 'the mode of constitution of the concepts of temporality and history in the theory of Capital' (ibid., p.296).

239 'Pre-Capitalist Modes of Production', London, Routledge & Kegan Paul, 1975, p.310.
240 Ibid., p.311.
241 Ibid., pp.311f.
242 Ibid., p.322.
243 In particular, 'Mode of Production and Social Formation', subtitled 'An Auto-Critique of Pre-Capitalist Modes of Production', London, Macmillan, 1977; Barry

Hindess, 'Philosophy and Methodology in the Social Sciences'; and A. Cutler, B. Hindess, P. Hirst and A. Hussain, 'Marx's "Capital" and Capitalism Today', 2 vols, London, Routledge & Kegan Paul, 1977, 1978.
244 Hindess, 'Philosophy and Methodology', p.5. Cf. 'Mode of Production', ch.1.
245 Cf. 'Mode of Production', pp.15f., 30f.
246 Ibid., pp.19f. Cf. pp.31ff.
247 For a critique of this Hindess-Hirst position, see Andrew Collier, In Defence of Epistemology, in John Mepham and D.-H. Ruben, op.cit., vol.III.
248 Cf. Hollis, 'Models of Man', esp. pp.178f.
249 See in particular J. Habermas, 'Knowledge and Human Interests', and Karl-Otto Apel, 'Transformation der Philosophie', 2 vols, Frankfurt, Suhrkamp, 1976. Of the two, Habermas concentrates more on social theory, especially Marxism - see especially the essay Toward a Reconstruction of Historical Materialism in 'Communication and the Evolution of Society', Boston, Beacon Press, 1979. Apel is more concerned with the 'transcendental pragmatics of language', the object of what he calls the 'transformation of philosophy'. In the present discussion the differences of emphasis between the two writers are largely ignored, since it would take a long time to elucidate them and is not very relevant in this context. See, however, 'Transformation', vol.II, pp.152ff. (This essay is not in the English translation.)
250 'Knowledge and Human Interests', Preface, p.vii. Cf. 'Postscript', p.165.
251 Ibid., p.4.
252 Apel, though not Habermas, tends to call this strategy 'the anthropology of knowledge' ('Erkenntnisanthropologie') - anthropology being here understood, of course, in the sense of philosophical anthropology concerned with universal features of human life. Cf. his introduction to 'Transformation der Philosophie', vol.I, pp.30f. and nn. 36 and 37. For Habermas's objection to the term, see 'Postscript', pp.160f.
253 Loc.cit.
254 Op.cit., p.136. Cf. pp.25ff. where Apel contrasts the 'old' view of Verstehen as an alternative method of explanation with the recent 'hermeneutic' demonstration 'dass das "Verstehen" als Weise des menschlichen In-der-Welt-Seins schon fur die Konstitution von Erfahrungs-Daten und somit fur die Beantwortung der *Was*-Frage in der Erkenntnistheorie vorausgesetzt wird'.
255 'Knowledge and Human Interests', Appendix, p.309.

256 A Postscript to 'Knowledge and Human Interests', 'Philosophy of the Social Sciences', vol.3, no.2, 1973, pp.157-89.
257 P.7.
258 'Knowledge and Human Interests', p.68. On the next page, Habermas uses the Husserlian term 'objectivism' to describe this process: 'Objectivism deludes the sciences with the image of a self-subsistent world of facts structured in a lawlike manner; it thus conceals the a priori constitution of these facts.' Cf. Apel's reference to the need to 'reverse' the abstractions of individual scientific theories, ('Transformation der Philosophie', vol.I, p.11), and Habermas's new introduction to 'Theorie und Praxis', 4th edn, Frankfurt, Suhrkamp, 1971, p.10.
259 'Knowledge and Human Interests', p.191.
260 Ibid., p.192.
261 Ibid., p.193. Cf. Schutz's dictum: 'The thought objects constructed by the social scientist refer to and are founded upon the thought of man living his everyday life among his fellow-men' (Common-sense and Scientific Interpretation of Human Action, I, 2, vol.I, pp.5ff.).
262 Ibid., p.193.
263 See, in particular, 'Philosophy of the Social Sciences', p.174.
264 'Theory and Practice', p.9.
265 Pp.8f. Cf. p.20f.
266 'Knowledge and Human Interests', p.194.
267 Ibid., p.197.
268 Ibid., p.194. Cf. Apel, 'Transformation der Philosophie', vol.I, pp.24f., 38, 61, 374, vol.II, pp. 255, 389.
269 'Theory and Practice', p.14. Cf. the excellent discussion of this problem in Thomas McCarthy, op. cit., pp.110-25.
270 Ibid., p.21. See also note 38. This empirical aspect of the cognitive interests is to be clarified by an investigation of evolutionary theory and ethology. ('Communication').
271 I am referring here to 'Legitimation Crisis' and to some of the later essays in 'Communication'.
272 'Theory and Practice', pp.19f. Cf. Postscript, pp. 166, 168-74. On this shift in Habermas's thought, see McCarthy, op.cit., esp. pp.293-9 and John Thompson, 'Critical Hermeneutics. A Study in the Thought of Paul Ricoeur and Jürgen Habermas', Cambridge University Press, 1981, esp. pp.96ff.
273 Theorie der Gesellschaft oder Sozialtechnologie? in

J. Habermas and N. Luhmann, 'Theorie der Gesellschaft oder Sozialtechnologie - Was Leistet die Systemforschung?', Frankfurt, Suhrkamp, 1971, pp.202-15.
274 P.205.
275 P.206. It is perhaps significant that Habermas cites in this connection the 'Erlangen school' of 'protophysics' rather than his own earlier work (ibid., n.7).
276 P.212.
277 P.215.
278 Krahl, one of the leading theorists of the West German SDS, was killed in a car accident in 1970. His collected papers have been published under the title 'Konstitution und Klassenkampf', Frankfurt, Verlag Neue Kritik, 1971. See also Heinrich Brinkmann (ed.), 'Sinnlichkeit und Abstraktion', Wiesbaden, Focus-Verlag, 1973, which contains a fascinating transcript of a discussion which took place over Christmas in 1967.
279 The importance he attached to the concept is indicated by the title which the editors gave to his papers - see their introduction. Cf. Manfred Lauermann's Nachwort in Brinkmann, op.cit., pp.216-43, esp. pp.226f. Lauermann suggests that Krahl's use of the concept reflected the contemporary emphasis on questions of ideology and false consciousness. Krahl also draws a satirical connection with the juridical concept of constitution: 'The transcendental logic of constitution is ... the constituent national assembly of the French Revolution projected onto the level of epistemology' ('Konstitution und Klassenkampf', pp.324f.).
280 Ibid., p.61.
281 Cf. pp.37, 59f.
282 Ibid., p.49.
283 P.323.
284 P.403.
285 Ibid., p.328. Habermas can, of course, retort that it is the Marxian concept which is vitiated by its 'latent positivism'. Cf. Labor and Interaction, in 'Theory and Practice', pp.142-69, esp. pp.168f.; and Albrecht Wellmer, 'Critical Theory of Society', New York, Herder & Herder, 1971, ch.2.
286 Cf. above, ch.3, n.99.
287 'A Realist Theory of Science', pp.16f.
288 'The Possibility of Naturalism', ch.1, pp.48f.
289 There is, of course, a partial historical justification for this restriction in that Habermas's 'target' is not so much natural science itself as positivist scientism; cf. 'Knowledge and Human Interests', pp.4f. and Postscript, p.158.

205 Notes

290 See, for example, N. Lobkowitz, Interest and Objectivity, 'Philosophy of the Social Sciences', vol.2, 1972, and Habermas's reply in his Postscript. Cf. McCarthy, op.cit., pp.65ff. The discussion below is indebted to an unpublished paper by Norman Stockman, What is Positivism, Anyway?
291 Norman Stockman, Positivism & Antipositivism in Sociological Metatheory, PhD thesis, Aberdeen, 1979, p.22.
292 Habermas might not accept this suggestion; he writes that 'any transcendental approach, in the last analysis, precludes that there can be such a thing as truthfulness to reality in the sense postulated by philosophical realism' (Postscript, p.180).
293 This, however, is controversial to the extent that Habermas's derivation of this interest rests on an incorrect (positivist) conception of natural science.
294 Above, p.110.
295 Cf. Thompson, 'Critical Hermeneutics'.
296 I shall not rehearse the arguments for this claim, from Popper onwards; a moment's reflection on the history and current state of the social sciences is enough to indicate its pertinence. However, the implied equation of découpage and constitution requires some justification, since it clearly departs from the more traditionally transcendentalist framework which Habermas seemed to invoke and which Stockman uses in defence of Habermas against realism. All I can say here is that I do not find the stronger formulations convincing and that I suspect Habermas saw his own concept of constitution in the more informal way in which I have presented it here.
297 Cf. Martin Hollis, 'Models of Man', pp.178f. (quoted above, p.45.
298 And also present, of course, in more general formulations such as those of Horkheimer (see p.66 above).
299 On the last of these, between 'meaning-imputation' and 'interaction', see Thomason, op.cit., p.184.
300 Cf. the related discussion of the concept of social relations of production in Sayer, op.cit., pp.80-7.
301 I do not want to deny that a serious case can be made for the opposite view, that reality can only be made meaningful under the simplifying perspective of, say, conflict/consensus theory. But this is merely to pass the buck to some sort of attempt at a synthesis.
302 Beyleveld, op.cit., pp.498-504. Beyleveld's 'rationalist actionism' relies on constitution$_e$ by a transcendental subject; this seems to me to be an unsatis-

factory basis for social theory unless rationalist types of theory (rational choice theory, decision theory, etc.) can be extended to cover the whole field of social theory.
303 Qualified along the lines suggested by Bhaskar in 'Naturalism'.
304 See in particular, Giddens's notion of 'a *double hermeneutic*', relating both to entering and grasping the frames of meaning involved in the production of social life by lay actors, and reconstituting these within the new frames of meaning involved in technical conceptual schemes' ('New Rules of Sociological Method', p.79). Cf. Apel, Sprechakttheorie und transzendentale Sprachpragmatik zur Frage ethischer Normen, in K.-O. Apel (ed.), 'Sprachpragmatik und Philosophie', Frankfurt, Suhrkamp, 1976, pp.36f. and Types of Social Science, p.10.
305 Hollis, 'Models of Man', p.179.

CHAPTER 4 MAX WEBER AND CONCEPT FORMATION IN SOCIOLOGY

1 GAW, p.208; translation, p.106. Cf. Eduard Baumgarten (ed.), 'Max Weber. Werk und Person', Tübingen, Mohr, 1964, p.593.
2 GAW, p.17, n.6; 'Roscher and Knies', p.220, n.37.
3 Dieter Henrich, 'Die Einheit der Wissenschaftslehre Max Webers', p.35. Cf. p.2. In other words, there is no need for objectivity to be guaranteed by a general theory of knowledge of the sort advanced by Rickert, or later by Habermas.
4 Ibid., p.103. Cf. Horst Baier, 'Von der Erkenntnistheorie zur Wirklichkeitswissenschaft', Habilitationsschrift, University of Münster, 1969.
5 Max Weber: Methods and the Man.
6 Cf. Albrecht Wellmer, 'Methodologie als Erkenntnistheorie', Frankfurt, Suhrkamp, 1967.
7 Cf. Guy Oakes's introduction to 'Roscher and Knies', pp.12ff. The title of the Shils-Finch translation of three of Weber's essays, The Methodology of the Social Sciences, is probably nearer to Weber's intentions than the more portentous 'Gesammelte Aufsätze zur Wissenschaftslehre' chosen by Marianne Weber for the posthumous publication of the essays.
8 GAW, p.208, translation, p.106: 'The greatest advances in the sphere of the social sciences are substantially tied up with the shift in practical cultural problems and take the guise of a critique of concept-construction.' Cf. GAW, p.214, transla-

tion, p.112: 'There comes a moment when the atmosphere changes.... The light of the great cultural problems moves on. Then science too prepares to change its standpoint and its analytical apparatus.' Also GAW, p.218. Cf. Thomas Kuhn, 'The Structure of Scientific Revolutions, vol.2, no.2, University of Chicago Press, 1962, 1970.
9   GAW, p.208, translation, p.106 (translation modified). Cf. GAW, pp.148f., translation, p.52, where the separation of 'is' and 'ought' is presented with similar assurance; Weber is declaring his allegiance to what he sees as the obviously correct (if not yet universally accepted) view. This does not mean, however, that Weber saw it as purely a matter of logic; it is clear that his views on this and other 'methodological' issues were deeply linked to his characterisation of the general development of Western history. See pp.132f. below.
10 GAW, pp.15f; 'Roscher and Knies', pp.66f. Weber notes that 'Roscher himself was quite familiar with the problems raised by this metaphysical proposition' (loc.cit.). As a result, his work is both incoherent and yet, in partially escaping from Hegel, 'represents *progress* in the objectivity of scientific inquiry' (GAW, p.41, 'Roscher and Knies', p.90).
11 Loc.cit.
12 GAW, p.195, translation, p.94.
13 Henrich, 'Die Einheit', p.89. This, Henrich argues, is the only philosophical claim which Weber makes in his methodology; anyone who accepts Weber's view on this point can discuss other aspects of his theories as questions of methodology, 'without paying attention to philosophical problems' (ibid., p.91). I find this sharp distinction unconvincing.
14 The argument seems to apply to science in general, though Weber often presents it with other arguments for ideal types, such as reference to values and cultural meaning, which are specific to the cultural sciences. See, for example, the passage quoted in the next paragraph.
15 Henrich, 'Die Einheit', p.91.
16 GAW, p.195; translation, pp.93f.
17 Above, p.14.
18 'A Realist Theory of Science', p.26. In other words, they equate the world with the world of experience, mistaking the contingent relation between the world as it is and our experience of it for an essential property of the world itself (ibid., p.28).

19 Ibid., p.24.
20 P.25.
21 P.25.
22 Cf. p.24.
23 P.27.
24 P.28.
25 See, in particular, Arato, op.cit., and Burger, op. cit.; Gillian Rose ('Hegel contra Sociology') provides a brilliant critique of neo-Kantian influences on sociology as a whole.
26 GAW, p.287; translation, pp.185f.
27 See, for example, the passage quoted below.
28 GAW, pp.194f.; translation, pp.93f. The translation here is taken from Burger, op.cit., p.123. Cf. GAW, p.202; translation, p.100, where Weber gives a similar analysis of the concept of exchange.
29 Above, pp.49ff.
30 Burger, op.cit., p.29.
31 GAW, p.191; translation, p.90. Cf. Burger, op.cit., pp.116, 127f.
32 GAW, p.170; translation, p.72. I have again used Burger's translation, op.cit., p.88.
33 Henrich, 'Die Einheit', pp.87f. Henrich and Burger agree that Weber is after real definitions of what he calls genetic conepts. They differ with regard to Weber's account of the specification of classificatory concepts. Henrich (pp.85f.) sees this as a process of nominal definition, while Burger (pp.126f.) insists that, as with genetic concepts, real definition is also involved here. There is a further complication that 'meaningfully adequate' ideal types of action, as opposed to the causal ideal types discussed above, will correspond to reality in so far as social action itself tends towards a meaningfully adequate form, such as that of purposive-rational action. Cf. Johannes Weiss, 'Max Webers Grundlegung der Soziologie', p.66; GAW, p.195; translation pp. 94f.; also Stages and Directions of Religious Rejections of the World, 'Gesammelte Aufsätze zur Religionssoziologie', vol.I, pp.536ff.; H. Gerth and C.W. Mills (eds), 'From Max Weber', Oxford University Press, 1958, pp.323f.
34 Above, p.50.
35 Cf. GAW, pp.193ff.; translation, pp.92ff.
36 'Economy and Society', vol.I, p.3.
37 See his letter to Robert Liefmann mentioned above in chapter 2 (p.28, n.28).
38 Free Press, New York, 1977, esp. chs 1 and 3.
39 Cf. K. Löwith, Die Entzauberung der Welt durch

Wissenschaft, 'Merkur', vol.18, 1964, p.514, para.2.
40 This inconsistency is perhaps less surprising if one bears in mind the general uncertainty of much discussion of nominal versus real definitions and the fact that, for example, a professional philosopher like Russell can plausibly be charged with a similar inconsistency. (Cf. p.38 above.) On the apparent lack of order and system in Weber's work, see Andreas Walther, Max Weber als Soziologe, 'Jahrbuch für Soziologie',vol.II, 1926, section VII, pp.52-65.
41 At the same time, there remains a powerful influence of empirical realism on the construction of the ideal types; the typology of action, for example, with its central distinction between rational and non-rational action, seems to be dictated by epistemological and methodological considerations. Cf. Walther, op.cit., pp.53, 64f. (I should say that, although Walther's article contains some stimulating arguments, it also displays a number of serious misunderstandings.)
42 David Papineau, Ideal Types and Empirical Theories, 'British Journal for the Philosophy of Science', vol. 27, no.2, 1976, esp. pp.142ff. Papineau points out the problems of this account.
43 C.G. Hempel and P. Oppenheim, 'Der Typusbegriff im Lichte der Neuen Logik', Leiden, Sijthoffs Uitgeversmaatschappij, 1936, pp.83ff.
44 Ibid., p.113.
45 'The Phenomenology', p.234.
46 Ibid., p.9.
47 P.8.
48 Ibid., p.10; CP, vol.I, p.6.
49 As we saw above (pp.63ff.), however, Schutz is by no means unequivocal about this.
50 GAW, p.439 (Über einige Kategorien der verstehende Soziologie, section III); my translation. Cf. 'Economy and Society', vol.I, ch.1, section 1, part 9 (pp.13ff.)
51 At least for what are presented as its foundations. It has frequently been argued that Weber's ostensible starting-points with the concepts of action, legitimacy, etc., become irrelevant once he gets under way. Cf. Paul Lazarsfeld, Max Weber and Empirical Social Research, 'American Sociological Review', vol.30, 1965, and Historical Notes on the Empirical Study of Action. Also E. Manheim's Comment on Vatro Murvar, Some Reflections on Weber's Typology of Herrschaft, 'Sociological Quarterly', vol.5, 1964.
52 Cf. GAW, p.48n; 'Roscher und Knies', p.239, n.13.
53 'Economy and Society', vol.I, p.20.

54 'Religionssoziologie', vol.II, pp.120f.; translated as 'The Religion of India' by H. Gerth and D. Martindale, Chicago, Free Press, 1958, p.121.
55 'Economy and Society', vol.I, p.21.
56 Ibid., p.31. Cf. p.213, n.1, and vol.III, p.953.
57 Cf. Paul Hirst, 'Social Evolution and Sociological Categories', London, Allen & Unwin, 1976, esp. pp.82f. Peter Blau, whose general orientation is very different from Hirst's, makes a similar point: Weber's 'focus on types of legitimacy leads him to take the existence of legitimate authority for granted and never systematically to examine the structural conditions under which it emerges out of other forms of power' (Critical Remarks on Weber's Theory of Authority, 'American Political Science Review', vol.57, no.2, 1963, p.307).
58 Alasdair MacIntyre, Is a Science of Comparative Politics Possible?, in Alan Ryan (ed.), 'The Philosophy of Social Explanation', Oxford University Press, 1973, pp.187f.
59 Compare the related anxiety expressed by Blau and other American commentators that Weber lacks a category of 'democratic authority' (Blau, op.cit., pp.314ff.).
60 Martin Albrow, 'Bureaucracy', London, Macmillan, 1970, esp. ch.3.
61 'Economy and Society', vol.III, ch.XI, part 6, pp.973ff. The use of the term 'efficiency' must be qualified; see Albrow, op.cit., pp.61-6.
62 Cf. Blau, op.cit., p.311.
63 John Schaar, Reflections on Authority, 'New American Review', vol.8, 1970. Reprinted as Legitimacy in the Modern State, in Philip Green and Stanford Levinson (eds), 'Power and Community', New York and Toronto, Random House, 1970. Hanna Pitkin, 'Wittgenstein and Justice', pp.280-6.
64 'Economy and Society', vol.I, p.31 (translation modified).
65 Ibid., p.214. It therefore seems odd to say, as Pitkin does (p.280), 'that Weber did not intend any substantial redefinition'. Cf. Giddens, 'Studies in Social and Political Theory', p.92.
66 Politik als Beruf, 'Gesammelte Politische Schriften', p.493; H. Gerth and C.W. Mills, op.cit., p.78.
67 Pitkin, op.cit., p.282.
68 Cf. above, p.210, ch.4, n.57 (Blau).
69 This has recently been attacked in interesting ways by Giddens, in 'Studies in Social and Political Theory', and by Bhaskar, in 'Naturalism'.

70 Pitkin, op.cit., p.285. Cf. p.284: 'an uninitiated student dropping in on the middle of a political science course may be startled to hear such propositions as that a government may become increasingly legitimate by the judicious and effective use of secret police and propaganda.'
71 Loc.cit.
72 A recent critical 'reader' thus rejects the term 'legitimacy' in favour of 'mass loyalty' as a description of political opinion in advanced capitalist societies (Wolf-Dieter Narr and Claus Offe (eds), 'Wohlfahrtsstaat und Massenloyalität', Cologne, Kiepenheuer & Witsch, 1975).
73 Pitkin, op.cit., pp.285f.
74 'British Journal of Sociology', vol.29, no.1, March 1978.
75 Ibid., pp.58f. Note that most of these elements can be ascribed equally to beliefs and to actions.
76 Ibid., p.61.
77 'Economy and Society', vol.I, p.85. Weber also distinguishes between formal and substantive rationality in the law (ibid., vol.II, pp.656f.). Here again, 'substantive rationality' 'means that the decision of legal problems is influenced by norms ... [such as] ... ethical imperatives, utilitarian and other expediential rules, and political maxims'.
78 But not rationality in general, since, as Roy Edgley has shown, anyone who thinks, argues or believes something for a reason is committed to using the concept of rationality in an evaluative sense. See Marx's Revolutionary Science, in Mepham and Ruben, op.cit., vol.3, esp. pp.17f.
79 Alternatively, he may simply have been following through a parallel with substantive rationality in the legal sense (see note 77 above).
80 Cf. Eisen, op.cit., pp.63f.: 'We need only glance at the six elements which we have identified to pinpoint the source of the problem. A thing of process can ultimately be judged efficient, purposive or systematic only relative to some end. The standard must come from outside. Considerations of substance are not extraneous to "formal" ones but rather built in unavoidably.' See also p.65: 'Weber's intention in ... separating technical efficiency from normative measures is evident, but his distinction effectively obscures the relativity of even formal evaluations. Only at a general level is monetary calculation optimally rational regardless of our provisioning standard: at a more specific level, the particular calcula-

tion or policy used will vary in utility depending on our specific goals.'
81 'Negations', Harmondsworth, Penguin, 1968, p.202.
82 'Economy and Society', vol.II, pp.918ff. Cf. Eisen, op.cit., pp.65f. and Wolfgang Schluchter, 'Wertfreiheit und Verantwortungsethik', Tübingen, Mohr, 1971, reprinted in Schluchter, 'The Rise of Western Rationalism', University of California Press, 1981.
83 Cf. 'Economy and Society, vol.I, pp.107ff. on the substantive conditions of the formal 'rationality' of monetary calculation.
84 David Beetham, 'Max Weber and the Theory of Modern Politics', London, Allen & Unwin, 1974, p.274.
85 Eisen, op.cit., pp.67ff.
86 Max Weber und Karl Marx, 'Archiv für Sozialwissenschaft und Sozialpolitik', vol.67, 1932. Reprinted in Löwith, 'Gesammelte Abhandlungen', Stuttgart, Kohlhammer, 1960; translation ed. T. Bottomore and W. Outhwaite, London, Allen & Unwin, 1982. Cf. a later article in 'Merkur', vol.18, 1964: Die Entzauberung der Welt durch Wissenschaft.
87 Cf. (in relation to the last of these characteristics) Nietzsche's concept of 'scientific atheism' ('Archiv', p.70).
88 Ibid., p.65.
89 GAW, p.41; Löwith, 'Archiv', p.72.
90 'Archiv', p.74.
91 Ibid., p.75, Cf. p.212: 'The immense casuistry of his conceptual definitions in *Economy and Society* also has a double purpose: to capture and establish reality within definitions, but also and above all the opposite aim of establishing an open system of "possibilities".'
92 E.g. 'Economy and Society', vol.I, p.18.
93 This individualist concept of the state coexists in Weber's work with his strong positive commitment to German nationalism.
94 Cf. Ernst Topitsch, Max Webers Geschichtsauffassung, 'Wissenschaft und Weltbild, vol.III, 1950.
95 Cf. 'Grundrisse', Penguin edn, pp.100ff.
96 For a very sophisticated discussion of this question and others raised here, see Jürgen Kocka, Karl Marx und Max Weber im Vergleich. Sozialwissenschaften zwischen Dogmatismus und Dezisionismus, in H.-U. Wehler (ed.), 'Geschichte und Ökonomie', Cologne, Kiepenheuer & Witsch 1972.
97 GAW, pp.181, 213.
98 See the opening sentence of the 'Introduction' appended to 'The Protestant Ethic', p.13, for an example of the

213 Notes

former and, for the latter, his closing remarks about rationalisation and bureaucratisation.
99 Cf. H.T. Wilson, 'The American Ideology: Science, Technology and Organisation as Modes of Rationality', London, Routledge & Kegan Paul, 1976.
100 In a similar way, Durkheim's 'conscience collective' does not conflict with realism directly though it is perhaps incompatible with, for example, Bhaskar's transformational model of society which he attempts to derive from a realist philosophy of science.
101 Cf. A. Schutz, 'The Phenomenology', ch.1.

CHAPTER 5 CONCEPTS OF SOCIETY

1 Cf. Adorno, 'Vorlesung', p.87; Introduction to Durkheim, GS, vol.8, pp.258ff.
2 'Practical' is intended here in the German sense which relates to morality and ethical action.
3 Cited by Adorno in 'Aspects of Sociology', p.17 and n.2, pp.33f.
4 H. Schoeck, 'Die Soziologie und die Gesellschaften', Freiburg, Alber Verlag, 1964, pp.107f. Cited by P. Kaupp in his article Gesellschaft, in Joachim Ritter (ed.), 'Historisches Wörterbuch der Philosophie', Darmstadt, Wissenschaftliche Buchgesellschaft, 1974, p.461. See also J. Habermas, 'Strukturwandel der Öffentlichkeit', Neuwied and Berlin, Luchterhand, 1962.
5 Paine, 'Common Sense', 1776.
6 The Baden minister of culture, commenting unfavourably on Simmel's work. Cited in Lewis Coser (ed.), 'Georg Simmel', Englewood Cliffs, New Jersey, Prentice-Hall, 1965, p.39.
7 Cf. Hans Müller, 'Ursprung und Geschichte des Wortes Sozialismus und seiner Verwandten', Hanover, Dietz, 1967. See also R.W. Outhwaite, Social Thought and Social Science, 'New Cambridge Modern History', vol.XIII - companion volume, ed. by Peter Burke, Cambridge University Press, 1979.
8 Alan Dawe, Theories of Social Action, in Bottomore and Nisbet, op.cit. This is a revised and expanded version of Dawe's earlier article The Two Sociologies, 'British Journal of Sociology', vol.21, no.2, 1970. See also Dawe's book, also entitled 'The Two Sociologies', New York, Harper & Row; London, Longman, 1982.
9 Cf. Bhaskar, 'Naturalism', p.16. The terms 'empirical realism' and 'transcendental idealism' should be

taken with a pinch of salt. I am concerned here to point to tendencies in the analysis of society, and not, for example, to argue that Simmel (still less Adler) was committed to transcendental idealism of a Kantian kind.
10 'Theories of Social Action', p.362. Dawe argues more boldly that this has 'always and everywhere' been the case.
11 Cf. 'Aspects of Sociology', ch.II, esp. p.3?
12 'The Language of Sociology', p.34.
13 Ibid., p.36.
14 P.55.
15 Loc.cit.
16 Connections of this kind are, however, not always clear: it will be remembered that Radcliffe-Brown's structural-functionalist theory appeals to a highly empiricist conception of social structure (cf. p.2 above).
17 David Papineau, 'For Science in the Social Sciences', London, Macmillan, 1978, p.47.
18 P.108. Cf. ch.1, passim.
19 P.109.
20 P.118.
21 Pp.116f.
22 P.117.
23 Pp.48f. Where Papineau involves social psychology as the foundation of the social sciences, Runciman has suggested relying on psychology tout court, 'Sociology in its Place', Cambridge University Press, 1970.
24 P.49.
25 Cf. my discussion in chapter 1, above, p.14.
26 'System of Positive Polity', vol.2, London, Longmans, 1875, p.153.
27 See Karl Mannheim, The Concept of the State as an Organism, in 'Essays on Sociology and Social Psychology', London, Routledge & Kegan Paul, 1953.
28 Op.cit., p.173. Cf. ibid., pp.177f.
29 'The Principles of Sociology', vol.I, part II, ch.II, London, Williams & Norgate, 1893, p.437.
30 Ibid., pp.557f.
31 'Principles', para.269, p.580.
32 See, for example, Weber's comments on Schäffle and Spann in 'Economy and Society', vol.I, pp.14ff. Up to about 1909, his references to 'sociology' itself are generally pejorative.
33 Cf. Walter Buckley, 'Sociology and Modern Systems Theory', Englewood Cliffs, New Jersey, Prentice-Hall, 1967, esp. chapter 2. I shall return to this theme a little later.

34 'The Study of Sociology', 9th edn, London, Williams & Norgate, 1880, p.50. John Peel in 'Herbert Spencer', London, Heinemann, 1971, pp.185-91, seems to me to exaggerate Spencer's leanings to methodological individualism.
35 'Rules', pp.100f.
36 Cf. John Peel, op.cit., p.189.
37 Cf. Lukes, 'Durkheim', p.227: 'it was precisely in its treatment of the nature of social phenomena that *The Rules* was least probing and decisive'.
38 London, Allen & Unwin, 1915, p.347. Cf. H. Alpert, 'Emile Durkheim and His Sociology', New York, Russell, 1961, p.151.
39 Cf. Lukes, 'Durkheim', esp. pp.20ff.
40 'Rules', ch.IV.
41 Cf. Lukes, 'Durkheim', pp.81f.
42 'Rules', pp.76f.
43 P.76.
44 Cf. Paul Hirst, Morphology and Pathology, 'Economy and Society', vol.2, no.1, 1973.
45 Alpert, loc.cit.
46 Stark, op.cit., ch.V.
47 Op.cit., p.1.
48 Ibid., p.4.
49 P.15.
50 P.94.
51 P.18.
52 Cf. p.2 above.
53 P.36.
54 'The Structure of Social Action', New York, Free Press, 1968, p.23.
55 Ibid., p.730.
56 P.733. For an interpretation which emphasises this aspect of Parsons's work, see Harold Bershady, 'Ideology and Social Knowledge', Oxford, Blackwell, 1973. Cf. Rene König's formulations, discussed in ch.2, above.
57 'The Social System', Chicago, Free Press, 1951, ch.I.
58 Cf. ch.3, pp.86f.
59 This is clearly one way of reading Simmel's assertion that 'the consciousness of constituting with the others a unity is actually all there is to this unity'. (Cf. p.86 of ch.3.)
60 Max Adler offers the more limited interpretation that Simmel was diverted from the crucial epistemological question to the 'psychological preconditions of social interaction'. (Cf. p.102 of ch.3.)
61 Cf. How is Society Possible?, Wolff, 'Sociology', pp.341f. On this theme, see Uta Gerhardt, op.cit., pl39.

62 'The Sociology of Georg Simmel', ed. K. Wolff, Chicago, Free Press, 1950, pp.10f. (The Field of Society). Cf. Wolff's Introduction, pp.xxvii ff. on the ambiguities of Simmel's concept of society. Cf. also Max Adler's assertion that 'the central concept of Marxist sociology is not society but socialised humanity' (Bottomore and Goode, op.cit., p.65: The Relation of Marxism to Classical German Philosophy).
63 Leipzig, Duncker & Humblot, 1890, p.10.
64 In Wolff, 'The Sociology of Georg Simmel'.
65 Ibid., pp.11f. Cf. Schrader-Klebert, op.cit., passim.
66 'Soziologische Vorlesungen von Georg Simmel', Society for Social Research, University of Chicago, 1931, p.4.
67 P.107.
68 The Problem of Sociology, in Wolff, 'Georg Simmel', p.316.
69 Cf. p.28 , n.28 , above.
70 Letter of 9.3.20, cited by Wolfgang Mommsen, Max Weber's Political Sociology and his Philosophy of World History, in D. Wrong (ed.), 'Max Weber', Englewood Cliffs, New Jersey, Prentice-Hall, 1970, p.192, n.12.
71 Emerich Francis, Kultur und Gesellschaft in der Soziologie Max Webers, in 'Max Weber, Gedächtnisschrift der Ludwig-Maximilians-Universität München', Berlin, Duncker & Humblot, 1966, esp. pp.100f.
72 My Relation to Sociology, p.10, in Ferdinand Tönnies, 'On Sociology: Pure, Applied and Empirical', University of Chicago Press, 1971.
73 Cf. chapter 3, p.89.
74 Cf. Theodor Geiger's assertion, reported by Raymond Aron, that there is agreement within German sociology 'on giving the concept of society an increasingly abstract and rational character' ('German Sociology', Chicago, Free Press, 1964, p.35). A French book by Jules Monnerot, 'Les faits sociaux ne sont pas des choses', Paris, Gallimard, 1946, relies heavily on German sources.
75 My Relation to Sociology, p.6.
76 Cf. Buckley, op.cit., pp.17-23.
77 Herbert Blumer, Psychological Import of the Human Group, cited by Buckley, op.cit., pp.21f.
78 'The Phenomenology', p.4.
79 'The Social Construction of Reality', pp.208f.
80 Ibid., p.30.
81 Cf. chapter 3, pp.70ff.
82 Anton Zijderveld, 'The Abstract Society', London,

Notes

Allen Lane, 1972, pp.48f. See also the same author's 'On Clichés', London, Routledge & Kegan Paul, 1979.
83 Paris, Seuil, 1977, p.7.
84 Max Adler, 'Die Staatsauffassung des Marxismus', Darmstadt, Wissenschaftliche Buchgesellschaft, 1973, pp.42f. First published in 'Marx-Studien', IV, 1922. Cf. Marx and Engels, 'The Holy Family','Marx-Engels Collected Works', vol.IV, London, Lawrence & Wishart, 1975.
85 See, in particular, 'Aspects of Sociology', ch.2 and the essay in 'Gesammelte Schriften', vol.8, translated in the journal 'Salmagundi', nos 10-11, 1969-70.
86 Adorno, 'Vorlesung', pp.31f.
87 Cf. 'The Sociology of Georg Simmel', p.10. Adorno also calls 'society' a 'category of mediation' ('Vorlesung', p.112). Karin Schrader-Klebert's article brings out the parallels between Simmel and critical theory in this respect. Adorno, of course, rejects Simmel's 'formal sociology' (cf. 'Vorlesung', pp.7f.).
88 Society, p.145. Cf. GS, vol.8, pp.238ff. (Notiz über sozialwissenschaftlicher Objektivität.)
89 This is, of course, precisely the objection raised by Popper and Albert in the Positivismusstreit, that Adorno was 'simply talking trivialities in high sounding language' ('The Positivist Dispute in German Sociology', London, Heinemann, 1976, p.296).
90 'Vorlesung', pp.33ff: Society, pp.148f.
91 'The Positivist Dispute', pp.79f.
92 See, for example, the last paragraph of Society (translation, pp.152f.). Cf. 'Vorlesung', p.47 on the 'principle of individuation'.
93 'Vorlesung', pp.156f.
94 See, in particular, Sociology and Psychology, 'New Left Review', nos 46 and 47.
95 'New Left Review', no.46, p.68.
96 P.68.
97 P.69.
98 P.77.
99 P.70.
100 P.73. Compare this with the desiccated theme of 'methodological individualism', which nevertheless has been discussed with a vehemence which shows that wider issues were in the minds of the protagonists.
101 Society, pp.146f.
102 'The Positivist Dispute', p.74.
103 See Adorno's introduction to Durkheim's 'Sociology and Philosophy', reprinted in GS, vol.8 (esp. pp. 250f.).

104 'Vorlesung', p.92.
105 Society, p.146.
106 GS, vol.8, pp.184f. (Anmerkungen zum sozialen Konflikt heute).
107 See, for example, 'Dissonanzen', 4th edn, Göttingen, Vandenhoeck & Ruprecht, 1969, pp.18ff.
108 'Aspects of Sociology', p.121.
109 A European Scholar in America, in D. Fleming and B. Bailyn (eds), 'The Intellectual Migration', Harvard University Press, 1969, p.346.
110 'Naturalism', ch.2.
111 Ibid., pp.18f.
112 Keat and Urry suggest that Lévi-Strauss's general theory of structure may also contain realist elements, if there are binary structures in the human mind which generate binary oppositions elsewhere ('Social Theory', p.131).
113 Bhaskar, 'A Realist Theory of Science', p.182.
114 Ted Benton, for example, makes it one of the conditions of a materialist theory that 'it recognise[s] the existence of "thought", "ideas", "knowledge" as realities in their own right,' 'The Philosophical Foundations of the Three Sociologies', p.171. Cf. the recent metapsychological discussion of the unconscious.
115 Cf. Lukes, 'Durkheim', pp.4ff.
116 As, of course, Weber himself did, when he insisted that 'it is not ideas but interests - material and ideal - which directly govern people's action' (Gerth and Mills, op.cit., p.280).
117 Cf. Benton, loc.cit.
118 Rom Harré, 'Social Being', ch.5. Harré says he is concerned with social psychological processes, rather than 'the great traditional problems of sociology' (p.349). This is slightly disingenuous - in fact the book exudes considerable scepticism about macro-theory. Be that as it may, the book is discussed here only by way of comparison with the more prevalent Marxist versions of social scientific realism.
119 'Naturalism', p.31.
120 Pp.42f.
121 'The Social Construction of Reality', p.30.
122 'Naturalism', p.42.
123 Loc.cit.
124 P. Berger and S. Pullberg, Reification and the Social Critique of Consciousness, 'New Left Review', vol.35, 1966. Cf. Bhaskar's definition of emancipation as the shift 'from an unwanted to a wanted source of

determination' (Scientific Explanation and Human Emancipation, 'Radical Philosophy', no.26, 1980).
125 'Naturalism', p.47. Berger's 'reification' corresponds to the traditional concept of 'alienation'. (Cf. 'Social Construction', p.225, n.58.)
126 'Naturalism', p.43. Bhaskar refers here (p.44, n.31) to Giddens's concept of the 'duality of structure' - cf. 'New Rules', p.121; 'Central Problems', p.5.
127 'Naturalism', p.42.
128 Ibid., pp.48f. Cf. chapter 1, above, pp.
129 'Naturalism', pp.34ff.
130 Ibid. Cf. Giddens, 'Central Problems', pp.117f.
131 Ibid., p.52.
132 'Central Problems', p.91.
133 This is the sub-title of 'Naturalism'.
134 Cf. also Thompson, 'Critical Hermeneutics'.
135 See for example, the different characterisations of classical sociologists given by Keat and Urry, op. cit., and by Ted Benton, op.cit. Similar examples can easily be found in more conventional philosophies of science.

Bibliography

ABEL, THEODORE, The Operation Called *Verstehen*, 'American Journal of Sociology', 54, 1948.
ACHINSTEIN, P., 'Concepts of Science', Baltimore, Johns Hopkins Press, 1968.
ACHINSTEIN, P. and BARKER, S., (eds), 'The Legacy of Logical Positivism', Baltimore, Johns Hopkins Press, 1969.
ADLER, MAX, 'Kausalität und Teleologie im Streite um die Wissenschaft', in 'Marx-Studien', vol.I, eds M.A. and R. Hilferding, Vienna, Ignaz Brand, 1904.
ADLER, MAX, 'Die Staatsauffassung des Marxismus', in 'Marx-Studien', vol.IV, eds M.A. and R. Hilferding, Vienna, 1922, reprinted Darmstadt, Wissenschaftliche Buchgesellschaft, 1973.
ADLER, MAX, 'Kant und der Marxismus', Berlin, E. Laub, 1925.
ADLER, MAX, 'Das Rätsel der Gesellschaft. Zur Erkenntniskritischen Grundlegung der Sozialwissenschaft', Vienna, Saturn-Verlag, 1936.
ADORNO, THEODOR W., 'Dissonanzen', 4th edn, Göttingen, Vandenhoeck & Ruprecht, 1969.
ADORNO, THEODOR W., A European Scholar in America in D. Fleming and B. Bailyn (eds), 'The Intellectual Migration', Harvard University Press, 1969.
ADORNO, THEODOR W., 'Gesammelte Schriften', vol.8, Frankfurt, Suhrkamp, 1972.
ADORNO, THEODOR W., 'Negative Dialectics', New York, Seabury Press, 1973.
ADORNO, THEODOR W., 'Vorlesung zur Einleitung in die Soziologie', Frankfurt, Junius-Drucke, 1973.
ADORNO, THEODOR W., Sociology and Psychology, 'New Left Review', nos 46 and 47, 1967 and 1968.
ADORNO, THEODOR W., DAHRENDORF, R., ALBERT, H., HABERMAS, J., PILOT, H., and POPPER, K.R., 'The Positivist Dispute in German Sociology', London, Heinemann, 1976.

Bibliography

AJDUKIEWICZ, K., Three Concepts of Definition, in T.M. Olshewsky (ed.), 'Problems in the Philosophy of Language', New York, Holt, Reinhart & Winston, 1969.
ALBROW, MARTIN, 'Bureaucracy', London, Macmillan, 1970.
ALPERT, H., 'Emile Durkheim and His Sociology', New York, Russell, 1961.
ALTHUSSER, L., 'For Marx', London, Allen Lane, 1969.
ALTHUSSER, L., 'Essays in Self-Criticism', London, New Left Books, 1976.
ALTHUSSER, L., and BALIBAR, E., 'Reading Capital', London, New Left Books, 1970.
ANSCOMBE, E., On Brute Facts, 'Analysis', 18, 1958, pp.69-72.
APEL, KARL-OTTO, 'Analytic Philosophy of Language and the Geisteswissenschaften', Dordrecht, Reidel, 1967.
APEL, KARL-OTTO, Szientistik, Hermeneutik, Ideologiekritik in Apel et al., 'Hermeneutik und Ideologiekritik', 1971.
APEL, KARL-OTTO, The Apriori of Communication', 'Acta Sociologica', vol.13, no.1, 1972.
APEL, KARL-OTTO (ed.), 'Sprachpragmatik und Philosophie', Frankfurt, Suhrkamp, 1976.
APEL, KARL-OTTO, 'Transformation der Philosophie', 2 vols, Frankfurt, Suhrkamp, 1976.
APEL, KARL-OTTO, Types of Social Science in the Light of Human Cognitive Interests in S.C. Brown (ed.), 'Philosophical Disputes in the Social Sciences', Brighton, Harvester Press, 1979.
APEL, KARL-OTTO, 'Towards a Transformation of Philosophy', London, Routledge & Kegan Paul, 1980.
APEL, KARL-OTTO, BORMANN, C.V., BUBNER, R., GODAMER, H.-G., GIEGEL, H.J., and HABERMAS, J., 'Hermeneutik und Ideologiekritik: Theorie-Diskussion', Frankfurt, Suhrkamp, 1971.
ARATO, ANDREW, The Neo-Idealist Defense of Subjectivity, 'Telos', no.1, 1974.
ARON, R., 'German Sociology', Chicago, Free Press, 1964.
ARON, R., 'D'une sainte famille à l'autre', Paris, Gallimard, 1969.
ARON, R., 'La Philosophie critique de l'histoire', Paris, NRF, 1969.
AUSTIN, J.L., 'Philosophical Papers', 2nd edn, Oxford, Clarendon Press, 1970.
AYER, A.J., 'Language, Truth and Logic', London, Gollancz, 1936.
BACHELARD, GASTON, 'Le Nouvel Esprit scientifique', Paris, Presses Universitaires de France, 1934.
BACHELARD, GASTON, 'La Philosophie du non', Paris, Presses Universitaires de France, 1966.
BAIER, HORST, 'Von der Erkenntnistheorie zur Wirklichkeitswissenschaft', Habilitationsschrift, University of Münster, 1969.

BALDAMUS, G., 'The Structure of Sociological Inference', London, Martin Robertson, 1976.
BALIBAR, ETIENNE, From Bachelard to Althusser: The Concept of 'Epistemological Break', 'Economy and Society',vol.7, no.3, 1978.
BARNES, H.E., and BECKER, H. (eds), 'Contemporary Social Theory', New York, Appleton Century, 1940.
BAUMAN, ZYGMUNT, 'Hermeneutics and Social Science', London, Hutchinson, 1978.
BAUMGARTEN, EDUARD, 'Max Weber. Werk und Person', Tübingen, Mohr, 1964.
BEETHAM, DAVID, 'Max Weber and the Theory of Modern Politics', London, Allen & Unwin, 1974.
BENDIX, REINHARD, and BERGER, BENNETT, Images of Society and Problems of Concept Formation in Sociology, in Llewellyn Gross (ed.), 'Symposium on Sociological Theory', Evanston, Illinois; Row, Peterson, 1959.
BENDIX, REINHARD, and ROTH, GÜNTHER, 'Scholarship and Partisanship: Essays on Max Weber', University of California Press, 1971.
BENN, S.I., and MORTIMORE, G.W., 'Rationality and the Social Sciences', London, Routledge & Kegan Paul, 1977.
BENTON, TED, 'The Philosophical Foundations of the Three Sociologies', London, Routledge & Kegan Paul, 1977.
BENTON, TED, Realism and Social Science, 'Radical Philosophy', no.27, 1981.
BERGER, JOHANNES, Intersubjektive Sinnkonstitution und Sozialstruktur. Zur Kritik handlungstheoretischer Ansätze der Soziologie, 'Zeitschrift für Soziologie', 7, 4, 1978.
BERGER, PETER, and LUCKMANN, THOMAS, 'The Social Construction of Reality', Harmondsworth, Penguin, 1967.
BERGER, PETER, and PULLBERG, S., Reification and the Social Critique of Consciousness, 'New Left Review', vol.35, 1966.
BERLIN, ISAIAH, A Note on Vico's Concept of Knowledge, in G. Tagliacozzo and H. White (eds), 'Giambattista Vico. An International Symposium', Baltimore, Johns Hopkins Press, 1969.
BERLIN, ISAIAH, 'Vico and Herder', London, Hogarth, 1976.
BERSHADY, HAROLD, 'Ideology and Social Knowledge', Oxford, Blackwell, 1973.
BETTI, EMILIO, 'Die Hermeneutik als Allgemeine Methodik der Geisteswissenschaften', 2nd edn, Tübingen, Mohr, 1972.
BEYLEVELD, DERYCK, Epistemological Foundations of Sociological Theory, An Examination of Recent Critiques of Positivism, PhD thesis, University of East Anglia, 1975.
BHASKAR, ROY, 'A Realist Theory of Science', 2nd edn, Brighton, Harvester Press, 1978.
BHASKAR, ROY, 'The Possibility of Naturalism', Brighton, Harvester Press, 1979.

BIERSTEDT, ROBERT, Logic, Language and Sociology, PhD thesis, Columbia University, 1950.
BIERSTEDT, ROBERT, Nominal and Real Definitions in Sociological Theory, in L. Gross (ed.), 'Symposium on Sociological Theory', Evanston, Illinois, Row, Peterson, 1959; reprinted in 'Power and Progress. Essays on Sociological Theory', New York, McGraw-Hill, 1974.
BLACKBURN, ROBIN, 'Ideology in Social Science', London, Fontana, 1972.
BLAU, PETER, Critical Remarks on Weber's Theory of Authority, 'American Political Science Review', vol.57, no.2, 1963.
BLUMER, HERBERT, The Problem of the Concept in Social Psychology, 'American Journal of Sociology', vol.44, 1940.
BÖHME, GERNOT, Die Ausdifferenzierung wissenschaftlicher Diskurse, in N. Stehr and R. König (eds), 'Wissenschaftssoziologie', Sonderheft 18, 'Kölner Zeitschrift', Opladen, Westdeutscher Verlag, 1975.
BÖHME, GERNOT, The Social Function of Cognitive Structures: A Concept of the Scientific Community Within a Theory of Action, in K. Knorr, H. Strasser and H.G. Zilian (eds), 'Determinants and Controls of Scientific Development', Dordrecht and Boston, Reidel, 1975.
BÖHME, GERNOT (ed.), 'Protophysik. Für und wider eine konstruktive wissenschaftstheorie der Physik', Frankfurt, Suhrkamp, 1976.
BÖHME, GERNOT, and ENGELHARDT, M.V. (eds), 'Entfremdete Wissenschaft', Frankfurt, Suhrkamp, 1979.
BOSL, KARL, Der 'soziologische Aspekt' in der Geschichte, 'Historische Zeitschrift', vol.20, 1965.
BOTTOMORE, TOM, and GOODE, PATRICK (eds), 'Austro-Marxism', Oxford, Clarendon Press, 1978.
BOTTOMORE, TOM, and NISBET, ROBERT (eds), 'A History of Sociological Analysis', London, Heinemann, 1978.
BOUDON, RAYMOND, 'La crise de la sociologie', Geneva, Droz, 1971.
BOURDIEU, PIERRE, et al., 'Le métier de sociologue', 3rd edn, Paris and The Hague, Mouton, 1973.
BOURDIEU, PIERRE, Structuralism and the Theory of Sociological Knowledge, 'Social Research', vol.35, 1968, p.69.
BRENNAN, J.M., 'The Open-Texture of Moral Concepts', London, Macmillan, 1977.
BRIDGMAN, P.W., 'The Logic of Modern Physics', New York, Macmillan, 1954.
BRINCKMANN, HEINRICH (ed.), 'Sinnlichkeit und Abstraktion', Wiesbaden, Focus-Verlag, 1973.
BROWN, RICHARD, 'A Poetic for Sociology', Cambridge University Press, 1977.
BROWN, S.C. (ed.), 'Philosophical Disputes in the Social Sciences', Brighton, Harvester Press, 1979.

BRUUN, H.H., 'Science, Values and Politics in Max Weber's Methodology', Copenhagen, Munksgaard, 1972.
BRUYN, SEVERYN T., Rhetorical Devices in Sociological Theory, 'Sociological Quarterly', vol.5, 1964.
BUBNER, RÜDIGER, 'Dialektik und Wissenschaft', Frankfurt, Suhrkamp, 1973, 2nd edn, 1974.
BUBNER, RÜDIGER, KRAMER, K., and WIEHL, R. (eds), 'Neue Hefte für Philosophie', vol.9, 1976.
BUCKLEY, WALTER, 'Sociology and Modern Systems Theory', Englewood Cliffs, New Jersey, Prentice-Hall, 1967.
BUCK-MORSS, SUSAN, 'The Origin of Negative Dialectics', Brighton, Harvester Press, 1977.
BURGER, THOMAS, 'Max Weber's Theory of Concept Formation', Duke University Press, 1976.
BURKE, KENNETH, 'A Grammar of Motives', New York, Prentice-Hall, 1952.
CALVEZ, JEAN-YVES, 'La Pensée de Karl Marx', Paris, Seuil, 1956.
CARNAP, RUDOLF, 'The Logical Syntax of Language', London, Kegan Paul, Trench Trübner, 1937.
CARNAP, RUDOLF, Logical Foundations of the Unity of Science, 'International Encyclopedia of Unified Science', vol.1, no.1, University of Chicago Press, 1938.
CARNAP, RUDOLF, 'The Logical Structure of the World', London, Routledge & Kegan Paul, 1967.
SCHILPP, P.A. (ed.), 'The Philosophy of Rudolf Carnap' (see under Schilpp).
CARROLL, LEWIS, 'Alice', Oxford University Press, 1971
CARVER, T. (ed.), 'Karl Marx, Texts on Method', Oxford, Blackwell, 1975.
CASSIRER, ERNST, Transcendentalism, 'Encyclopedia Britannica', 14th edn, 1928.
CASSIRER, ERNST, Zur Theorie des Begriffs, 'Kant-Studien', vol.33, 1928.
CASSIRER, ERNST, The Influence of Language upon the Development of Scientific Thought, 'Journal of Philosophy', vol.39, 1942.
CASSIRER, ERNST, 'The Philosophy of Symbolic Forms', New Haven, Yale University Press, 1953.
SCHILPP, P.A. (ed.), 'The Philosophy of Ernst Cassirer' (see under Schilpp).
CASSIRER, H.W., 'A Commentary on Kant's "Critique of Judgement"', London, Methuen, 1938.
CERRUTTI, FURIO, Hegel, Lukács, Korsch, in O. Negt (ed.), 'Aktualität und Folgen der Philosophie Hegels', Frankfurt, Suhrkamp, 1970.
CHASE, STUART, 'The Tyranny of Words', London, Methuen, 1938.
COHEN, G.A., Review of Schmidt, 'Nature', in 'Radical

Philosophy', no.2, 1972.
COLLIER, ANDREW, In Defence of Epistemology, in John
Mepham and David Rub n (eds), 'Issues in Marxist Philo-
sophy', vol.III, Brighton, Harvester, 1979.
COMTE, AUGUSTE, 'System of Positive Polity', vol.2,
London, Longmans, 1875.
CONNOLLY, WILLIAM E., 'Political Science and Ideology',
New York, Atherton Press, 1967.
CONNOLLY, WILLIAM E., 'The Terms of Political Discourse',
Lexington, Mass., D.C. Heath, 1974.
COSER, LEWIS (ed.), 'Georg Simmel', Englewood Cliffs,
New Jersey, Prentice-Hall, 1965.
CROSLAND, MAURICE O., 'Historical Studies in the Language
of Chemistry', London, Heinemann, 1962.
CUTLER, ANTHONY, HINDESS, BARRY, HIRST, PAUL, and HUSSAIN,
ATHAR, 'Marx's Capital and Capitalism Today', London,
Routledge & Kegan Paul, vol.1, 1977; vol.2, 1978.
DALLMAYR, F. and McCARTHY, T. (eds), 'Understanding and
Social Inquiry', Notre Dame University Press, 1977.
DAWE, ALAN, Theories of Social Action, in Tom Bottomore
and Robert Nisbet (eds), 'A History of Sociological
Analysis', London, Heinemann, 1978.
DÖBERT, R., HABERMAS, J. and NUNNER-WINKLER, C. (eds),
'Die Entwicklung des Ichs', Cologne, Hain/KNO, 1977.
DRUCKER, H.M., Just Analogies? The Place of Analogies
in Political Thinking, 'Political Studies', 18, 4, 1970.
DUMONT, RICHARD G., and WILSON, W.J., Aspects of Concept
Formation, Explication and Theory Construction in Socio-
logy, 'American Sociological Review', vol.32, no.6, 1967.
DURKHEIM, EMILE, 'The Elementary Forms of the Religious
Life', London, Allen & Unwin, 1915.
DURKHEIM, 'The Rules of Sociological Method', Chicago,
Free Press, 1964.
DURKHEIM, EMILE, 'Les règles de la méthode sociologique',
Paris, Presses Universitaires de France, 1973.
DURKHEIM, EMILE, L'état actuel des études sociologiques
en France, 'La Riforma sociale', 1895, reprinted in
'Textes 1. Eléments d'une théorie sociale', ed. V.
Karady, Paris, Minuit, 1976.
EASLEA, BRIAN, 'Liberation and the Aims of Science. An
Essay on Obstacles to the Making of a Beautiful World',
Chatto & Windus for Sussex University Press, 1973.
EISEN, ARNOLD, The Meanings and Confusions of Weberian
'Rationality', 'British Journal of Sociology', vol.29,
no.1, March 1978.
EMBREE, LESTER (ed.), 'Life World and Consciousness.
Essays in memory of Aron Gurvitsch', Northwestern Univer-
sity Press, 1972.
ESAER, ERIC, Les principaux concepts pour une science

sociale, 'Revue de l'Institut de Sociologie', vol.49, no.1, 1976.
EUBANK, E.E., The Conceptual Approach to Sociology, in H.E. Barnes and H. Becker (eds), 'Contemporary Social Theory', New York, Appleton Century, 1940.
EUCKEN, WALTER, Wissenschaft im Stile Schmollers, 'Weltwirtschaftliches Archiv', 52, 2, 1940.
EUCKEN, WALTER, 'The Foundations of Economics', London, William Hodge, 1950.
FAIRCHILD, H.P., 'Dictionary of Sociology', New York, Philosophical Library, 1944.
FARIS, E., Review of 'The Social System', 'American Sociological Review', vol.18, 1953.
FEIGL, HERBERT, The Origin and Spirit of Logical Positivism, in P. Achinstein and S. Barker, 'The Legacy of Logical Positivism', Baltimore, Johns Hopkins Press, 1969.
FEYERABEND, PAUL, 'Against Method', London, New Left Books, 1975.
FILMER, PAUL, PHILLIPSON, MICHAEL, SILVERMAN, DAVID, and WALSH, DAVID, 'New Directions in Sociological Theory', London, Collier-Macmillan, 1972.
FINER, S.E., The Vocabulary of Political Science, 'Political Studies', vol.XXIII, nos 2-3, 1975.
FLECK, LUDWIK, 'Enstehung und Entwicklung einer Wissenschaftlichen Tatsache', Basel, B. Schwabe, 1935.
FLEMING, D., and BAILYN, B. (eds), 'The Intellectual Migration', Harvard University Press, 1969.
FORMAN, PAUL, Weimar Culture, Causality and Quantum Theory, 'Historical Studies in the Physical Sciences', vol.3, 1971.
FOUCAULT, M., 'The Order of Things', London, Tavistock, 1970.
FOUCAULT, M., 'The Archeology of Knowledge', London, Tavistock, 1972.
FRANCIS, EMERICH, Kultur und Gesellschaft in der Soziologie Max Webers, in 'Max Weber. Gedächtnisschrift der Ludwig-Maximilians-Universität München', Berlin, Duncker & Humblot, 1966.
FRANKFURT INSTITUTE FOR SOCIAL RESEARCH, 'Aspects of Sociology', London, Heinemann, 1973.
FREUD, SIGMUND, 'An Autobiographical Study', 2nd edn, London, Hogarth, 1946.
FREYER, HANS, 'Soziologie als Wirklichkeitswissenschaft', Leipzig and Berlin, Teubner, 1930.
GADAMER, HANS-GEORG, 'Truth and Method', London, Sheed & Ward, 1975.
GADAMER, HANS-GEORG, 'Philosophical Hermeneutics', University of California Press, 1976.
GALLIE, D., Essentially Contested Concepts, 'Proceedings

of the Aristotelian Society', New Series, LVI, 1955-6.
GARFINKEL, HAROLD, A Comparison of Decisions Made on
Four 'Pre-Theoretical' Problems by Talcott Parsons and
Alfred Schutz, unpublished paper, c.1960.
GARFINKEL, HAROLD, 'Studies in Ethnomethodology',
Englewood Cliffs, New Jersey, Prentice-Hall, 1967.
GASSEN, KURT, and LANDMANN, MICHAEL (eds), 'Buch des
Dankes an Georg Simmel', Berlin, Duncker & Humblot, 1958.
GEERTZ, CLIFFORD, 'The Interpretation of Cultures',
London, Hutchinson, 1975.
GERAS, NORMAN, Marx and the Critique of Classical Political Economy, in R. Blackburn (ed.), 'Ideology in Social
Science', London, Fontana, 1972.
GERHARDT, UTA, 'Rollenanalyse als kritische Soziologie',
Neuwied and Berlin, Luchterhand, 1971.
GIDDENS, A., 'New Rules of Sociological Method', London,
Hutchinson, 1976.
GIDDENS, A., 'Studies in Social and Political Theory',
London, Hutchinson, 1977.
GIDDENS, A., Positivism and its Critics, in Tom Bottomore
and Robert Nisbet (eds), 'A History of Sociological
Analysis', London, Heinemann, 1978.
GIDDENS, A., 'Central Problems in Social Theory', London,
Macmillan, 1979.
GODDARD, DAVID, Max Weber and the Objectivity of Social
Science, 'History and Theory', vol.12, 1973.
GODELIER, MAURICE, Qu'est-ce que définir une 'formation
économique et sociale'? L'exemple des Incas, 'La Pensée',
159, October 1971, translated in his 'Perspectives in
Marxist Anthropology', Cambridge University Press, 1977.
GOLDMANN, LUCIEN, 'Marxisme et sciences humaines', Paris,
Gallimard, 1970.
GOODFIELD, JUNE, and TOULMIN, STEPHEN, 'The Architecture
of Matter', London, Hutchinson, 1962.
GORMAN, RICHARD, 'The Dual Vision. Alfred Schutz and the
Myth of a Phenomenological Social Science', London,
Routledge & Kegan Paul, 1977.
GRAB, HERMANN, 'Der Begriff des Rationalen in der
Soziologie Max Webers', Karlsruhe, Braun, 1927.
GRANGER, G.-G., 'Pensée formelle et sciences de l'homme',
Paris, Aubier-Montagne, 1968.
GRATHOFF, RICHARD, Ansätze zu einer Theorie sozialen
Handelns bei Alfred Schutz, in R. Bubner et al., 'Neue
Hefte für Philosophie', vol.9, 1976.
GRATHOFF, RICHARD (ed.), 'The Theory of Social Action',
Indiana University Press, 1978.
GRAY, JOHN, On the Contestability of Social and Political
Concepts, 'Political Theory', vol.5, no.3, 1977.
GREEN, PHILIP, and LEVINSON, STANFORD (eds), 'Power and

Community', New York and Toronto, Random House, 1970.
GROSS, LL. (ed.), 'Symposium on Sociological Theory',
Evanston, Illinois, Row, Peterson, 1959.
GUSFIELD, JOSEPH R., 'Community. A Critical Response',
Oxford, Blackwell, 1975.
HABERMAS, J., 'Strukturwandel der Öffentlichkeit',
Neuwied and Berlin, Luchterhand, 1962.
HABERMAS, J., Der Universalitätsanspruch der Hermeneutik,
in K.-O. Apel et al, 'Hermeneutik und Ideologiekritik:
Theorie-Diskussion', Frankfurt, Suhrkamp, 1971.
HABERMAS, J., 'Toward a Rational Society', London, Heinemann, 1971.
HABERMAS, J., Zu Gadamers 'Wahrheit und Methode', in
K.-O. Apel et al., 'Hermeneutik und Ideologiekritik:
Theorie-Diskussion', Frankfurt, Suhrkamp, 1971.
HABERMAS, J., 'Zur Logik der Sozialwissenschaften', 2nd
edn, Frankfurt, Suhrkamp, 1971.
HABERMAS, J., 'Knowledge and Human Interests', London,
Heinemann, 1972.
HABERMAS, J., A Postscript to 'Knowledge and Human Interests', 'Philosophy of the Social Sciences', vol.3, no.2,
1973.
HABERMAS, J., 'Theory and Practice', London, Heinemann,
1974.
HABERMAS, J., 'Zur Rekonstruktion des Historischen
Materialismus', Frankfurt, Suhrkamp, 1976.
HABERMAS, J., 'Theorie und Praxis', Frankfurt, Suhrkamp,
1978.
HABERMAS, J., 'Communication and the Evolution of
Society', Boston, Beacon Press, 1979.
HABERMAS, J., 'Die Entwicklung des Ichs', see R. Döbert.
HABERMAS, J., and LUHMANN, N., 'Theorie der Gesellschaft
oder Sozialtechnologie - Was Leistet die Systemforschung?',
Frankfurt, Suhrkamp, 1971.
HALFPENNY, PETER, 'Explanations in Sociology: Positivist
and Interpretivist Models', PhD thesis, Essex, 1976;
Manchester University Press, forthcoming.
HANSON, N.R., Logical Positivism and the Interpretation
of Scientific Theories, in P. Achinstein and S. Barker
(eds), 'The Legacy of Logical Positivism', Baltimore,
Johns Hopkins Press, 1969.
HARRE, R., 'The Principles of Scientific Thinking',
London, Macmillan, 1970.
HARRE, R., 'The Philosophies of Science', Oxford University Press, 1972.
HARRE, R., 'Social Being', Oxford, Blackwell, 1979.
HARRE, R., and MADDEN, E.H., 'Causal Powers', Oxford,
Blackwell, 1975.
HARRE, R., and SECORD, P.F., 'The Explanation of Social

Behaviour, Oxford, Blackwell, 1972.
HARRIS, C.C., 'Fundamental Concepts and the Sociological Enterprise', London, Croom Helm, 1980.
HART, HORNELL, Abridged Report of the Sub-Committee on the Definition of Definition, 'American Sociological Review', vol.8, 1943.
HAVRILESKY, THOMAS, On Definitional Controversy in Economics, 'American Journal of Economics and Sociology', 27, 1, 1968.
HEGEL, G.W.F., 'Lectures on the History of Philosophy', London, Kegan Paul, 1895.
HEGEL, G.W.F., 'Wissenschaft der Logik', Hamburg, Meiner, 1978, translated as 'Science of Logic', London, Allen & Unwin, 1929.
HEGEL, G.W.F., 'Encyclopedia of the Philosophical Sciences', New York, Philosophical Library, 1959.
HEGEL, G.W.F., 'The Phenomenology of Spirit', trans. A. Miller, Oxford, Clarendon Press, 1977.
HEGEL, G.W.F., 'Phänomenologie des Geistes', Hamburg, Meiner, 1952.
HEGEL, G.W.F., 'The Philosophy of History', trans. J. Sibnee, London, Constable, 1956.
HEINTEL, ERICH, Gegenstandskonstitution und Sprachliches Weltbild, in Helmut Gipper (ed.), 'Sprache, Schlüssel zur Welt. Festschrift für Leo Weisgerber', Dusseldorf, Schwann, 1959.
HEMPEL, C.G., Fundamentals of Concept Formation in Empirical Science, 'International Encyclopedia', vol.II, no.7, 1952.
HEMPEL, C.G., Reduction: Ontological and Linguistic Facets, in S. Morgenbesser et al., 'Philosophy, Science and Method. Essays in Honor of Ernest Nagel', New York, St Martin's Press, 1969.
HEMPEL, C.G. and OPPENHEIM, P., 'Der Typusbegriff im Lichte der Neuen Logik', Leiden, Sijthoff, 1936.
HENRICH, DIETER, 'Die Einheit der Wissenschaftslehre Max Webers', Tübingen, Mohr, 1952.
HENRICH, DIETER (ed.), 'Hegel im Kontext', Frankfurt, Suhrkamp, 1971.
HESSE, MARY, 'The Structure of Scientific Inference', London, Macmillan, 1974.
HEYMANS, GERARD, Zur Cassirerschen Reform der Begriffslehre, 'Kant-Studien', 33, 1928.
HICKS, J.R. and WEBER, W., 'Carl Menger and the Austrian School of Economics', Oxford, Clarendon Press, 1973.
HINDESS, BARRY, 'Mode of Production and Social Formation', London, Macmillan, 1977.
HINDESS, BARRY, 'Philosophy and Methodology in the Social Sciences', Brighton, Harvester, 1977.

HINDESS, BARRY, 'Sociological Theories of the Economy', London, Macmillan, 1977.
HINDESS, BARRY, and HIRST, PAUL, 'Pre-Capitalist Modes of Production', London, Routledge & Kegan Paul, 1975.
HINTIKKA, JAAKO (ed.), 'Rudolf Carnap. Logical Empiricist', Synthese Library, vol.73, Dordrecht and Boston, Reidel, 1975.
HIRST, PAUL, Morphology and Pathology, 'Economy and Society', vol.2, no.1, 1973.
HIRST, PAUL, 'Durkheim, Bernard and Epistemology', London, Routledge & Kegan Paul, 1975.
HIRST, PAUL, 'Social Evolution and Sociological Categories', London, Allen & Unwin, 1976.
HOGREBE, W., 'Historisches Worterbuch der Philosophie', Darmstadt, Wissenschaftliche Buchgesellschaft, 1976.
HOGREBE, W., Konstitution, 'Historisches Worterbuch der Philosophie', Darmstadt, Wissenschaftliche Buchgesellschaft, 1976.
HOLLIS, MARTIN, The Limits of Irrationality, 'Archieves Européennes de Sociologie VIII 2', 1967, reprinted in Bryan Wilson (ed.), 'Rationality', Oxford, Blackwell, 1974.
HOLLIS, MARTIN, and NELL, EDWARD, 'Rational Economic Man. A Philosophical Critique of Neo-Classical Economics', Cambridge University Press, 1975.
HOLLIS, MARTIN, 'Models of Man', Cambridge University Press, 1977.
HORKHEIMER, MAX, Zum Rationalismusstreit in der gegenwärtigen Philosophie, in 'Kritische Theorie', I, Frankfurt, Fischer, 1968.
HUSSERL, EDMUND, Phenomenology, 'Encyclopedia Britannica', 14th edn, 1946.
HUSSERL, EDMUND, 'Ideen zu einer reinen Phänomenolgie und phänomenologischen Philosophie', vol.III, 'Husserliana', vol.V, The Hague, Nijhoff, 1952.
HUSSERL, EDMUND, 'Cartesian Meditations', The Hague, Nijhoff, 1960.
HUSSERL, EDMUND, 'The Crisis of European Sciences and Transcendental Phenomenology', Northwestern University Press, 1970.
HUTTEN, ERNEST H., 'The Language of Modern Physics', London, Allen & Unwin, 1956.
ITZKOFF, S.M., 'Ernst Cassirer: Scientific Knowledge and the Concept of Man', University of Notre Dame Press, 1971.
JÄCKEL, E., and WEYMAR, E. (eds), 'Die Funktion der Geschichte in Unserer Zeit', Stuttgart, Klett, 1975.
JAMMER, MAX, 'Concepts of Force. A Study in the Foundations of Dynamics', Harvard University Press, 1957.
JAY, MARTIN, 'The Dialectical Imagination. A History of

the Frankfurt School and the Institute for Social Research 1923-1950', London, Heinemann, 1973.
JENKS, CHRIS (ed.), 'Rationality, Education and the Social Organisation of Knowledge', London, Routledge & Kegan Paul, 1977.
KALLEBERG, ARTHUR L., Concept Formation in Normative and Empirical Studies: Toward Reconciliation in Political Theory, 'American Political Science Review', vol.63, 1969.
KANT, I., 'Critique of Judgement', trans. J.C. Meredith, Oxford University Press, 1952.
KANT, I., 'Critique of Pure Reason', trans. Kemp Smith, London, Macmillan, 1964.
KAPLAN, ABRAHAM, 'The Conduct of Inquiry', San Francisco, Chandler, 1964.
KAPLAN, DAVID, Significance and Analyticity, in Jaako Hintikka (ed.), 'Rudulf Carnap, Logical Empiricist', Synthese Library, vol.73, Dordrecht and Boston, Reidel, 1975.
KARRENBERG, F. and ALBERT, H. (eds), 'Sozialwissenschaft und Gesellschaftsgestaltung. Festschrift für G. Weisser', Berlin, Duncker & Humblot, 1963.
KAUFMANN, FELIX, Logik und Wirtschaftswissenschaft, 'Archiv für Sozialwissenschaft und Sozialpolitik', vol. 54, no.3, 1925.
KAUFMANN, FELIX, 'Methodenlehre der Sozialwissenschaften', Vienna, Springer, 1936. Abridged as 'Methodology of the Social Sciences', New York, Humanities Press, 1958.
KAUFMANN, FRITZ, Cassirer, Neo-Kantianism and Phenomenology, in P.A. Schilpp (ed.), 'The Philosophy of Ernst Cassirer', the Library of Living Philosophers, vol.VI, Evanston, Illinois, 1949.
KEAT, RUSSELL, and URRY, JOHN, 'Social Theory as Science', London, Routledge & Kegan Paul, 1975.
KENNY, A.J., 'Action, Emotion and Will', London, Routledge & Kegan Paul, 1963.
KEPPLINGER, H.M., Probleme der Begriffsbildung in den Sozialwissenschaften: Begriff und Gegenstand Öffentliche Meinung, 'Kölner Zeitschrift für Soziologie und Sozialpsychologie', 29, 1977.
KERN, ISO, 'Husserl und Kant. Eine Untersuchung über Husserls Verhältnis zu Kant und zum Neukantianismus', The Hague, Nijhoff, 1964.
KOCKA, JÜRGEN, Karl Marx und Max Weber im Vergleich. Sozialwissenschaft zwischen Dogmatismus und Dezisionismus, in H.-U. Wehler (ed.), 'Geschichte und Ökonomie', Cologne, Kiepenheuer & Witsch, 1972.
KOLAKOWSKI, L., 'Marxism and Beyond', London, Pall Mall Press, 1969; Paladin, 1971.
KOLAKOWSKI, L., 'Positivist Philosophy. From Hume to the Vienna Circle', Harmondsworth, Penguin, 1972.

KOLAKOWSKI, L., 'Husserl and the Search for Certitude', New Haven and London, Yale University Press, 1975.
KÖNIG, RENE, Grundlagenprobleme der soziologischen Forschungsmethoden (Modelle, Theorien, Kategorien), in F. Karrenberg and Hans Albert (eds), 'Sozialwissenschaft und Gesellschaftsgestaltung. Festschrift für G. Weisser', Berlin Duncker & Humblot, 1963.
KÖNIG, RENE (ed.), 'Handbuch der empirischen Sozialforschung', 2nd edn, Stuttgart, Enke, 1967.
KORZYBSKI, ALFRED, 'Science and Sanity', Lakeland, Conn., International Non-Aristotelian Publishing Company, 1958.
KRAHL, HANS-JÜRGEN, 'Konstitution und Klassenkampf', Frankfurt, Verlag Neue Kritik, 1971. See also Brinkmann.
KRECKEL, REINHART, 'Soziologische Erkenntnis und Geschichte', Opladen, Westdeutscher Verlag, 1972.
KUHN, THOMAS, 'The Structure of Scientific Revolutions', University of Chicago Press, 1962, 1970.
LACHENMEYER, CHARLES, 'The Language of Sociology', Columbia University Press, 1971.
LACLAU, ERNESTO, 'Politics and Ideology in Marxist Theory', London, New Left Books, 1977.
LAVINE, T.Z., Knowledge as Interpretation: An Historical Survey, 'Philosophy and Phenomenological Research', vols 10 and 11, 1950, pp.526-40, 88-102.
LAZARSFELD, PAUL, and BOUDON, RAYMOND, Les fonctions de la formalisation en sociologie, 'Archives Européennes de Sociologie', vol.4, 1963.
LAZARSFELD, PAUL, and ROSENBERG, (eds), 'The Language of Social Research', Chicago, Free Press, 1955.
LAZARSFELD, PAUL, Max Weber and Empirical Social Research, 'American Sociological Review', vol.30, 1965.
LAZARSFELD, PAUL, Historical Notes on the Empirical Study of Action, 'American Sociological Review', 1965. Reprinted in Lazarsfeld, 'Qualitative Analysis', Boston, Alleyn & Bacon, 1972.
LEACH, EDMUND, 'Political Systems of Highland Burma', London, Bell, 1954.
LEFEVRE, WOLFGANG, 'Zum historischen Charakter und zur historischen Funktion bürgerlicher Soziologie', Frankfurt, Suhrkamp, 1971.
LEVI-STRAUSS, CLAUDE, 'Structural Anthropology', London, Allen Lane, 1968.
LEVI-STRAUSS, CLAUDE, 'Tristes Tropiques, London, Cape,1973.
LIEBER, H.-J., and FURTH, P., Zur Dialektik der Simmelschen Konzeption einer Formalen Soziologie, in K. Gassen and M. Landmann (eds), 'Buch des Dankes an Georg Simmel', Berlin, Dunker & Humblot, 1958.
LIPP, WOLFGANG, Handlung und Herrschaft - Systemkategorien bei V. Pareto, M. Weber und T. Parsons, 'Jahrbuch für Soziologie', 19, 3, 1968.

LOBKOWITZ, NICHOLAS, Interest and Objectivity, 'Philosophy of the Social Sciences', vol.2, 1972.
LÖWE, ADOLF, Uber den Sinn und die Grenzen verstehender Nationalökonomie, 'Weltwirtschaftliches Archiv', 36, 2, 1932.
LÖWE, ADOLF, 'Economics and Sociology', London, Allen & Unwin, 1935.
LÖWITH, KARL, Max Weber und Karl Marx, 'Archiv für Sozialwissenschaft und Sozialpolitik', vol.67, 1932. Reprinted in Löwith, 'Gesammelte Abhandlungen', Stuttgart, Kohlhammer, 1960. Partially translated in D. Wrong (ed.), 'Max Weber', Englewood Cliffs, New Jersey, Prentice-Hall, 1970. Translation ed. T. Bottomore and W. Outhwaite, London, Allen & Unwin, 1982.
LÖWITH, KARL, Die Entzauberung der Welt durch Wissenschaft, 'Merkur', vol.18, 1964.
LÜBBE, HERMANN, Positivism and Phenomenology - Mach and Husserl, in T. Luckmann (ed.), 'Phenomenology and Sociology', Harmondsworth, Penguin, 1978.
LUCKMANN, THOMAS, On the Boundaries of the Social World, in M. Natanson (ed.), 'Phenomenology and Social Reality. Essays in Memory of Alfred Schutz', The Hague, Nijhoff, 1970.
LUCKMANN, THOMAS (ed.), 'Phenomenology and Sociology', Harmondsworth, Penguin, 1978.
LUKACS, GEORG, 'History and Class Consciousness', London, Merlin, 1971.
LUKACS, GEORG, Die Ontologischen Grundlagen des Menschlichen Denkens und Handelns, in 'Autorität - Organisation - Revolution', The Hague, von Eversdijck, 1972.
LUKACS, GEORG, 'Zur Ontologie des Gesellschaftlichen Seins. Die Arbeit', Neuwied and Darmstadt, Luchterhand, 1973.
LUKACS, GEORG, 'The Ontology of Social Being', 2 vols: 'Hegel's False and His Genuine Ontology'; 'Marx's Basic Ontological Principles'; London, Merlin, 1978.
LUKES, STEVEN, Some Problems About Rationality, 'Archives Européennes de Sociologie VIII 2', 1967, reprinted in Bryan Wilson (ed.), 'Rationality', Oxford, Blackwell, 1974.
LUKES, STEVEN, 'Emile Durkheim', London, Allen Lane, 1973.
LUKES, STEVEN, 'Power. A Radical View', London, Macmillan, 1974.
LUKES, STEVEN, Relativism, Cognitive and Moral, 'Proceedings of the Aristotelian Society', Supplementary Volume, 1974.
LUKES, STEVEN, On the Relativity of Power, in S.C. Brown (ed.), 'Philosophical Disputes in the Social Sciences', Brighton, Harvester Press, 1979.
LUNDBERG, GEORGE, Operational Definitions in the Social Sciences, 'American Journal of Sociology', vol.47, no.5, 1942.

LUNDBERG, GEORGE, 'Sociology', 3th edn, New York, Harper & Row, 1968.
McCARTHY, THOMAS, 'The Critical Theory of Jürgen Habermas', London, Hutchinson, 1978.
MACHLUP, FRITZ, Idealtypus, Wirklichkeit und Konstruktion, 'Ordo', vol.12, 1960-1.
MACHLUP, FRITZ, 'Essays on Economic Semantics', Englewood Cliffs, New Jersey, Prentice-Hall, 1963.
MacINTYRE, ALASDAIR, Is a Science of Comparative Politics Possible?, in Alan Ryan (ed.), 'The Philosophy of Social Explanation', Oxford University Press, 1973.
MANNHEIM, KARL, 'Essays on Sociology and Social Psychology', London, Routledge & Kegan Paul, 1953.
MARCUSE, HERBERT, 'Reason and Revolution', 2nd edn, London, Routledge & Kegan Paul, 1955.
MARCUSE, HERBERT, 'One Dimensional Man', London, Routledge & Kegan Paul, 1964.
MARCUSE, HERBERT, 'Negations', London, Allen Lane, 1968.
MARGENAU, HENRY, 'The Nature of Physical Reality', New York, McGraw-Hill, 1950.
MARGOLIS MICHAEL, The New Language of Political Science, 'Polity', vol.3, part 3, 1971.
MARX, KARL, 'The German Ideology', London, Lawrence & Wishart, 1965.
MARX, KARL, 'Capital', vol.III, Harmondsworth, Penguin, 1981.
MARX, KARL, 'Grundrisse', Harmondsworth, Penguin, 1973.
MARX, KARL, 'The German Ideology', part I, ed. Chris Arthur, London, Lawrence & Wishart, 1974.
MARX, KARL, 'Karl Marx. Early Writings', Harmondsworth, Penguin, 1975.
MARX, KARL, 'Capital', vol.I, Harmondsworth, Penguin, 1976.
MARX, KARL, and ENGELS, FRIEDRICH, 'Marx-Engels Selected Correspondence', London, Lawrence & Wishart, 1941.
MELDEN, A.I., 'Free Action', London, Routledge & Kegan Paul, 1961.
MENGER, C., 'Untersuchungen über die Methode der Sozialwissenschaften und der Politischen Ökonomie insbesondere', Leipzig, 1883.
MENGER, C., 'Kleinere Schriften zur Methode und Geschichte der Volkswirtschaftslehre', 'Collected Works', vol.III, London School of Economics, 1935.
MENGER, C., 'Problems of Economics and Sociology', University of Illinois Press, 1963.
MEPHAM, JOHN, and RUBEN, D.-H. (eds), 'Issues in Marxist Philosophy', 3 vols, Brighton, Harvester Press, 1979.
MERTON, ROBERT, 'Social Theory and Social Structure', Chicago, Free Press, 1957.

MEYERSON, EMILE, 'La déduction relativiste', Paris, Payot, 1925.
MILL, JOHN STUART, 'A System of Logic', 2 vols, London, Longmans, 1868.
MOMMSEN, WOLFGANG, Max Weber's Political Sociology and Philosophy of World History, 'International Social Science Journal', vol.17, 1965. 'Historische Zeitschrift', vol.201, 1965.
MOMMSEN, WOLFGANG, 'The Age of Bureaucracy', Oxford, Blackwell, 1974.
MONNEROT, JULES, 'Les faits sociaux ne sont pas des choses', Paris, Gallimard, 1946.
MORGAN, GARETH (ed.), 'Beyond Method' (forthcoming).
MORGENBESSER, S., SUPPES, P., and WHITE, M. (eds), 'Philosophy, Science and Method. Essays in Honor of Ernest Nagel', New York, St Martin's Press, 1969.
MÜHLMANN, WILHELM, 'Max Weber und die Rationale Soziologie', Tübingen, Mohr, 1966.
MULKAY, M., 'Science and the Sociology of Knowledge', London, Allen & Unwin, 1979.
MÜLLER, GERT H., The Notion of Rationality in the Work of Max Weber, 'Archives Européennes de Sociologie', vol.XX, 1979.
MÜLLER, HANS, 'Ursprung und Geschichte des Wortes Sozialismus und seiner Verwandten', Hanover, Dietz, 1967.
MURVAR, VATRO, Some Reflections on Weber's Typology of Herrschaft, 'Sociological Quarterly', vol.5, 1964.
NAGEL, E., 'The Structure of Science', London, Routledge & Kegan Paul, 1961.
NARR, WOLF-DIETER, and OFFE, CLAUS (eds), 'Wohlfahrtsstaat und Massenloyalität', Cologne, Kiepenheuer & Witsch, 1975.
NATANSON, MAURICE, 'Philosophy of the Social Sciences', New York, Random House, 1963.
NATANSON, MAURICE (ed.), 'Phenomenology and Social Reality. Essays in Memory of Alfred Schutz', The Hague, Nijhoff, 1970.
NATORP, PAUL, Kant und die Marburger Schule, 'Kant-Studien', vol.17, 1912.
NATORP, PAUL, 'Allgemeine Psychologie', Tübingen, Mohr, 1921.
NATORP, PAUL, 'Platons Ideenlehre', 2nd edn, Leipzig, F. Meiner, 1921.
NEGT, OSKAR (ed.), 'Aktualität und Folgen der Philosophie Hegels', Frankfurt, Suhrkamp, 1970.
NEISSER, HANS, Der Gegensatz von 'anschaulich' und 'rational' in der Geschichte der Volkswirtschaftslehre, 'Archiv für Soziologie und Sozialpolitik', vol.65, no.2, 1931.
NEURATH, OTTO, 'Empiricism and Sociology', ed. M. Neurath and R.S. Cohen, Dordrecht and Boston, Reidel, 1973.

NIETZSCHE, F., 'The Will to Power', ed. O. Levy, Edinburgh and London, Foulis, 1910.
NIETZSCHE, F., 'The Genealogy of Morals: an Attack', New York, Doubleday, 1966.
NIETZSCHE, F., 'Erkenntnistheoretische Schriften', Frankfurt, Suhrkamp, 1968.
NIETZSCHE, F., 'The Gay Science', New York, Random House, 1974.
NORMAND, CLAUDINE, 'Métaphore et Concept', Brussels, Edition Complexe, 1976; distributed by Presses Universitaires de France.
OGDEN, C.R., and RICHARDS, I.A., 'The Meaning of Meaning', London, Kegan Paul, 1923.
OLLMAN, B., Marx's Use of 'Class', 'American Journal of Sociology', 73, 5, 1968.
OLLMAN, G., 'Alienation', Cambridge University Press, 1971.
OLSHEWSKY, T.M. (ed.), 'Problems in the Philosophy of Language', New York, Holt, Reinhart & Winston, 1969.
OPPENHEIM, FELIX, 'Political Concepts. A Reconstruction', Oxford, Blackwell, 1981.
OPPENHEIM, P., Die Denkfläche. Statische und Dynamische Grundgesetze der Wissenschaftlichen Begriffsbildung, Kant-Studien, Erganzungsheft, 62, 1928.
OPPENHEIM, P. and PUTNAM, H., Unity of Science as a Working Hypothesis, in H. Feigl, M. Scriven and G. Maxwell (eds), 'Concepts, Theories and the Mind-Body Problem', Minnesota Studies in the Philosophy of Science, vol.II, University of Minnesota Press, 1958.
See also C.G. Hempel and P. Oppenheim, 'Typusbegriff'.
OPPENHEIMER, HANS, 'Die Logik der Soziologischen Begriffsbildung mit Besonderer Berücksichtigung von Max Weber', Tübingen, Mohr, 1925.
OSSOWSKI, STANISLAW, 'Class Structure in the Social Consciousness', London, Routledge & Kegan Paul, 1963.
OUTHWAITE, WILLIAM, 'Understanding Social Life. The Method Called Verstehen', London, Allen & Unwin, 1975.
OUTHWAITE, WILLIAM, Social Thought and Social Science, 'New Cambridge Modern History', vol.XIII, companion vol., ed. Peter Burke, Cambridge University Press, 1979.
PAP, ARTHUR, 'Semantics and Necessary Truth', Yale University Press, 1958.
PAPINEAU, DAVID, Ideal Types and Empirical Theories, 'British Journal for Philosophy of Science', vol.27, no.2, 1976.
PAPINEAU, DAVID, 'For Science in the Social Sciences', London, Macmillan, 1978.
PARETO, V., 'The Mind and Society', London, Cape, 1935.
PARSONS, ARTHUR S., Interpretive Sociology: The Theoretical Significance of Verstehen in the Constitution of

Social Reality, 'Human Studies', 1, 1978.
PARSONS, TALCOTT, 'The Social System', Chicago, Free Press, 1951.
PARSONS, TALCOTT, 'The Structure of Social Action', New York, Free Press, 1968.
PASSMORE, JOHN, 'A Hundred Years of Philosophy', Harmondsworth, Penguin, 1968.
PEEL, JOHN D.Y., 'Herbert Spencer', London, Heinemann, 1971.
PERMAN, DAVID, Metaphor, Cliche & Social Theory: An Analysis of the Connection between Images & Sociological Concepts, University of Birmingham, Faculty of Commerce and Social Science, Discussion Papers Series E, no.21, 1973.
PERMAN, DAVID, The Artful Face of Sociology, 'Sociology', vol.12, no.13, 1978.
PERRY, CHARNER, The Semantics of Political Science, 'American Political Science Review', vol.44, no.2, 1950.
PITKIN, HANNA, 'Wittgenstein and Justice', University of California Press, 1972.
PIVCEVIC, EDO, Concepts, Phenomenology and Philosophical Understanding, in Pivčević (ed.), 'Phenomenology and Philosophical Understanding', Cambridge University Press, 1975.
POMPA, LEON, 'Vico', Cambridge University Press, 1975.
POPPER, KARL, 'Conjectures and Refutations', 3rd edn, London, Routledge & Kegan Paul, 1969.
POPPER, KARL, 'Objective Knowledge', Oxford University Press, 1972.
POPPER, KARL, 'The Logic of Scientific Discovery', London, Hutchinson, 6th impression, 1972.
QUINE, W.V.O., 'Ontological Relativity and Other Essays', New York and London, Columbia University Press, 1969.
RADCLIFFE-BROWN, A.R., 'A Natural Science of Society', 2nd edn, Chicago, Free Press, 1957.
RADNITZSKY, GERARD, 'Contemporary Schools of Metascience', vol.I, Akademiförlaget Göteborg, 1968.
RANCIERE, JACQUES, 'Lire le Capital', vol.III, Paris, Maspéro, 1973.
RANCIERE, JACQUES, On the theory of ideology, 'Radical Philosophy', no.7, Spring 1974.
RASMUSSEN, DAVID, Towards a Theory of Social Constitution, unpublished paper, c.1978.
RICKERT, HEINRICH, 'Der Gegenstand der Erkenntnis', Tübingen, Mohr, 1892.
RICKERT, HENRICH, 'Die Grenzen der Naturwissenschaftlichen Begriffsbildung', Tübingen, Mohr, 1902, 1921.
RICKERT, HEINRICH, 'Naturwissenschaft und Geisteswissenschaft', Tübingen, Mohr, 1899, 1926. Translated as 'Science and History', New York, Van Nostrand, 1962.

RICOEUR, PAUL, Herméneutique et critique des ideologies, tr. in Paul Ricoeur, 'Essays on Hermeneutics', ed. John Thompson, Cambridge University Press, 1981.
RITTER, JOACHIM, 'Historisches Wörterbuch der Philosophie', Darmstadt, Wissenschaftliche Buchgesellschaft, 1974.
ROBINSON, RICHARD, 'Definition', Oxford University Press, 1954, reprinted 1962.
ROHLFES, JOACHIM, Beobachtungen zur Begriffsbildung in den Geschichtswissenschaften, in E. Jäckel and E. Weymar (eds), 'Die Funktion der Geschichte in Unserer Zeit', Stuttgart, Klett, 1975.
RORTY, RICHARD (ed.), 'The Linguistic Turn', University of Chicago Press, 1967.
ROSE, GILLIAN, 'The Melancholy Science', London, Macmillan, 1978.
ROSE, GILLIAN, 'Hegel contra Sociology', London, Athlone Press, 1981.
RUBEN, DAVID-HILLEL, 'Marxism and Materialism: A Study in Marxist Theory of Knowledge', 2nd edn, Brighton, Harvester Press, 1979.
RUDNER, M., 'Philosophy of Social Science', Englewood Cliffs, New Jersey, Prentice-Hall, 1966.
RUDNER, M. and WINOKUR, S. (eds), 'Analyses of Theories and Methods of Physics and Psychology', Minnesota Studies in the Philosophy of Science, vol.4, University of Minnesota Press, 1970.
RUNCIMAN, W.G., 'Sociology in its Place', Cambridge University Press, 1970.
RUNCIMAN, W.G., Describing, 'Mind', 81, 1972.
RUNCIMAN, W.G., 'A Critique of Max Weber's Philosophy of Science', Cambridge University Press, 1972.
RUNCIMAN, W.G. (ed.), 'Max Weber. Selections in Translation', Cambridge University Press, 1978.
RUSSELL, B. and WHITEHEAD, A.N., 'Principia Mathematica', Cambridge University Press, 1910.
RYAN, ALAN, Deductive Explanation in the Social Sciences, part II, 'Proceedings of the Aristotelian Society', supplementary volume XLVII, 1973.
RYAN, ALAN (ed.), 'The Philosophy of Social Explanation', Oxford University Press, 1973.
SALIN, EDGAR (ed.), 'Synopsis. Festgabe für Alfred Weber', Heidelberg, L. Schneider, 1948.
SALIN, EDGAR, 'Politische Ökonomie', Tübingen, Mohr, 1967.
SALOMON, GOTTFRIED, 'Historischer Materialismus und Ideologienlehre', vol.I, 'Jahrbuch für Soziologie II', Karlsruhe, 1926.
SANDER, FRITZ, Der Gegenstand der reinen Gesellschaftslehre, 'Archiv für Sozialwissenschaft', vol.54, no.2, 1925.
de SANTILLANA, GEORGE, Aspects of Scientific Rationalism

in the Nineteenth Century, 'International Encyclopedia of Unified Science', vol.II, no.8, University of Chicago Press, 1941.
SARTORI, GIOVANNI, RIGGS, FRED W., and TEUNE, HENRY, 'Tower of Babel. On the Definition and Analysis of Concepts in the Social Sciences', International Studies Association, Occasional Paper no.6, University of Pittsburgh, 1975.
SAYER, DEREK, 'Marx's Method. Ideology, Science and Critique in "Capital"', Brighton, Harvester Press, 1979.
SCHAAF, J.J., 'Geschichte und Begriff. Eine Kritische Studie zur Geschichtsmethodologie von E. Troeltsch und Max Weber', Tübingen, Mohr, 1946.
SCHAAR, JOHN, Reflections on Authority, 'New American Review', vol.8, 1970. Reprinted in P. Green and S. Levinson (eds), 'Power and Community', New York and Toronto, Random House, 1970.
SCHELER, MAX, 'Die Wissensformen und die Gesellschaft', 'Werke', 2nd edn, vol.8, Bern, Francke Verlag, 1960.
SCHELER, MAX, 'Problems of the Sociology of Knowledge', ed. Kenneth Stikkers, London, Routledge & Kegan Paul, 1980.
SCHEUCH, ERWIN K., and KUTSCH, TH., 'Grundbegriffe der Soziologie', vol.I, Stuttgart, Teubner, 2nd edn, 1975.
SCHILPP, P.A. (ed.), 'The Philosophy of Ernst Cassirer', The Library of Living Philosophers, vol.VI, New York, Tudor Press, 1949.
SCHILPP, P.A. (ed.), 'The Philosophy of Bertrand Russell', The Library of Living Philosophers, New York, Tudor Press, 1944, 1951.
SCHILPP, P.A. (ed.), 'The Philosophy of Rudolf Carnap', The Library of Living Philosophers, vol.XI, New York, Tudor Press, 1963.
SCHLICK, MORITZ, 'Allgemeine Erkenntnislehre', 2nd edn, Berlin, Springer, 1925.
SCHLUCHTER, WOLFGANG, 'Wertfreiheit und Verantwortungsethik', Tübingen, Mohr, 1971.
SCHMIDT, ALFRED (ed.), 'Beiträge zur Marxistischen Erkenntnistheorie', Frankfurt, Suhrkamp, 1969.
SCHMIDT, ALFRED, 'The Concept of Nature in Marx', London, New Left Books, 1971.
SCHOLZ, HENRICH, and SCHWEITZER, HERMANN, 'Die Sogenannten Definitionen durch Abstraktion', Leipzig, Meiner, 1935.
SCHRADER-KLEBERT, KARIN, Der Begriff der Gesellschaft als Regulative Idee. Zur Transzendentalen Begründung der Soziologie bei Georg Simmel, 'Soziale Welt', 19, 2, 1968.
SCHUTZ, A., 'Collected Papers', vol.I, 'The Problem of Social Reality', ed. M. Natanson, The Hague, Nijhoff, 1962.
SCHUTZ, A., 'Collected Papers', vol.II, 'Studies in Social Theory', ed. Arvid Brodersen, The Hague, Nijhoff, 1964.

SCHUTZ, A., Choice and the Social Sciences, in L.E. Embree (ed.), 'The Phenomenology of the Social World', London, Heinemann, 1972.
SCHUTZ, A., Subjective Action and Objective Interpretation, in 'The Annals of Phenomenological Sociology', vol.I, 1976.
SCRIVEN, MICHAEL, Definitions, Explanations and Theories, in 'Minnesota Studies in the Philosophy of Science', vol.II, University of Minnesota Press, 1958.
SCHULZ, WALTER, 'Philosophie in der Veränderten Welt', Pfüllingen, Neske, 1972.
'La Sémantique dans les Sciences', Colloque de l'Académie Internationale de Philosophie des Sciences, Rixensart, 1974, Paris, Beauchesne, 1978.
SHANIN, TEODOR, Units of Sociological Analysis, 'Sociology', 6, 3, 1972.
SHAPERE, DUDLEY, Toward a Post-Positivistic Interpretation of Science, in P. Achinstein and S. Barker (eds), 'The Legacy of Logical Positivism', Baltimore, Johns Hopkins Press, 1969.
SIMMEL, GEORG, 'Über soziale Differenzierung', Leipzig, Duncker & Humblot, 1890.
SIMMEL, GEORG, 'Soziologische Vorlesungen von Georg Simmel', University of Chicago, Society for Social Research, 1931.
SIMMEL, GEORG, 'Fragmente und Aufsätze', Hildesheim, G. Olms, 1967.
SIMMEL, GEORG, 'The Problems of the Philosophy of History', New York, the Free Press, 1977.
SIMMEL, GEORG, 'Buch des Dankes an Georg Simmel', see Gassen and Landmann.
SOCIAL SCIENCE RESEARCH COUNCIL (US), Bulletin 54, 1946.
SOHN-RETHEL, ALFRED, 'Intellectual and Manual Labour', London, Macmillan, 1978.
SOKOLOWSKI, ROBERT, 'The Formation of Husserl's Concept of Constitution', The Hague, Nijhoff, 1964.
SPEIER, MATTHEW, Phenomenology and Social Theory, 'Berkeley Journal of Sociology', vol.12, 1967.
SPENCER, HERBERT, 'The Study of Sociology', 9th edn, London, Williams & Norgate, 1880.
SPENCER, HERBERT, 'The Principles of Sociology', London, Williams & Norgate, 1893.
SPIEGELBERG, HERBERT, 'The Phenomenological Movement', 2 vols, The Hague, Nijhoff, 1960.
SPIETHOFF, ARTHUR, Anschauliche und reine Volkswirtschaftstheorie, in E. Salin (ed.), 'Synopsis. Festgabe für Alfred Weber', Heidelberg, L. Schneider, 1949.
STARK, WERNER, 'The Fundamental.Forms of Social Thought', London, Routledge & Kegan Paul, 1962.

STEHR, N. and KÖNIG, R. (eds), 'Wissenschaftssoziologie', Sonderheft 18, 'Kölner Zeitschrift für Soziologie und Sozialpsychologie', Opladen, Westdeutscher Verlag, 1975.
STOCKMAN, NORMAN, Positivism and Antipositivism in Sociological Metatheory, PhD thesis, Aberdeen, 1979.
STRASSER, STEPHEN, Grundgedanken der Sozialontologie E. Husserls, 'Zeitschrift für philosophische Forschung', vol.29, no.1, 1975.
TAGLIACOZZO, G. and WHITE, H. (eds), 'Giambattista Vico. An International Symposium', Baltimore, Johns Hopkins Press, 1969.
TAYLOR, CHARLES, Interpretation and the Sciences of Man, 'Review of Metaphysics', vol.25, 1971.
THERBORN, GÖRAN, Social Practice, Social Action, Social Magic, 'Acta Sociologica', vol.16, no.3, 1973.
THERBORN, GÖRAN, 'Science, Class and Society', London, New Left Books, 1976.
THOMAS, PAUL, Marx and Science, 'Political Studies', vol. 24, no.1, 1976.
THOMAS, W.I. and D.S., 'The Child in America', New York, Knopf, 1928.
THOMASON, BURKE, 'The Social Reality of Reification', PhD thesis, University of Sussex, 1978. 'Making Sense of Reification', London, Macmillan, 1982.
THOMPSON, JOHN, Critical Hermeneutics. A Study in the Thought of Paul Ricoeur and Jürgen Habermas, Cambridge University Press, 1981.
TÖNNIES, FERDINAND, 'Philosophische Terminologie in Psychologische-soziologischer Absicht', Leipzig, Thomas, 1906.
TÖNNIES, FERDINAND, 'On Sociology: Pure, Applied and Empirical', University of Chicago Press, 1971.
TOPITSCH, ERNST, Max Webers Geschichtsauffassung, 'Wissenschaft und Weltbild', vol.III, 1950.
TORRANCE, JOHN, Max Weber: Methods and the Man, 'Archives Européennes de Sociologie', vol.XV, 1974.
TOULEMONT, R., 'L'Essence de la société selon Husserl', Paris, Presses Universitaires de France, 1962.
TOULMIN, STEPHEN, From Logical Analysis to Conceptual History, in P. Achinstein and S. Barker (eds), 'The Legacy of Logical Positivism', Baltimore, Johns Hopkins Press, 1969.
TOULMIN, STEPHEN, 'Human Understanding', Oxford, Clarendon Press, 1972.
TOULMIN, STEPHEN, and BAIER, K., On Describing, 'Mind', vol.61, 1952.
TOULMIN, STEPHEN, and GOODFIELD, JUNE, 'The Architecture of Matter', London, Hutchinson, 1962.
TOURAINE, ALAIN, 'Sociologie de l'action', Paris, Seuil, 1965.

TRENDELENBURG, F.A., 'Geschichte der Kategorienlehre', Berlin, 1846.
URRY, JOHN, and KEAT, RUSSELL, 'Social Theory as Science', London, Routledge & Kegan Paul, 1975.
VADEE, MICHEL, La critique de l'abstraction par Marx, in Jacques d'Hondt (ed.), 'La Logique de Marx', Paris, Presses Universitaires de France, 1974.
VAIHINGER, H., 'The Philosophy of "As If"', London, Kegan Paul, 1925.
VORLÄNDER, KARL, 'Kant und der Sozialismus', Berlin, Reuter & Reichard, 1900.
WALSH, DAVID, Sociology and the Social World, in Paul Filmer et al., 'New Directions in Sociological Theory', London, Collier-Macmillan, 1972.
WALSH, DAVID, Varieties of Positivism, in P. Filmer, et al., 1972.
WALSH, DAVID, Science, Sociology and Everyday Life, in Chris Jenks (ed.), 'Rationality, Education and the Social Organisation of Knowledge', London, Routledge & Kegan Paul, 1977.
WALTHER, ANDREAS, Max Weber als Soziologe, 'Jahrbuch für Soziologie', vol.II, 1926.
WAXWEILER, EMILE, 'Esquisse d'une sociologie', Brussels and Leipzig, Misch & Thron, 1906.
WEBER, MAX, 'Gesammelte Aufsätze zur Religionssoziologie', Tübingen, Mohr, vol.I, 1920; vol.2, 1921.
WEBER, MAX, 'The Methodology of the Social Sciences', Chicago, Free Press, 1949.
WEBER, MAX, 'From Max Weber', ed. H. Gerth and C.W. Mills, Oxford University Press, 1958.
WEBER, MAX, 'Gesammelte Politische Schriften', Tübingen, Mohr, 1958.
WEBER, MAX, 'Gesammelte Aufsätze zur Wissenschaftslehre', 3rd edn, Tübingen, Mohr, 1963.
WEBER, MAX, 'Economy and Society', 3 vols, New Jersey, Bedminster Press, 1968.
WEBER, MAX, 'Roscher and Knies', New York, Free Press, 1975.
WEBER, MAX, 'The Protestant Ethic and the "Spirit" of Capitalism', London, Allen & Unwin, 1976.
WEIPPERT, GEORG, Die idealtypische Sinn- und Wesenserfassung, 'Zeitschrift für die gesamte Staatswissenschaft', vol.33, 1940.
WEISS, JOHANNES, 'Max Webers Grundlegung der Soziologie', Munich, UTB Verlag Dokumentation, 1975.
WEISS, JOHANNES, On the Marxist Reception and Critique of Max Weber, paper for the 1979 congress of the International Political Science Association.
WEISS, JOHANNES, 'Das Werk Max Webers in der marxistischen Rezeption und Kritik', Opladen, Westdeutscher Verlag, 1981.
WEITZ, MORRIS, Analysis and the Unity of Russell's Philo-

sophy, in P.A. Schilpp (ed.), 'The Philosophy of Bertrand Russell', The Library of Living Philosophers, New York, 1944, 1951.
WEIZSÄCKER, C.F. von, 'The World View of Physics', London, Routledge & Kegan Paul, 1952.
WELLMER, ALBRECHT, 'Methodologie als Erkenntnistheorie', Frankfurt, Suhrkamp, 1967.
WELLMER, ALBRECHT, 'Critical Theory of Society', New York, Herder & Herder, 1971.
WERKMEISTER, W.H., Cassirer's Advance Beyond Neo-Kantianism, in P.A. Schilpp (ed.), 'The Philosophy of Ernst Cassirer', The Library of Living Philosophers, vol.VI, New York, Tudor Press, 1949.
WIESE, L.V. and BECKER, H.E., 'Systematic Sociology', London, Chapman & Hall, 1932.
WILSON, BRYAN (ed.), 'Rationality',Oxford, Blackwell, 1974.
WILSON, H.T., 'The American Ideology: Science, Technology and Organisation as Modes of Rationality', London, Routledge & Kegan Paul, 1976.
WINCH, PETER, 'The Idea of a Social Science', London, Routledge & Kegan Paul, 1972.
WINCH, PETER, Understanding a Primitive Society, 'American Philosophical Quarterly', 1964. Reprinted in 'Ethics and Action', London, Routledge & Kegan Paul, 1972.
WINCH, PETER, Language, Belief and Relativism, in H.D. Lewis (ed.), 'Contemporary British Philosophy', London, Allen & Unwin, 1976.
WISDOM, JOHN, Scientific Theory, Embedded Ontology, and Weltanschauung, 'Philosophy and Phenomenological Research', vol.33, 1972.
WITTGENSTEIN, L., 'Tractatus Logico-Philosophicus', London, Routledge & Kegan Paul, 1922.
WOLFF, KURT (ed.), 'The Sociology of Georg Simmel', Chicago, Free Press, 1956.
WOLFF, KURT (ed.), 'Georg Simmel', Columbus, Ohio State University Press, 1959.
WRIGHT, G.H. von, 'Explanation and Understanding', London, Routledge & Kegan Paul, 1971.
WRONG, D. (ed.), 'Max Weber', Englewood Cliffs, New Jersey, Prentice-Hall, 1970.
ZELENY, JINDRICH, 'The Logic of Marx', Oxford, Blackwell, 1980.
ZETTERBERG, HANS L., 'On Theory and Verification in Sociology', 3rd edn, New Jersey, Bedminster Press, 1965.
ZIJDERVELD, ANTON, 'The Abstract Society', London, Allen Lane, 1972.
ZIJDERVELD, ANTON, The Problem of Adequacy, 'Archives Européennes de Sociologie', vol.13, no.1, 1972.
ZIJDERVELD, ANTON, 'On Clichés', London, Routledge & Kegan Paul, 1979.

Subject index

Abstraction, 34, 44, 56-7, 65, 94, 99, 104, 137, 144-5, 147-8, 151, 154, 176-7, 199, 203, 216
Action, social action, 11, 14-16, 20, 32-5, 53, 57-8, 63-5, 67, 89-90, 94-6, 106, 110-11, 113-14, 118, 126-8, 130, 134, 136-7, 143, 146, 151-4, 161, 163-5, 181, 183, 190-2, 205, 208-9, 211, 218
Actor, agency, see action
Adequacy, 12, 43, 59, 63-5, 126; causal and meaningful, 58, 64, 179, 181, 208
Analytic philosophy, 3, 10, 27, 29, 36, 39, 41, 43-4, 158, 161; see also Ordinary language
Anthropology, 2, 54, 161; of knowledge, 113, 202; philosophical, 180, 202
a priori, 13, 15-19, 34, 55, 76-7, 85, 102, 144, 158, 162-4, 172, 185, 188, 198, 203

Capitalism, 17, 20, 34, 131-4, 178
Cause, causal, causality, 11, 16-17, 20, 45, 48, 50, 63, 85, 87, 103-4, 123-4, 133, 151, 153, 161, 163, 181, 185, 199, 208
Cognitive interests, 4, 11, 21, 59, 66, 87, 109-14, 116, 119, 145, 203, 205
Commodity, 34, 47, 101
Common sense, 1, 53, 57-60, 62-4, 67, 94; see also Lebenswelt, Ordinary language
Concepts, 1, 5, 10, 21, 24, 27, 73, 78-9, 101, 120, 122, 138, 148-50, 156, 164, 167, 176; choice of, 2-3, 13, 22, 28-36, 117; definition of, 2, 4, 13, 36, 39-50, 169-70, 173-6, 208; scientific, theoretical, 3, 6-7, 11, 14, 20, 26, 58, 62-3, 67, 81-4, 87, 90, 105, 107, 115, 124-35, 142-4, 154, 159-60, 171, 199, 201, 206; everyday, 11, 52, 59, 67; concept-dependence, 116; critique of, 121, 206; of society, 135, 138, 142-4, 148-50, 153-5; see also Abstraction, Ideal type, Lebenswelt, Ordinary language, Observation, Theory

Subject Index

Constitution, 4, 30, 32, 62-3, 68-119, 134, 148, 185, 188, 205; epistemic and ontological, 21, 49, 61, 66-7, 143-4, 154, 180, 183, 189, 191-3, 200-3; of the subject, 73, 195; in juridical sense, 204; see also Transcendental
'Continuism', 51, 56, 65, 67, 111-12
Conventionalism, 2-3, 13-14, 38, 45, 54, 80, 116, 125, 127, 134, 142-3, 163, 194
Correspondence rules, 7, 8, 42; see also Observation, Theory, Empiricism, Positivism
Correspondence theory of reality, 193
Correspondence theory of truth, 164
Critical theory, 4, 10, 36, 51, 65, 68, 74, 109, 117, 217
Critique, 20-1, 44, 99, 102, 109, 114, 121, 154, 166, 195, 199, 206

Definition, 2, 4, 8, 13, 17-18, 24, 32, 35-51, 60, 64, 122, 124-5, 128-9, 133-4, 136, 138, 144-5, 149-50, 154, 171-6, 208-10, 212
Description, 5, 9, 11, 14-15, 17-18, 21, 29, 61, 115, 119, 126, 131, 160-1, 173, 183
Dialectic, 20, 43-4, 46, 84, 101, 133, 136, 143, 150

Economics, 13, 39, 47, 51, 56-9, 65, 87-8, 107, 126, 130-1, 164, 176-9
Empirical realism, 14, 21, 123-4, 136, 138, 152, 209, 213
Empiricism, 2, 7, 13, 22, 29, 50, 100, 108-9, 123, 127, 133-4, 136, 138, 142, 155, 159-60, 163, 172, 183-4, 196, 214
Epistemic constitution, see Constitution
Epistemic fallacy, 138, 207
Epistemology, 43, 47, 74, 86, 98-111, 114, 117-21, 125, 133, 147, 153, 163, 166, 188, 197, 199-202, 204, 206, 209, 215
Ethnomethodology, 10, 30, 97, 169, 195
Existentialism, 10, 74, 82, 87, 89, 90, 126, 153, 180, 195
Experimentation, 15, 17
Explanation, explanatory, 9, 11, 12, 14, 15, 17-19, 22, 58-9, 61, 137-40, 149, 152, 160, 178, 202
Extensionalism, 7, 40, 50, 173

Fact, 8, 13, 44, 48-9, 52, 56, 61-3, 71, 85, 87, 94, 117, 123, 148-9, 159-60, 163, 203; see also Social fact
Fact/value distinction, 129-31, 138, 207
Falsification, 8, 44
Formalisation, 3, 8, 39, 41-2
Functionalism, 17, 18

Hermeneutics, 3-5, 10-12, 15, 22-3, 27, 29, 32, 36, 41-3, 45, 54, 66-7, 111, 118-19, 125-6, 155, 161, 202, 206

History, 49-50, 55, 59,
  81-7, 107-8, 122, 127,
  133, 140-1, 175, 179,
  186-91, 199-201, 207
Holism, 2, 125, 136-7, 140,
  145, 150
Human sciences, see Social
  science

Idealism, 6, 29, 39, 68-9,
  86, 106, 116, 118, 128,
  134, 144, 148, 152, 183,
  186; see also Transcendental idealism
Ideal type, 32, 36, 49-50,
  59, 61, 89, 90, 120,
  122, 124-8, 134, 146,
  171, 176, 207-9
Identity theory, 21, 99,
  199, 200
Ideology, 1, 5, 12, 51, 57,
  64, 109, 115, 118, 121,
  129-30, 134, 150, 154,
  201, 204
Immanent method, 27, 44
Individualism, 2, 57-8,
  125-6, 132, 136-40, 143,
  145, 147-9, 150, 212,
  215, 217
Instrumentalism, see
  Conventionalism
Interpretation, 11, 12, 22,
  30, 42, 53, 62-4, 68-9,
  71, 95, 126, 181, 184;
  see also Hermeneutics,
  Verstehen
Intransitive objects, see
  Transitive objects

Knowledge-guiding interests,
  see Cognitive interests

Language, 3-4, 6, 24-31,
  37, 39, 42-3, 47, 67,
  85, 111, 114, 135,
  158-60, 167-9, 184, 186,
  192, 198, 202
Laws, 9-11, 14, 56, 59, 63,
  77-80, 126, 143, 148,
  151, 157, 159-60, 163,
  176, 203
Lebenswelt, 'life-world',
  11, 39, 52, 54, 58, 60-1,
  63-7, 85, 94, 126, 192-3
Legitimacy, 128-30, 134-5,
  209-11
Linguistic philosophy, see
  Analytic philosophy
Logic, 7, 8, 12, 13, 29,
  41-2, 46, 112, 121, 169,
  181, 186, 198, 204, 207
Logical empiricism, logical
  positivism, 3, 7, 10, 29,
  159-60, 163

Marxism, 5, 9, 13, 20, 22,
  29, 32-5, 68-9, 73-4, 87,
  101-2, 107-9, 114-16,
  118, 120, 131, 148-9,
  166, 177, 197, 200-2,
  216, 218; see also Marx,
  Materialism
Materialism, 4, 6, 9, 21,
  29, 39, 73, 105-6, 114,
  116-17, 119, 134, 151-2,
  160, 166, 183, 200-1,
  218
Meaning, 2, 7, 11, 12, 17,
  24-5, 31, 40, 42, 58,
  60-2, 68-9, 72-3, 89, 90,
  92-7, 114, 116, 118-19,
  124, 126-8, 134, 142,
  146, 156, 158, 160, 173,
  181, 190-2, 194, 205-7
Metaphysics, 6-8, 13, 29,
  64, 95, 122, 158-60, 207
Method, methodology, 10, 88,
  94-5, 100, 111-12, 120-1,
  126, 132-4, 149, 161,
  167, 170, 190, 192, 196,
  201, 207, 209

Naturalism, 3, 16, 20, 54,
  67, 73, 116-17, 119,
  122, 155, 161, 165, 186,
  188
Natural science, 1, 3,
  10-11, 16, 30, 45, 51,
  54-5, 59, 62, 74, 81-2,
  84, 109, 112-13, 116,
  148, 161, 164, 167-8,
  197, 204-5; see also
  Science, Social science
Neo-Kantianism, 14, 52, 68,
  73-4, 79-80, 83-4, 91-2,
  123, 186, 194, 197, 208
Nominalism, 6, 13, 38-9,
  45, 47, 50, 54, 132, 140,
  142, 151, 172
Normal science, 1, 121

Objectivism, 60, 62, 117,
  183, 203
Observation (language, sentences, statements,
  terms, etc.), 3, 7-9, 22,
  29, 34, 40, 42, 44, 48,
  62, 160, 163; see also
  Empiricism, Positivism,
  Theory
Ontology, 4, 6, 35, 43, 46,
  86, 91, 94, 96-8, 102-7,
  119, 123, 126, 134,
  136-8, 140-1, 152-4, 163,
  184, 194, 199
Open systems, 14, 16
Operationalism, 2, 3, 40,
  43, 136, 169, 174
Ordinary (everyday) language, usage, etc., 2, 4,
  6, 7, 11, 24, 29, 30,
  36, 42-3, 51-2, 59, 67-8,
  112, 167
Ordinary language philosophy, see Analytic
  philosophy

Phenomenalism, 38
Phenomenology, 52, 60, 68,
  74-5, 91-7, 180, 186,
  192, 194-5, 197
Phenomenological sociology,
  12, 17, 22, 61, 67, 69,
  72, 116, 118, 134, 138,
  146, 179
Philosophy, 7, 12, 13, 25,
  34, 35, 36, 38, 41, 42,
  43, 44, 60, 68, 69, 71,
  74, 77, 97-103, 106, 109,
  120-1, 123, 140-1, 146,
  148, 153-5, 157-8, 161,
  168, 177, 186, 197, 199,
  202, 205, 207, 209, see
  also Analytic philosophy;
  of Science, social science, 2, 5, 6, 10, 12,
  13, 19, 21, 22, 34, 39,
  41, 44, 59, 110, 115-16,
  119, 126-7, 134, 164-5,
  173, 201, 213, 219
Physicalism, 7, 9, 11, 28,
  39, 158, 160
Physics, 7-10, 170
Positivism, 2-6, 8-11, 13,
  15, 22-5, 29, 32,
  39-42, 52, 54, 58, 66,
  72-3, 80, 91, 111, 116,
  121, 125-6, 136, 138,
  142, 148, 155, 157,
  160-1, 163, 165, 169,
  186, 194, 204-5, 217;
  see also Logical positivism
Power, 12, 18-19, 26-7, 45,
  71, 118, 124, 153, 156,
  165, 210
Practice, praxis, 4, 54,
  68-9, 74, 99, 106, 108,
  114, 118-19, 143-4, 183,
  196, 200, 206
Protocol sentences, see
  Observation statements

Rationalism, 3-5, 10, 12-15,
  19, 23, 29, 33, 36, 39,
  44, 72, 103, 108-9,

248 Subject Index

117-18, 162-4, 166, 192, 205-6, 213
Rationality, 13-16, 19, 33, 43, 57-8, 60, 113, 127, 129-32, 134-5, 163-4, 178, 208-9, 211-12, 216
Realism, 3-6, 9-10, 12-15, 19, 21-3, 36, 38-9, 43-4, 47-8, 68, 73, 75, 84, 101, 109, 115-17, 119-20, 123-5, 127, 132-4, 136, 138, 140, 142-3, 147-8, 151-2, 154-5, 157, 162-6, 173, 177, 181, 183, 188, 205, 213, 218
Reality, 2, 4, 21, 34, 43, 47-50, 53, 59, 72, 86-7, 92, 99, 104, 108, 111-12, 115, 117, 120-2, 125, 132-3, 138, 144, 146, 148-9, 154, 158, 163, 171, 176-7, 183-4, 189-90, 193, 195, 200, 205, 218; social, 20, 88, 96, 100, 142, 145-6, 151-2, 194
Reduction(ism), 7, 9, 28-9, 39, 125, 127, 134, 137-8, 154, 159-60
Reification, 33, 44, 105, 114-15, 136, 139-40, 142, 147, 149-51, 153-4, 219
Relations, internal, 46, 175; real, 47, 100, 118, 151, 177-8, 196; social, 127, 136, 144, 152-3
Relativism, 12, 15, 19, 23, 87-8, 190, 192, 194
Role, 33, 137, 146-7

Science, 1, 8, 10, 14, 19, 34, 40, 52-6, 59-63, 65-6, 68, 75, 79-81, 84-5, 90, 95, 100, 102, 104-5, 108-12, 115-17, 119-21, 123, 126, 128, 132, 136, 142, 145, 149, 151, 159, 173, 177, 180-1, 192, 194-5, 197, 203, 207; and language, 24-32, 36, 39, 42-7, 51, 67, 129, 159, 167, 170; and philosophy, 5-7, 71, 93, 97, 158, 164, 169, 201; see also Philosophy of social science, Natural science, Social science
Semantics, 2, 25-6, 40, 167
'Separatism', 51, 53, 56, 59, 60, 111, 177
Social facts, 28, 35, 49, 55, 136-8, 140, 148; see also Facts
Social science, 1-4, 6-11, 13-20, 22-5, 30, 32-3, 38, 41, 50-2, 54-5, 57, 61-2, 65-7, 88, 94, 96, 109, 113, 116-18, 121, 125-6, 129-30, 134-6, 150, 154-5, 157, 164, 167-8, 181-2, 186, 190, 192, 197, 203, 205-7, 214
Social structure, 2, 15-17, 26, 34, 44-5, 53, 72, 89, 127, 136-7, 140, 142, 146, 150-3, 156, 214
Society, 2-4, 12, 20, 34, 55, 68-9, 85-6, 117, 135-55, 175, 183, 198-9, 213-14, 216-17
Sociology, 2, 4, 5, 9, 10, 13, 19, 26, 30, 32-3, 35-6, 38-9, 44, 47-50, 52-3, 55, 58-9, 61, 63, 67, 74, 85-6, 89-90, 97, 118-19, 121, 125-7, 133-7, 141, 143-9, 152-4, 160-1, 165, 173-4, 176, 179, 189-90, 194, 208, 214, 216-19
State, 28, 83, 89, 125, 132, 135, 212
Structure, 9, 14-15, 20-1, 35, 45, 69, 75, 85, 107, 115, 123, 134, 137, 139-40, 142, 145, 152-4,

249 Subject Index

163, 165, 170, 183, 200, 218-19

Theory, 1-8, 10, 13-15, 17-19, 21-2, 25-6, 29, 31, 34, 40-2, 44-5, 47, 49, 56, 58-9, 65-6, 88, 90-1, 112, 117, 119, 122, 125-7, 132-4, 138, 142-3, 150-2, 154-6, 160, 163-4, 166, 168, 171-2, 177, 183, 190, 201, 203, 206, 218; of knowledge, see Epistemology
Transcendental, 4, 13, 14, 17, 29, 32-4, 60-1, 66, 70, 76, 78-80, 83, 86, 90-1, 93-4, 101-2, 106, 110-15, 145, 180, 182, 185, 189, 192, 198, 204-5; idealism, 4, 14, 22, 91, 123, 136, 143-4, 146-7, 151-2, 166, 294; realism, see Realism
Transitive objects, 14, 115-17, 119, 183, 196

Truth, truth-conditions, 7, 13, 19, 30, 45, 69, 71, 87, 90, 106, 112, 117, 119, 122, 136, 156, 163-4, 190-1, 193

Unified Science, 9, 159
Universals, 6
Understanding, see Verstehen

Value(s), 28, 59, 81-3, 87-90, 109, 128-33, 135, 190-1, 207; see also Fact/value distinction, Wertbeziehung
Verstehen, 5, 10-13, 33, 51, 53-5, 57-8, 61, 69, 72, 85, 89-90, 126-7, 150, 160, 178, 189, 198, 202
Vienna Circle, 6, 7, 52, 159

Wertbeziehung, value-reference, 59, 81-3, 87-90, 115, 124, 133, 187, 189-90

Name index

Abel, T., 11, 161
Achinstein, P., 25, 169
Adler, M., 32, 74, 101-2,
　104-5, 136, 143-4, 147,
　185, 188, 196-8, 214-17
Adorno, T., 21, 27, 43-4,
　65-6, 147-51, 166, 175,
　181, 213, 217-18
Ajdukiewicz, K., 171-2
Albert, H., 217
Albrow, M., 210
Alpert, H., 141, 215
Althusser, L., 34-5, 45-6,
　51, 107-9, 170-1, 175,
　200
Apel, K.O., 65, 68, 74,
　101, 109-10, 157, 161,
　192, 202-3, 206
Arato, A., 83, 184, 187,
　189, 191, 208
Aristotle, 25, 27
Aron, R., 107, 170, 187,
　201, 216
Austin, J.L., 10, 29, 158,
　169
Ayer, A.J., 157

Bachelard, G., 51, 176
Baier, H., 206
Baldamus, W.G., 26, 38,
　167, 172
Balibar, E., 35, 46, 107-8,
　170-1, 175, 201

Bauman, Z., 194
Baumgartner, E., 206
Beard, C., 174
Becker, H.E., 174
Beetham, D., 131, 212
Bendix, R., 168
Benton, T., 162, 164, 166,
　218-19
Berger, P., 146, 152-3,
　194, 216, 218-19
Bergmann, T., 25
Bergson, E., 94
Berlin, I., 55, 177
Bershady, H., 215
Berzelius, J.J., 25
Beyleveld, D., 12-13, 87,
　93, 95-6, 118, 162-4,
　166, 184, 189, 192-4,
　205
Bhaskar, R., 3, 13-16,
　18-20, 22, 34, 45, 68,
　73, 115-17, 119, 122-3,
　127, 136, 138, 143,
　151-3, 157, 159, 162-6,
　175, 182-4, 194, 196,
　206-7, 210, 213, 218-19
Bierstedt, R., 38, 50, 172-3
Blau, P., 210
Blum, A., 195
Blumer, H., 41, 146, 173,
　216
Bluntschli, J.C., 135, 141
Böhm-Bawerk, E., 179
Böhme, G., 164, 167, 177

Name Index

Bormann, C. von, 162
Bosl, K., 176
Boudon, R., 25, 156, 167, 173
Bourdieu, P., 52-3, 177
Boyle, R., 25
Brennan, J.M., 160
Bridgman, P.W., 40, 169, 174
Brinkmann, H., 204
Brown, R., 167
Bubner, R., 162
Buckley, W., 141-2, 214, 216
Buck-Morss, S., 166
Burger, T., 50, 124, 170-1, 176, 178, 187, 189-90, 208

Calvez, J.Y., 200
Carnap, R., 6, 7, 11, 28-9, 40, 42, 158-9
Carroll, L., 167
Carver, T., 170, 175
Cassirer, E., 25, 79-80, 167, 184-6
Cassirer, H.W., 77, 79, 185
Cerrutti, F., 195
Chamboredon, J.C., 53
Chase, S., 174
COCTA, 174
Cohen, G.A., 200
Cohen, H., 73, 79-80, 186
Collier, A., 202
Comte, A., 139-40
Condillac, E., 25
Connolly, W.E., 26-7, 165
Coser, L., 18, 213
Crosland, M., 25, 167
Cutler, A., 166

Dawe, A., 136, 143, 213-14
Descartes, R., 43, 55, 106
Dewey, J., 94
Dilthey, W., 55, 110, 177
Döbert, R., 182
Droysen, J.G., 10, 55
Durkheim, E., 1-2, 22, 28, 33, 35-6, 45, 47-9, 51-2, 54-6, 59, 63, 121, 138, 140-1, 150, 152, 154, 156, 176-7, 213, 215, 217

Easlea, B., 199
Edgley, R., 33, 166, 211
Eisen, A., 130-1, 211-12
Engels, F., 46; see also Marx
Erlangen School, 177, 204
Esaer, E., 171
Eubank, E.E., 41, 173-4
Eucken, W., 39

Fairchild, H.P., 174
Faris, E., 170
Feigl, H., 159
Feuerbach, L., 200
Feyerabend, P., 18, 27
Fichte, J.G., 102, 197
Filmer, P., 184
Fink, E., 92
Fireman, P., 46
Forman, P., 176
Francis, E., 145, 156, 216
Frankfurt Institute for Social Research, 175, 214
Franklin, B., 134
Frege, G., 29, 192
Freud, S., 39
Furth, P., 188

Gadamer, H.G., 10, 12, 25, 27, 29-30, 32, 42-3, 66, 162, 185
Galileo, 60, 199
Gallie, W.B., 165
Garfinkel, H., 71-2, 96, 169, 184, 193, 195
Geertz, C., 161
Geiger, T., 216
Geras, N., 168
Gerhardt, U., 189, 215
Giddens, A., 67, 153, 157, 159, 161, 182, 194, 206, 210, 219

Goddard, D., 186, 189
Godelier, M., 177
Goldmann, L., 115, 190
Gorman, R., 94, 179-80, 193-5
Granger, G.G., 182, 201
Grathoff, R., 180-1, 194
Gusfield, J., 168

Habermas, J., 12, 21, 60, 65-8, 74, 101, 109-18, 161-2, 181-2, 184-5, 187, 192, 195, 197, 199, 202-6, 213
Haldane, J.B.S., 195
Halfpenny, P., 157
Harré, R., 117, 152, 163, 165, 194, 218
Hart, H., 174
Hegel, G.W.F., 20, 34, 46, 56, 74, 98-100, 102, 105-6, 109, 120, 122, 147, 175, 195-9, 207
Heidegger, M., 27, 30, 192, 195
Hempel, C.G., 40, 158, 160, 173, 209
Henrich, D., 120, 122, 124, 189, 200, 206-8
Hesse, M., 160, 163-4
Hicks, J.R., 177
Hilferding, R., 179
Hindess, B, 108, 166, 192-3, 200-2
Hirst, P., 48-9, 108, 166, 176, 200-2, 210, 215
Hogrebe, W., 182-3, 185
Hollis, M., 12-13, 15-16, 18-20, 44, 119, 159, 162-5, 170, 202, 205-6
Hook, S., 174
Horkheimer, M., 65-6, 200, 205
Humboldt, W. von, 25, 31
Hume, D., 159
Humpty Dumpty, 25, 36, 174
Hussain, A., 166
Husserl, E., 43, 51, 60-1, 66, 68, 73, 75-6, 91-5, 179-80, 184, 191-2, 195, 203

Itzhoff, S.M., 186

James, W., 63, 94
Jay, M., 196

Kant, I., 68-9, 73-80, 86, 91-2, 98-102, 105-6, 109, 111, 114, 121, 144-5, 184-5, 188-9, 194-7, 199, 200, 214
Kaplan, D., 159
Kaufmann, Felix, 72, 178, 194
Kaufmann, Fritz, 80, 91, 184-6, 191
Keat, R., 20, 162, 166, 177, 218-19
Kecskemeti, P., 190
Kenny, A., 169
Kern, I., 184-6, 191
Knies, K., 120-1, 132, 171
Kocka, J., 212
Kolakowski, L., 21, 93, 166, 173, 191-2, 196
König, R., 32-3, 170, 215
Korsch, K., 195
Korzybski, A., 40, 174
Krahl, H.J., 114-15, 197, 204
Kuhn, T., 1, 18, 121, 207

Lachenmeyer, C., 136-7, 169
Landgrebe, L., 92
Lange, F.A., 80, 186
Lask, E., 74
Lauerman, M., 204
Lavine, T., 69, 73
Lavoisier, A.L., 25
Lazarsfeld, P., 25, 156, 167, 173, 190, 209
Leach, E., 152, 156

Name Index

Lévi-Strauss, C., 2, 52-3, 142, 152, 156, 177, 218
Lieber, H.J., 188
Liefmann, R., 145, 168, 208
Lilienfeld, P. von, 141
Lobkowitz, N., 205
Locke, J., 157
Löwith, K., 132, 208, 212
Lübbe, H., 186
Luckmann, T., 146, 152, 193-4, 216
Luhmann, N., 113, 204
Lukács, G., 70, 102-4, 187, 195-6, 198-9
Lukes, S., 13, 18-19, 153, 163, 165, 176, 190, 215, 218
Lundberg, G., 25, 39-41, 161, 173-4

McCarthy, T., 182, 203, 205
Mach, E., 52, 159
Machlup, F., 57
McHugh, P., 195
MacIntyre, A., 210
Maison des Sciences de l'Homme, 174
Manheim, E., 209
Mannheim, K., 12, 139, 214
Marcuse, H., 105, 131, 196, 199, 212
Marx, K., 17, 20-2, 26, 28, 34-5, 38, 45-7, 54, 56, 69-70, 74, 98-101, 103-7, 109, 115, 132-3, 143, 147, 172, 177-8, 183, 196-7, 199-201, 204, 216-17
Melden, A.I., 169
Menger, C., 56-7, 59, 173, 178
Meyerson, E., 51, 176
Mill, J.S., 25, 35, 37-8
Mises, L. von, 57
Mommsen, W., 168, 216
Monnerot, J., 216
Morgan, G., 157
Mulkay, M., 167

Müller, H., 213
Murvar, V., 209

Nadel, S.F., 152
Nagel, E., 40, 163
Narr, W.D., 211
Natanson, M., 41, 167, 174, 180, 193
Natorp, P., 73, 79, 91, 184, 186
Negt, O., 195
Neisser, H., 178
Nell, E., 159-60
Neurath, O., 7, 9, 11, 29, 158-60
Newton, I., 44, 51
Nietzsche, F., 70-1, 73, 89, 175, 184, 212
Normand, C., 168, 173

Oakes, G., 206
Offe, C., 211
Ogden, C.R., 40, 174
Ollman, B., 45-6, 175
Oppenheim, P., 159, 174, 209
Ossowski, S., 26, 168
Outhwaite, W., 161-2, 187, 213

Paine, T., 135, 213
Pap, A., 172
Papineau, D., 137-8, 209, 214
Pareto, V., 24
Parsons, T., 17-18, 32-3, 38, 65, 96, 137, 142-3, 180-1, 215
Pascal, B., 47
Passeron, J.C., 53
Passmore, J., 186
Peel, J., 215
Perman, D., 168
Pierce, C.S., 110
Pitkin, H., 129, 169, 175, 181, 210-11

254 Name Index

Plato, 139
Poincaré, H., 53
Pompa, L., 177
Popper, K., 8, 156, 160,
  173, 205, 217
Poulantzas, N., 171
Pullberg, S., 218
Putnam, H., 159, 174

Quine, W.V.O., 137, 194

Radcliffe-Brown, A.R., 2,
  152, 156, 214
Radnitzsky, G., 7, 159
Rancière, J., 175, 200
Rasmussen, D., 185
Richards, I.A., 40, 174
Rickert, H., 50, 55, 74,
  80-3, 87, 89-90, 125,
  186-7, 189-91, 197, 206
Ricoeur, P., 12, 162
Riggs, F., 174
Robbins, L., 57
Robinson, R., 36-7, 171-2
Rohlfes, J., 174
Rorty, R., 158
Roscher, W., 120-1, 132, 207
Rose, G., 166, 175, 184,
  197, 208
Ruben, D.H., 184
Runciman, W.G., 90, 187,
  190-1, 214
Russell, B., 29, 38, 159,
  209
Ryan, A., 15, 164
Ryle, G., 161

Salin, E., 178
Salomon, G., 172
Sander, F., 180
Sartori, G., 174
Sartre, J.P., 153
Sayer, D., 101, 166, 170,
  175, 196, 205
Schaar, J., 129, 210
Schäffle, A., 141, 214

Scheler, M., 38, 110, 172
Schelling, F.W.J., 139
Schlick, M., 158
Schluchter, W., 212
Schmidt, A., 74, 105-7, 143,
  185, 199, 200
Schmoller, G., 57
Schoek, H., 213
Schopenhauer, A., 146
Schrader-Klebert, K., 86,
  144-5, 189, 216-17
Schutz, A., 6, 51, 57-8, 61,
  63-5, 68, 89, 91, 93-7,
  121, 126, 146, 178-81,
  188, 190-4, 203, 209,
  213, 216
Scriven, M., 41-2, 156, 173,
  175
Shapere, D., 159
Silverman, D., 72
Simmel, G., 64, 68-9, 80,
  83-6, 89, 102, 125, 136,
  139-40, 142-8, 151, 183,
  187-9, 213-17
Smelser, N., 18
Smith, A., 26
Social Science Research
  Council (US), 174
Sohn-Rethel, A., 104-5, 196
Sokolowski, R., 92, 183,
  185, 191
Spann, O., 214
Spencer, H., 139-41, 215
Spiegelberg, H., 191
Spiethoff, A., 181
Stark, W., 141, 215
Stockman, N., 119, 157, 205
Strasser, S., 179

Teune, H., 174
Therborn, G., 57, 178-9
Thomas, P., 178
Thomas, W.I., 69, 183
Thomason, B., 95, 193, 205
Thompson, J., 203, 205, 219
Tönnies, F., 38, 45, 47,
  146, 176, 216
Topitsch, E., 212

255 Name Index

Torrance, J., 120-1, 189
Toulemont, R., 179
Toulmin, S., 41-2, 159, 167, 173
Touraine, A., 52-3, 117, 147, 177
Trendelenburg, F.A., 25, 167
Troeltsch, E., 191

Urry, J., 20, 162, 166, 177, 218-19

Vaihinger, H., 80, 186
Vico, G., 54-5, 106, 143, 177
Vorländer, K., 197

Wagner, A., 34-5, 101, 175
Walsh, D., 72, 169, 184, 195
Walther, A., 209
Waxweiler, E., 41
Weber, Marianne, 206
Weber, Max, 1, 2, 6, 11, 22, 28, 32, 35-6, 38, 44-5, 49-51, 59, 61, 64-5, 74, 80-2, 87-90, 115, 120-35, 139-40, 143, 145-6, 150, 154, 156, 161, 168, 170-1, 173, 176, 179, 181, 186, 189-91, 206-12, 214, 218
Weber, W., 178
Weiss, J., 191, 208
Weitz, M., 172
Weizsäcker, C.F. von, 177
Wellmer, A., 161, 182, 204
Werkmeister, W.H., 184-6
Whewell, W., 41
Whitehead, A.M., 29, 38, 94, 159
Wickstead, P., 57
Wiese, L. von, 41, 142, 174
Wilson, H.T., 213
Winch, P., 9, 10, 12, 157, 184
Windelband, W., 74, 197
Wisdom, J., 194
Wittgenstein, L., 10, 36, 41, 158, 198
Wolff, K., 188-9, 216
Wright, G.H. von, 157, 161

Zetterberg, H., 12, 161
Želeny, J., 196
Zijderveld, A., 147, 181, 194, 216-17

For Product Safety Concerns and Information please contact our EU representative GPSR@taylorandfrancis.com
Taylor & Francis Verlag GmbH, Kaufingerstraße 24, 80331 München, Germany

www.ingramcontent.com/pod-product-compliance
Lightning Source LLC
Chambersburg PA
CBHW062130300426
44115CB00012BA/1869